ATTITUDE TOWARDS INFORMATION

CONCEPTS IN COMMUNICATION
INFORMATICS & LIBRARIANSHIP
(CICIL)

For a list of titles in this series, see pp. 289 at the end of the book

ABOUT THE AUTHOR

N.G. SATISH has an M.A. in English Literature and a Ph.D. in Library Science from the University of Mysore. He worked as a Documentation Officer in National Institute of Rural Development for over a decade. He is presently a Deputy Librarian at the American Studies Research Centre, Hyderabad.

Concepts in Communication
Informatics & Librarianship-17

General Editor: S.P. Agrawal

ATTITUDE TOWARDS INFORMATION

A Study of Social Scientists

N.G. SATISH
American Studies Research Centre
Hyderabad

CONCEPT PUBLISHING COMPANY, NEW DELHI 110059

ISBN 81-7022-513-2

First Published 1994

Published and Printed by
Ashok Kumar Mittal
Concept Publishing Company
A/15-16, Commercial Block, Mohan Garden
NEW DELHI 110059

Lasertypeset by
Printing Express
H-13, Bali Nagar
NEW DELHI 110015

ACKNOWLEDGEMENTS

My sincere and heartfelt thanks are due to Dr. H.A. Khan, Reader, Department of Library and Information Science, University of Mysore, Mysore, and Dr. B.C. Muthayya, Director (Psychology), National Institute of Rural Development, Hyderabad, for their valuable guidance at various stages of this work.

N.G. SATISH

GENERAL EDITOR'S INTRODUCTION

Most of the information user studies made over the decades are in the direction of science and technology. The quantum of the researches on humanities and social sciences is not much. Even those investigation that have been made about social scientists relate to the manifest aspect of information use. They shed light more on the sources of the information to be provided to the users than on the behaviour of the information users. Of late it has been increasingly realised that this behavioural aspect should receive more attention of the researches in this field and that there is a need to have more studies that deal with the attitude of the information users towards the communication information and library use.

On the basis of the researches carried out so far in the context of the social sciences it could well be said that the image that emerges of the social scientists is that they are not favourably drawn towards the conventional bibliographical tools and other library services. They are also generally not aware of the specialist information services available on their subjects in the libraries which they can utilise. As a matter of fact their apathetic attitude towards the library resources stems from the fact that they think that these are not of much help to them in their search for materials they need. This is all the more why it has become necessary to understand their information use behaviour so that remedial measures may be taken by the professionals concerned to bring about a change in the attitude of social scientists towards their information use.

In India a beginning has been made with a few user studies which have generally concentrated on the use of the individual libraries by the scientists and the general public. There is a scant data in regard to information use of the social scientists. Fewer are the studies on their information use behaviour. The present book is the outcome of the investigation made by the author regarding the attitude of social scientists, working in the university social science departments and research and training institutions, towards the information use. The study not only attempts to examine the attitude-behaviour relations, but also analyse the relation of the attitude towards information-seeking with various personal and psychological attributes of the social scientists. Besides, the study also explores the relation of the information source use with attitude towards information and makes endeavour to provide an answer to the question as to how far the attitude-behaviour relations are conditional to other personal and psychological attributes of the social scientists.

This information user study, though exploratory in nature, is an useful addition to the existing literature, on the subject in India, particularly in regard to the social scientists, inasmuch as it would help initiate further studies so as to make more empirical data available to enable concerned professionals to serve the information seekers more effectively.

S.P. AGRAWAL

CONTENTS

LIST OF TABLES

LIST OF FIGURES

1

INTRODUCTION

1.1 Introduction and Context of the Study

Information user studies over the years have assumed that the use of recorded knowledge is an essential and a continuing process of keeping up to date with new developments of with current progress in the field of one's primary interest or specialisation. This is specially so for those involved in research and teaching (Egan and Henkle, 1956).

The primary goal of research and to some extent teaching activities is to extend the boundaries of knowledge. Academicians involved in such activities are aware of the importance placed on originality and priority in their research contributions. Not only are they strongly oriented to provide and communicate scientific information, but are also determined to exert in seeking and using such information. Many studies have established the strongly motivated information seeking habit of the scientists and their persistent information search patterns. In fact, a full range of human needs are at the root of information seeking behaviour. These needs arise out of the roles an academician fills in the organizational environment.

Scientific information is used by academicians involved in research and teaching for various purposes (Garvey *et al.*, 1974). They are for:

(i) *Attainment of Professional Goals*

That is, for maintaining the visibility among the peers and to enhance the scientific career by identification with discoveries.

(ii) *Establishment of Scientific Body of Knowledge*

This is mostly done through archival depositing of the scientific work and by adding their findings to other recently generated information so that it becomes integrated into scientific knowledge.

(iii) *To Facilitate Day-to-day Work*

The scientists also use information to get a critical feedback, to act as quality control men and to disseminate information about their work.

Menzel (1966) observes that scientists have very high motivation to obtain information that is channelled in their direction through the system that is designed to serve them. They go out of their way to reach the information. They want this information to help in very specific activities that form essential parts of their professional roles and therefore of their lives. Because of both these facets, they have very well developed and they well structured behaviour patterns with regard to professional communications.

Thus, it has been acknowledged that information acquisition activity is a highly motivated one. The primary goal of a researcher is to extend the boundaries of knowledge. Not only are they strongly oriented to generate and communicate scientific information, but are also expected to persevere in seeking and using such information. Garvey and Griffith (1964) have described that one of the essential prerequisites of an active researcher is to make every effort to discover all possible means of obtaining information, especially on the work related to his own area of interest. In fact, scientific communication represents both a major input and an ultimate objective of scientific activity.

Science by its method of investigation contributes to the growth of knowledge. Knowledge grows by the addition of new material on top of a great edifice formed by earlier contributors. Any individual who is ignorant of what is already known has little chance of making worthwhile contribution.

Kent (1984) views scientific information as the raw material for academic activities. Paisley (1968) sees scientific productivity as a consequence of information use. Thus, information has been recognised as the functional component of the scientific work.

Garvey (1979), recognising the interactive flow of information as an inseparable part of research process, observes that the producer of research information must be continually reporting on it, seeking information relevant to it, reshaping its course and updating its potential relevance. Underlying these imperatives, he opines, are the combination of psychological and sociological factors which determine perceived need for information and also the motives of information seeking activity.

Wilson and Farid (1979), in their review on use of records of research, also express that the attempt to discover new knowledge requires the use of old knowledge. Research, thus, builds on prior research. Recognising three levels of familiarity with the prior research that the researchers generally aim at namely, expert familiarity, working familiarity and nodding familiarity, the authors observe that whatever be the sort of familiarity aimed at it is expected to be pursued through a regular and more or less systematic set of arrangements for gathering information.

Empirical observations and research on literature needs of scientists have revealed that this task is usually accomplished through the reading of relevant articles in a selected group of journals, scanning abstracts and the use of annual reviews of progress. Other sources for updating ones information are attendance at or participation in lectures, classes, seminars, professional conventions and informal conversation with colleagues. It is opined that an academician's esteem would drop quickly and sharply if he himself does not review the stock of knowledge through constant recourse to the published literature.

Arndt *et al* (1980) commenting on the information imperatives, observes that scientific performance is basically evaluated in terms of the research output. A common goal of scientists is to produce knowledge in their respective disciplines. In fact, publish or perish qualitative norms used by universities and research institutes make formal communication output a main criterion for career success. Communication is also a major input in the scientific process, since scientists add to the body of knowledge by building up and extending results achieved by colleagues either going through their research publications or through interacting frequently with colleagues with known interests. In case of those in teaching and research, there is likely to be additional emphasis on seeking professional recognition. The work demands of an academician not only supports this outlook of professional reputation, but it usually produces considerable pressure to seek and use information.

Thus, a persistent information seeking behaviour is viewed as a prerequisite for all the academicians and specially so for those engaged in research and other scholarly work. Much of the prior investigation into this aspect of academic work — information use behaviour — has concentrated on the manifest or what is overt and noticeable. Latent factors which modulate and influence the information use behaviour is less often touched upon, if not entirely absent. The present investigation focus on this issue of latent aspect namely, attitude towards information. This study enquires as to what uses do the social scientists perceive of the information seeking activity, what incentives or motives stimulate them, do they extend beyond the immediate utility in their academic work, what users perceive as the constraints. In sum, the evaluative opinion of social science information users about the information products and the need for information seeking activity, which reflect their attitude towards the information or readiness to involve in use behaviour is explored in the context of social scientists engaged in teaching at post graduate level in a universities and those affiliated to various social science research and training institutions.

The study attempts to examine the attitude-behaviour relations. In addition, it also explores how far the attitude towards information is in itself related to various personal and psychological attributes. It is often expressed that attitude though a determining factor for behaviour, its relationship will tend to improve when the situational factors are conducive to it. This latent aspect is viewed as the affective tendency which has a definite bearing on the overt information use behaviour viewed particularly in the context of enormous research literature output. Thus, the study explores the strength of attitude and its relationship with use behaviour in various contexts. It also goes into the relations of attitude towards information (ATI) with the personal and psychological attributes. The study is explorative in nature, as much research is not carried out on this topic.

1.2 Information User Studies

Information user studies over the years have attempted to explain the information use phenomena, to understand information use bahaviour, to predict this bahaviour, to control and improve the information use by manipulating essential conditions. One of the preliminaries to the attainment of this objective is the description of user behaviour in many aspects (Ford, 1977).

Information seeking behaviour results from the recognition of some need experienced by the user. That behaviour may take several forms, e.g. user may make the demands upon formal systems (libraries) or upon systems which may perform information functions in addition to a primary non-information function. Alternatively the user may seek information from other people. In this context user studies do not aim to pattern information seeking behaviour, but to draw interrelationships among concepts used in the field.

The data gathered in a user study may be categorised as demographic data, behaviour data and knowledge data. Of these, information seeking behaviour — including user needs, information availability, user preference etc., — is the central category of user analysis. Several doubts have been expressed about the ability of the users to express the needs as opposed to information requirements (Rees, 1963; Menzel, 1964; Line, 1969) and others have noted that the users may be in no position to specify complexity of their information requirements. It is argued by these writers that the user is able to give a rough guide to types and sources of information that he uses for research, but even here he often comes up with vague generalisations and is unable to relate the details of his information searches and information uses.

Despite the doubts expressed regarding the users' ability to convey their needs investigations concerning user needs have been pursued for their practical value. Paisley (1968) has pointed out that the earliest studies of information needs and uses took place within libraries, information centres and laboratories because librarians and administrators needed data for service decisions. Later many studies were sponsored by professional associations such as American Psychological Associations, American Institute of Physics, for the learned associations in general were examining their information programmes in the light of information explosion and the new technology. Thus, the vast majority of user studies in science and technology fall into one of the following categories: study of information requirements of a particular discipline like physics, chemistry, etc., or the ones limited to a particular research establishment or industry where they cut across subject boundaries.

Bernel (1959) stressing on the value of research on user communication behaviour senses a danger, and necessarily a growing one, of the scientific information developing as an activity entirely in its own right, even more and more competent to take in, store and hand out information regardless of whether it is superfluous, inaccurate and unwanted. In this context, it is important to ask not only how the information is to be dealt with but also what the information is, whom it is intended for and to what degree does the process of transmission of information help in the advancement of knowledge.

Meadows (1974), referring to major approaches used in these studies, opines that the basic intention in each case is to estimate as qualitatively as possible the relative importance of the various communication channels for the group under examination.

In recent times the studies aim to give a theoretical backing to the process of information use in a research context. This process can be fulfilled only with a vast amount of data so that a clear demarcation of a 'dynamic scientific information uscr' (Garvey *et al.,* 1974) or an understanding about 'information man', on the analogy of 'economic man', can be arrived at (Roberts, 1982).

1.2.1 *User Studies and the Nature of their Data*

User studies have a history going back to more than four decades. Two studies reported by Bernel (1948) and Urquhart (1948) are among the earliest examples of user studies, making what is generally regarded as the beginning of the research on user communication behaviour. Over the years the research on user behaviour has produced data on many aspects. Among the individual studies, on the more extensive side in coverage, is one conducted by Lin *et al* (1970), who, concentrating on the information generation and output behaviour, have explored as many as 37 personnel and situational variables in the biomedical field which included level of training, nature of work, workstyle, urgency, worksetting, reward/control system, peer communication, etc.

Line (1969) enumerates 15 characteristics that may influence information requirements and on which data need to be collected. They include age, experience in research, background, qualification, seniority, solitary or teamworker, persistence, thoroughness, orderliness, motivation, independence, willingness to accept help from others, breadth of approach, rate of absorption, awareness of sources, awareness of non-literary media of communication and storage and languages understood. Bourne (1962) has enumerated the possible variables as the search time and the amount of irrelevant material that can be tolerated, time available for searching, preferred form of search output, users input channel capacity, work habits, terminological idiosyncrasies etc.

The data collected in user studies in the past fall principally in the following categories:

Pattern of exposure to information sources, including studies in exposure to different sources are initiated chiefly to guide in the management of particular service and to facilitate the solution of local information problem. As such data do not give the understanding about motives of use, they contribute little to information exchange behaviour.

Preferences for and evaluation of information sources.

Prevalence of certain information skills and practices including facility in languages, maintenance and organization of personal files, the delegation of information gathering activities to assistants, library use and requests made to information centres etc. These data reveal idiosyncracies that characterise the researcher's use of information services and media. They also supply clues to the amount of indifference or resistance that must be overcome in effecting modifications or introducing new services.

The functions information perform for effective modifications of communication media (Menzel, 1960). Six categories of information functions are recognised (Herner, 1962) which include conceptual, empirical, procedural, simulation, policy and directive. American Psychological Association (APA) (Garvey and Compton, 1967) conducted various studies involving informal and formal media and on the basis of the results they experimented with the modification of certain media so that they would complement one another in the more effective performance of specific functions.

Impact of information on performance explored by Urquhart (1948) and Menzel (1958) in their studies in which they describe a number of instances wherein information was received too late to prevent losses of time or money or needless duplication. Such studies have been relatively few in the recent years.

And lastly, the emphasis on flow of information from generator to user. In the early 1960s APA studies (Garvey and Griffith, 1966) concentrated on this aspect of communication. In biomedical field, Orr (1961) has reported metabolism of information — defined as digestion, absorption and assimilation into the scientific community.

Studies have now extended to include theoretical aspects for purposes of model building and to visualise the typologies of dynamic information users and various situational and other attributes going along with that.

1.2.2 *User Study Methods*

Various methods adopted for the study of information use behaviour largely include survey methods used in social sciences, such as questionnaire, interview, participant observation and also experiments in field settings. Diary keeping by the researchers is also used extensively by the researchers in user behaviour. Connections among documents, rather than people, have been studied by citation analysis. A few studies have also tried participatory research, computer content analysis etc.

Most frequently used method is that of questionnaire. Paisley (1965) speaks of questionnaire as a compromise technique expedient to use when the sample is widely spread, but subject to such shortcomings as low response, respondents' understanding and interpretation of the questions and inability to clarify incomplete responses. Even with these drawbacks the self-administered questionnaire technique is more sounder with a high level of response for typical behaviour measurement.

1.2.3 *Trends in User Studies*

More than thirty years of research on scientific communication behaviour and hundreds of studies have produced relatively few findings that can be regarded as well established or generally accepted. One definite trend that is, however, discerned is towards comprehensive description of all facets of scientific communication in particular disciplines. In biomedical fields, Orr *et al* (1964) made an extensive study of scientific communication. APA project of scientific information exchange in psychology employed a variety of methods and approaches to develop a comprehensive picture of the flow of information in psychology and of the characteristics of all the major media used to acquire and disseminate information in the field. John Hopkins Centre for Research in Scientific Communication (Compton, 1973) has also produced, through surveys, comprehensive data in several major disciplines, such as physics for instance. INFROSS study of Bath University (Line *et al*., 1971) has through an extensive questionnaire survey filled up a gap in the understanding of user behaviour in the social sciences.

Another major trend is the growing awareness of the social character and social organisation of scientific communication as reflected in the studies of invisible college (Price and Beaver, 1966; Parker and Paisley, 1966; Garvey and Griffith, 1963, 1965). Since the information generators are also among the principal users, the system continuously feeds back on itself. With the adoption of systems approach to the study of scientific communications, interrelations and interdependence of various methods of communication systems have received increased attention. Current data on invisiblc college, 'information men', work teams and interpersonal communication networks show that informal person to person interactions play a vital part in scientific communication.

Another trend in the communication research is defining the role of the scientific meeting and enhancing its effectiveness as a means of information exchange. APA project is an intensive effort in this direction. This study dealt with meeting participants who were seeking specific information through their attendance, their success in obtaining it, the nature of information they sought or received and the factors affecting the value of meeting. John Hopkins Centre for Research in Scientific Communication (Compton, 1965) has also made large scale efforts to compare and contrast the effectiveness of annual meetings in various disciplines. The study reveals the effectiveness of meeting for each participating scientific group.

More recently, in social sciences, the studics have focused on practitioners such as clinical psychologists, social workers, policy-makers, administrators etc. As a part of the Bath University study, several services were produced to understand the needs of the social workers. Information Needs and Information Service in Local Authority Social Services Department Project (INISS) (Streatfield *et al.*, 1981) explored the information use generation in which it parted away from the custodial model of self prescription to the users prescription of their problem, Experimental Information Service in two Social Welfare Agencies (EISSWA) (Blake *et al.*, 1979) involves the practitioners themselves in the research process.

Wilson *et al* (1982) observe that the early models of user studies were more concerned with document seeking or library use than with the characteristics of behaviour which might usefully discriminate among information users and provide guidance to service planning. The produce of work under this model was a more complete description of the use made of library system and documents of various types. In the second phase of research in this area studies have sought to use models based on the information user as an organizational member and as a performer of different kinds of tasks, with different kinds of demands and so having different information requirements. The more recent studies, particularly those conducted in the organizational environment as a part of INISS etc., have explored the fundamental categories of human needs which, influenced by various environmental and role variables, act as motivation towards information seeking behaviour. It is now clear that only through more complex analysis of information seeking behaviour within an organizational and behavioural science framework can any real understanding of the user be had which leads to genuinely applicable results for information systems and services.

Wilson (1981) also recognises the necessity of identifying the ends served by the information seeking behaviour within the wider context of users totality of experiences or 'users life world' centred upon the individual as an information user. Within their 'life world' are world of work and various reference groups with which the user identifies, such as peer group, fellow professionals etc. He feels much of the user studies in the past have suffered from a concentration on the means by which people discover information, analysed in terms of how the users ought to have been seeking information.

1.3 User Studies in Social Sciences

The communication system associated with physical and social science is composed of essentially similar elements, but differ with respect to their operations and use. The flow of information is affected by time lags and filtering which differ according to the discipline so that the scientists behave differently to compensate them. Communication in social sciences is in early stages of development compared to that in the physical sciences. Thus, the system is more random. Studies (Garvey *et al.,* 1970; Skelton, 1971) have indicated lags in the communication as largest in social sciences (15 months) and dissemination process in the social sciences takes 80 per cent longer than in physical sciences. Further, sequential organization of events follow a much perfect pattern for physical scientists compared with their counterparts in social sciences. This calls for the understanding of social science communication against the background of the structure of communication and knowledge in social sciences.

1.3.1 *Structure of Communication and Knowledge in Social Sciences*

In social sciences there is less agreement about the way in which progress in made – the relative importance of communication channels, information requirements and so forth. It is difficult to show that social science progress by a series of building blocks where each generation builds upon achievements of the previous one. There is no general consensus about subject matter, procedures, methods and interpretation of data. The following characteristics of research and theory building are common in many areas of the social sciences (Brittain, 1979; Hogeweg-De Haart, 1983).

Theories about human behaviour, society, economy etc., are put forward by the social scientists, sometimes they are related to previous theories, sometimes not.

Many theories are not stated in a way that allow them to be verified.

Many social scientists pay only lip service to one of the classical methods of science, hypothetico-deductive method. As a result rival schools of thought flourish in social sciences.

Many theories, because of lack of consensus and problems of verification, are no more than theoretical points of view.

More because of these factors the orientation of the social scientists to bibliographic sources has to be much different from their counterparts in physical sciences. Guttsman (1966) commenting on the methods employed in social sciences namely, observation (including fact findings) and experimental, historical or comparative and philosophical or speculative – observes that only the first method is at all comparable to the types of investigation which are typical of the natural sciences, in the sense that there can be an element of the lab situation present. The second and third methods insofar as they are not entirely cognitive, use literature sources in the widest sense as the raw materials for the investigation itself. Whether the reading and the use of information contained in books and other materials is selective or whether data are systematically collected or used in an experimental way, the need to consult material is prolonged and often repetitive. Due to lack of concensus and problems of verification there is not one general body of information on various issues that is accepted by everybody. Information services in social sciences have to take into consideration the above factors and accordingly adjust their services to suit the structure of knowledge and the resultant communication pattern.

1.3.2 *Information needs of Social Scientists*

Very little is known about the information needs of social scientists compared to that of physical scientists. Nearly three decades back Paisley (1965) made the first attempt to review user studies in social sciences when he considered the literature on flow of behavioural science information. He concluded that there is no literature to review.

Uytterschaut (1966), in a study directed towards the methods used by social science researchers in searching the literature, has aimed to find out if researchers went about literature searching according to some general and uniform programme and to assess the researchers' attitude towards assistance from documentalists. Though the study was a novel one at that time, the sample studied constituted only twenty researchers in law and economics. Nonetheless, the study observes the different information seeking behaviours in central and peripheral areas. In peripheral areas the respondents were predisposed at the very beginning to contact experts. Another finding is that experienced researchers were certain of their ground and avoided redundancy at the outset. Respondents did not think in terms of sophisticated documentation and information centres.

By far the most thorough and extensive investigation of the information requirements of a social science discipline is that of American Psychological Association. This project was intended to encompass the full spectrum of communication. The fundamental approach adopted was that of viewing scientific communication as a large social system compounding on a variety of formal elements (e.g. journals) and informal elements (e.g. preprint exchange). The purpose of the study was to develop (a) a theory directed toward a process of decision as to what communication media are in need of innovation, the matter of effecting innovation in the system and the prediction of the affect of the innovation on the various elements in the overall system, and (b) a methodology for measuring the innovations throughout the entire system of dissemination (Griffith and Garvey, 1964; Garvey and Griffith, 1963, 1965).

The study programme was threefold:

Study of procedures and users of scientific information to provide data on dissemination pattern and user practices.

Study of informal exchange media – journals, books, abstracting and indexing services, technical reports and scientific meetings to establish the content conveyed, the extent and purpose of use and the role and interrelationship of these media in the scientific communication system.

The institution of innovations on an experimental trial basis and testing and follow up of such efforts.

The first two sets of studies made possible a map of the communication system for psychology. The studies further showed how elements in the system complemented one another and established the time intervals in the dissemination process. This map of system operation also revealed the points at which innovation can be introduced and would be likely to encounter resistance. The data derived from these studies gave a picture of the dissemination process of the 'average' research report appearing in a core psychological journal in the early 1960s. The outstanding characteristics of the picture were: (a) the small number of widely accessible media carrying relatively old information, and (b) the multiplicity of media serving restricted and typically small audience and carrying up to date information on recently completed or ongoing work.

Two innovations, viz., listing of articles accepted for publication in five APA journals published with considerable time lag and convention papers, were developed. These were viewed as social innovations in that they were imposed on a complex social system, i.e., scientific communication in psychology and that their effects are measured in terms of the changes in the communication behaviour which occurred within this system.

The study also revealed a number of functions of the informal system that could be fulfilled at less cost, by new and formal system. It identified a positive relationship between productivity and possession of a doctoral degree and noted that age had little to do with productivity. At the highest level of productivity, research was ranked as the first or second most information demanding activity. Research, research guidance and writing and editing increased in time consumption and information demands, as productivity increased. Applied and clinical activities plus administrative work and graduate study decreased as the measures of productivity increased. Journal use, meeting attendance and use of information contacts all increased as productivity level increased.

APA studies also included the information requirements of

university teachers. Data from 246 universities and colleges of U.S.A. revealed that teaching was regarded as a very time consuming activity and it was seen, by slightly less than half of the respondents, as the most information demanding activity (Garvey and Griffity, 1963, 1964a, 1964b, 1965a, 1965b).

Another major study in the area of social sciences, in the wake of Paisley's (1965) observation about the absence of user studies in social sciences, is an Investigation in to Information Requirements of Social Sciences (INFROSS) conducted in U.K. in 1969-71 (Line *et al.*, 1971c). This study commonly referred to as INFROSS has a wider canvas and covered several disciplines including anthropology, economics, education, politics, psychology and sociology. The study went on to consider the difficult problems of information needs, as opposed to information demands or information uses.

In the absence of any full scale survey of social science information problems INFROSS was designed to provide an aerial view of social sciences to see how far existing information systems and services meet the empirically determined requirements, and to make a preliminary formulation of the design requirements which future information system should satisfy. The sample for the study consisted of two in every seven identifiable researchers in U.K., which was about 2500, including researchers from universities, practitioners in industry, social work and government. The questionnaire survey was followed up by interview and observation of a small number of respondents.

This study among other things examined whether the basic pattern of information need is discipline-oriented or environment-oriented? Are there any patterns and trends detectable which could be associated with age, suggesting that the pattern of use and need was changing or likely to change in the near future? Did users certain blockages or preferences which should be taken into account in designing information systems? What particular aspects of the formal systems did they find difficult? What would happen if one created more abstracting journals? Would they be used as well or in preferences to existing ones, or not at all? Should abstracting journals aim to be general or comprehensive or specialised or smaller in size? and what information do social science researchers require for what they are doing?, in what form? With what speed of delivery? etc.

The study revealed that social scientists are still print-oriented, books and periodicals are used all types of need. The results included the following:

Twenty-five per cent of the respondents had never used abstracts or indexes, library catalogues, book reviews of searched on library shelves, 48% never consulted librarians.

Following up references in books and periodicals was found useful by 94% and 59% even rated this as the most useful method. Informal channels were quite commonly used for locating relevant references as well as for keeping abreast of new publications and for keeping up with current research.

Hard social sciences (Psychology, Geography) showed to be akin to physical sciences in abstract and index use with 63% of the psychologists and 95% of the Geographers using it.

Delegation of searching was rare, only 7% delegated extensively. Users involved in applied or experimental research were more willing to delegate than those who wanted theoretical or conceptual material.

The older, more senior and experienced researchers used fewer libraries. Library stacks tended to be adequate for teaching needs than research needs. Most common information problem was that of physical access to and availability of information published or unpublished.

Line (1971a) observes that social scientist as an information user is at a point along the continuum from hard to soft social sciences. The hard social sciences exhibit a number of characteristics that have been found in physical science studies and is distinguishable in a number of ways from the 'softer' social sciences.

The main conclusions that emerged from the experimental information service that was set up at Bath University in the framework of the INFROSS study were, that academic social scientists are not highly motivated to search for references, nor well equipped in the means of doing so. Library catalogues are little used. Most formal information comes through reading primary journals and press and publishers notices of books. Much information is converged through informal channels of various kinds. Personal files are organised in highly individualised ways (Bath University, 1972). This is also confirmed by Strenstrom and McBride (1979) in a later survey of serial use by a social science faculty, in which the faculty relied heavily (50-70%) on bibliographies and footnotes in journals and books to find references. They used the library as a supplementary source.

A sociometric study (Arndt, 1980) at University of Applied European Educators and Researchers in Marketing, explored with a structured questionnaire the motivations for social interactions particularly through informal channels such as exchange of working papers and discussing with colleagues at convention. Based on the Homains theory of social exchange (essence of which is that social interaction tends to be purposeful and motivated, including both of material goods and information as well as approval) the study establishes the relations of information exchange with geographical distance, cultural distance and the relative position of the scientists in professional ladder, i.e., scientists low in status are more likely to seek information from high status scientists and high status scientists are particularly active in information exchange.

Clark (1979) tests a theory of middle range concerning the variables influencing information seeking behaviour on a sample of psychologists and sociologists in applied and teaching capacities. The study reveals that high pressure to use literature, both self and role induced, will be associated with a high use of information, high level of users of information evaluate it more positively, be more open to it and make a greater effort to keep up with it.

A comprehensive investigation on the use of social science information by policy-makers was executed by Caplan (1975) at the University of Michigan. The study on the nature and degree of social science information utilization in decision-making among upper level government officials showed a high level of interest in and receptivity to social science information reports in policy level decisions, but little evidence that such information, either directly or indirectly, enters into decision-making activity. Studies to assess the information needs of town planners (White, 1969) and policy-makers (Lazarsfeld and Reitz, 1975) have also added to the understanding of the information needs of the practitioners.

Another significant research particularly in the context of developing countries has been carried out by Aiyepeku (1980). This pioneering study of the processes of information dissemination to and its utilization by policy-makers in Nigeria explores how the particular research for policy-making was initiated and conducted, how the results were presented and what comes in the way in the use of the results. This study casts light on the conventional assumption about the extent of such research and the point that there was comparatively less awareness of the results. The study identifies a total of

270 information perception/utilisation variables and dynamics of their relationship as reported by 384 policy makers.

As a deviation from the focus of the above mentioned studies and initiation of psychological methods in users research, Summers *et al*., (1983) have examined the affective response to information. An attitude scale based on the "Taxonomy of educational objectives" was administered to a sample of 1078 respondents of public school teachers and administrators in Canada. The study reveals that attitude towards information is a powerful psychological construct which differentiated the professional and personal characteristics of educators performing various work roles and relate significantly to several facets including years of experience, education, frequency of the source use and dissemination in the information seeking behaviour of the teachers, consultants and administrators pursuing those work roles.

Summers *et al* (1983a) have also examined the information habits of the educational practitioners within interacting cognitive, emotional and social systems. The study reveals that position, dissemination and attitude towards information are strong predictors of information use; education is a moderate predictor and experience and isolation from information accounted for low percentage of variance. The findings of the study offer support for information source use by educators is the result of a complex set of interaction of personal, professional and psychological attributes of users and provide an useful beginning in understanding the dimensions influencing the use of information sources.

The main points that emerge out of this brief survey of major studies may be summarised as follows:

Investigation in social science information started in the early sixties with research into the flow of social science information. From the late sixties onwards the focus of interest shifted towards the information requirements and information seeking behaviour of social science researchers. These were followed by investigations and experiments on the social scientists in non-research environment and the need for information by non-social scientists. These investigations have shown that there is a considerable difference in information requirements and use of information among the three groups.

Until recently social science information services have been concentrating on the information requirements of researchers, who however do not use these services to a great extent, but prefer references in the books etc. and informal contacts for their literature searches. Though they rarely delegate their searches, there seems to be a need for personal intermediaries to show the way through the mass of information. A start has been made, though late, in the use of standardised psychological tests to measure the user behaviour so that in the longer run, precise and needed services could be generated based on the results of such studies.

1.4 User Studies in India

A handful of user studies have also been conducted in India. These are more often than not case studies of the use of individual libraries by the scientists or the general public. The pattern of the information obtained by the surveys can be ascertained by a few which are typical of its nature.

Rajagopalan and Rajan (1984) presenting an account of programmes and activities on user studies in India with emphasis on success and shortfalls try to deduce from the five laws of library science propounded by S.R. Ranganathan a conceptual framework for use and user studies. Though the authors claim the existence of a good body of literature supporting user studies at the level of individual libraries it has not been substantiated with the relevant citations.

An extensive analysis of the use of Sapru House Library which serves social science teachers and research scholars has been made by Krishna Kumar (1973). This study of 147 respondents provides data regarding the average number of days library was used and number of hours per day, order of priority of information sources (books, periodicals, press cuttings, dissertations, microfilms, maps) etc.

Of much wider scope is an analysis of the information of Indian Industry (Karki, 1982) based on the queries received by the industrial information service of publications and Information Directorate. Falling in this area are the studies by Singh (1981) on 'Information needs of engineering scientists' and Sudhakara Rao and Subramanyam (1981) on 'Information for small scale industry'. The former was conducted with the objective to prepare the foundation for active documentation in the field of engineering science in India and provide guidelines for librarians in day-to-day operations. The study, with a citation analysis of two engineering journals of India and questionnaire survey of 42 respondents, observes that 87 per cent of the information needs are satisfied by foreign journals and only over 12 per cent are met by Indian Journal. English, multilingual and German language journals satisfy 99 per cent of the needs. The latter study conducted with an elaborately drawn questionnaire identifies the role of information in small scale industry, their information activities, sources used, role of industrial associations and information centres and the specific information services required. Data collected from 51 respondents revealed that the information generated within the organization in day-to-day work is considered important. In addition the entrepreneurs depend on sources such as people engaging in similar type of business, different associations, consultants, research institutions and special libraries. They procure information which has immediate bearing on their activities. Topics such as marketing, product diversification and development and various government regulations where they need regular information small entrepreneurs are conscious of utilizing library information services available.

Pruthi and Nagpaul (1978, 1979) report the communication patterns in two research projects of a national laboratory examining the relationship of communication patterns of individuals' status in the organizational hierarchy, education level and social relations. They also try to identify technological gate keepers and the role of formal and informal communication in problem solving and idea generation.

One striking feature of the studies in India is the existence of a large number of theoretical and review type papers repeatedly stressing the need for user studies, quoting the findings of the studies conducted either in U.K. or U.S.A. and suggesting further research in the area without any data or observation of their own. Another conspicuous feature is the emphasis on bibliometric studies in general and citations studies in particular.

A review of library science literature published in past five years by Amba and Raghavan (1985) reveals that only 4.69% of the articles deals with user studies and a review of ongoing doctoral research shows that there is just one study each in communication and use/user studies. The journal 'Library Science with a Slant to Documentation' has published more than 25 papers on information user studies. But a large majority of these papers do not deal with information behaviour despite some of the using the term.

By and large we have to subscribe to the observation of Singh (1979) about the non-availability of users studies in India, and those that are available lack in depth and innovative methodology resulting in hackneyed conclusions. There are, nonetheless, a few exceptions as mentioned above.

Most of the user studies have been conducted as a part of the masters degree requirement in various universities and as such they are relatively inaccessible and have narrower scope.

1.5 Drawbacks in User Studies and Need for Current Research

Thirty years of research on the information users have remained relatively unambitious, in that despite many studies there are no generally acceptable theoretical guidelines to make sense of the huge mass of the data accumulated. Brittain (1982) points out that the user studies have neglected potential users, information requirements assessed are of a more general nature, and few user studies have been concerned with the requirements of data or information as such. The research in this area is library and document-oriented and not user-oriented. They do not touch upon the users' ability to digest and appreciate the process of information generation and use. Results of the user studies, in short, have not accumulated to form a body of knowledge. He also observes (1970, p. 148) that user studies have neglected fundamental questions about the psychology of users.

Commenting on the methodology Brittain (1975) observes that questions in the study should reflect user priorities and not those of the enquirer. Questions that users are in a position to answer should be asked. He further points that relatively a few statistical tests of the significance to the findings have been applied with the result that only a very small proportion of the large amount of data that have appeared is worth reporting. Remarking that a point of saturation may have been reached with respect to collection of data about information requirements at a general level, he calls for methods which assist the user to formulate one's own information needs and providing indirect assessment of the needs.

Reviewers of the user studies have consistently observed a need for the behavioural science orientation to the users research. Parker and Paisley (1966), almost two decades back pointing the drawbacks in the user studies, have called for ways in which psychological research is essential to the accomplishment of the mission to provide an efficient flow of information to scientists. Information science mission, they opine, is to facilitate a peculiarly intellectual behaviour viz., research itself. Because of this essential difference an information system must be defined as a behavioural one. Psychological research is necessary to measure their skills and to instruct the designers and operators of information system. Psychological research is also necessary to test the behavioural assumptions of the system designers.

Marzocco (1975), reviewing on human dimensions of information need, observes that information science, no less than psychology, is a science of human behaviour, although it is more than that. He opines that learning, motivation, personality and other kinds of psychological variables affect all behaviour which needs to be explored.

Wilson (1981) feels that much of the user studies in the past have suffered from a concentration on the means by which people discover information and analysed in terms of researchers view of how the user aught to have been seeking information. He recognises the necessity of identifying the ends served by information seeking behaviour within the wider context of users totality of experiences or 'users life-world' centred upon individual as an information user. Within this 'life-world' are the world of work and various reference groups with which the user identified such as peer group, fellow professionals etc.

Atherton (1975) points out the needs for research in cognitive style and other personality variables of information seekers such as degree of motivation, attitudes, anxiety, frustration, need for reassurance and reward, work orientation and situational context such as time pressure, stimulus for obtaining information etc.

A few investigations have been carried out with a psychological orientation. Mick *et al* (1980), for instance, who have examined the information use by the scientists *vis-a-vis* a set of individual attributes, work environment attributes and task attributes conclude that environmental and situational constraints play a major role in determining information behaviour. This research also observes that variables studied provide one with the ability to design information services that conform to the attitudes and perception of the intended users.

Fine (1984) in her review – Research and the psychology of information use – observes that one of the broad questions concern the way in which people interact with information and under what environmental and psychological circumstances. She also states that there are studies, for example, of attitudes i.e., attitudes towards library services, tools and procedures. But the studies, she observes, treat attitude simplistically as though it is simply a like-dislike response.

More urgent is the need to examine the information traits assumed of the users. Roberts (1982) observes that user studies have been expecting characteristics such as:

Indulging in rational information acts i.e., possessing a knowledge of available information sources, allowing a selection of 'best' source for a specific purpose; accepting and applying information so that best decisions result, and living in a world shaped by the need to generate, obtain and use information, no other form of activity capable of influencing information behaviour is allowed to interlude.

He observes that such assumptions do not seem to take into account the individual variations in the information use behaviour and also narrow visualisation about information environments and information use dominate research design. Stability in information behaviour is postulated, motives for the use of information sources are rarely explored, causal factors are rarely handled with same rigour as measurable data. Admitting that the role of 'information man' is yet to be clearly established, he feels that human individuality has to be taken into account in research in this area of study.

Wersig and Wendel (1985), qualifying the above observations made by Robert, express that social, economic and cultural factors and also status, prestige, group dynamics also influence ongoing behaviour. They propose for a more complicated model of information action which includes individual, collective and process approaches, personal conditions and psychological factors, such as traits, values, motives, attitudes etc., and group dynamics like status of job, organizational necessities etc. However, information is not sought in all instances for more action. This is specially so for academicians who do not necessarily aim to solve a problem. It is more a questioning, reassessment and persuasion requiring a wider reading and awareness.

An investigation into the attitudes of the users towards information use would reveal how far the users are psychologically favourable to the process of information source use. As attitude is a predisposition or readiness towards a certain course of action, examination of various factors including personal and psychological attributes which are related to favourable attitude towards information would facilitate in better understanding of information behaviour of the users. In fact, studies dealing with the psychological constructs of the users *vis-a-vis* information source use with a well defined methodology, has been observed to be the direction in which user studies have to develop (Brittain, 1979).

The study of attitude towards information gains additional importance in the context of social sciences. As has been rightly observed by Brittain (195) nearly all social scientists exhibit some resistance to the use of conventional library and information tools in the social sciences. In addition, it was also found that they are ignorant of specialist information tools of potential value. Despite the increased user awareness education in 1970s, social scientists for the most part remain unsystematic and irregular in their use of bibliographic tools and other information services. It has also been noted that in 1960s and 1970s some information providers suggested that social science researchers and academics ought to make better use of existing network of services. These suggestions have met with very little success. Social science researchers/academics on the one hand and social science practitioners on the other continue to demonstrate a great deal of resistance to the use of conventional bibliographical and library services, and indeed in many instances the use of primary literature. Recognising the importance of changes in the attitude towards information and information services has in a way become imperative for understanding of the information use behaviour. This has been explicitly noted by Brittain (1982) in conclusions of a report to UNESCO concerning supply and demand of documentation and data in social sciences.

Thus, the observation of several of the reviewers, viz., the need for research with an orientation to users rather than the sources of information gains sufficient substantiation. The present investigation makes an attempt to enquire into information use aspect with the users as its main focus.

The study has a psychological orientation, in that it attempts to measure the attitude of the social scientists towards information. A favourable disposition to information is an important user trait assumed of the researchers and teachers alike. The present investigation attempts to throw more and better light on this aspect by empirically measuring the magnitude of the attitude.

The study also examines the relation of attitude towards information with various personal and psychological attributes of the social scientists, which gives an understanding of the factors that could possibly lead to the favourable attitude towards information use.

Information source use behaviour is also viewed in the context of this study from a new angle, in that it explores the relations of information source use with attitude towards information and how far the attitude-behaviour relations are conditional to other personal and psychological attributes of the social scientists.

Thus, the study acts as a fillip insofar as it explores the affective dimensions of the users as to the information use and the other factors which are not hitherto extensively considered in the context of user studies. With this understanding of the problem the following objectives are set-forth for investigation.

1.6 Objectives of the Study

To measure the attitude (ATI) of the social scientists towards information;

To know the extent of information source use of the social scientists;

To examine the extent to which ATI is related to overt behaviour in terms of information source use;

To study the nature of relationship of ATI with selected personal and psychological attributes, and also the job environment with which the social scientists are affiliated, taken individually and in meaningful combinations;

To understand the effect of variations in the level of personal, psychological attributes and the job environment on the ATI and source use relations. The research also has the objective of examining the constraints experienced in the information source use.

1.7 Scope

With the above said objectives in mind the study investigates variables such as:

Attitudes Towards Information (ATI);
Information Source Use;
Motivation;
Job satisfaction;
Dedication to job;
Level of aspiration;

Educational attainment;
Professional experience;
Position;
Constraints in information use; and
Institutional affiliation.

Data are also collected on the subject specialisation, current research activities and also use of various library services.

As the data are collected through self-administered questionnaire, to a certain extent they share the inherent limitations of the data collection tool. The respondents for the study are with different institutional affiliation observations of their information behaviour, either participative or otherwise, is not feasible. The scale for the measure of psychological attributes such as motivation, job satisfaction and dedication to job are largely borrowed from the scientific productivity studies conducted elsewhere. Due to relative absence of research on this topic the study is an explorative one.

1.8 Hypotheses

The study proposed to examine the following hypotheses:

1. Attitude towards information has positive relations with information source use.
2. Situational factors including psychological and personal attributes and also environments have a modifying/facilitating effect on ATI and information source use relations. That is, higher job satisfaction, motivation, dedication to work, level of aspiration and also personal attributes like higher educational attainment, professional experience, position in the hierarchy have a facilitating effect on the ATI and information source use relations. So also, the relations of ATI and source use tend to be modified by the different job environments.
3. ATI tends to differ for social scientists in two job environments viz., University Post-graduate departments and those in Research and Training Institutes.
4. Various personal and psychological attributes have a positive effect on ATI. That is, job satisfaction, motivation, dedication, level of aspiration and also higher educational attainment, professional experience and position in the hierarchy tends to

be positively related to the ATI.

5. Personal and psychological attributes show varying effect on ATI in two different job environments or interaction effect of the job environment and personal and psychological attributes taken individually tends to be significant on ATI. That is, trend of relationship of job satisfaction, motivation, dedication, level of aspiration and educational attainment, experience, position in the hierarchy tends to be different in two job environments.
6. Psychological attributes show significantly varying effect on ATI when considered together with one of the personal attributes or the interaction of psychological and personal attributes on ATI is significant. That is,

   (a) The trend of relationship of job satisfaction and ATI is different for experience and position groups and also for those with different educational attainment.
   (b) The trend of relationship of motivation and ATI is different for position, experience and education groups.
   (c) The trend of relationship of dedication and ATI is different for position, experience and education groups.
   (d) The trend of relationship of level of aspiration and ATI is different for position, experience and education groups.

7. Constraints in the information use hinder the use of information sources and also constraints affect the ATI and source use relations.

In Chapter 2 an attempt has been made for the detailed description of thc concepts used in the study and the related research conclusions to support the hypotheses formulated.

2

CONCEPTS USED IN THE STUDY

It has been noted in the previous chapter that information acquisition is an essential component in the research and teaching work. Various bibliographic and non-bibliographic sources of information are expected to be put to intense use in that process. In the present context the attitudinal disposition of social scientists towards information, that is, The users readiness to make use of available information are examined. the following sections give a description of the concepts used in the study and a brief review of available researches to substantiate the assumptions made therein.

2.1 Attitude

There are many definitions of attitude. These definitions vary in the relative emphasis they lay on the different features of attitude like preparation, adjustment, cognition, affection and action tendency. However, all of them rest on the pre-supposition that attitudes are learned through experience and that they are always acquired in specific socio-cultural context.

Initial use of the term attitude in psychology was in the field of experimental psychology while interpreting the subject's reaction to physical stimuli. More particularly attitude was conceived as readiness to discriminate or respond in a manner to a given set of stimuli.

In 1918 Thomas and Znaniecki gave a central and prominent position to attitudes in the study of social psychology. They recognised attitudes as individual mental processes which determine both the actual and potential responses of each person in the social world. Since then attitude has been the focus of many studies in the area of social psychology. Prominent researchers have viewed the concept attaching varying degrees of importance to its components.

Thurstone and Chave (1929) define attitude as a generalised reaction for or against a specific psychological object. The object may be a person or a group, a king of objects or living things, concepts or values, events or situation, institutions or systems.

According to Allport (1967) attitude is a mental or neural state of readiness, organised through experience, exerting a directive or dynamic influence upon the individual's response to all objects and situation with which it is related.

Newcomb (1952) views the individual's attitude towards something as his predisposition to perform, perceive, think and feel in relation to it.

According to Drever (1956) attitude is more or less stable set of disposition of opinion, interest or purpose, involving expectancy or a certain kind of experience and readiness with an appropriate response.

Kretch *et al* (1962) argue that man's social actions are directed by his attitudes. Attitudes are enduring systems of positive or negative evaluations, emotional feelings and pro and con action tendencies with respect to a psychological object. An attitude is a relatively stable organization of beliefs around an object or situation predisposing one to respond in some preferential manner.

Despite several definitions of attitude, limiting its scope and content by various researchers several common elements in all these views are noticeable. They are:

Attitude is a learned predisposition,

It is a hypothetical construct or an implicit response, not directly open to observation, but inferred from verbal expression,

It is anticipatory and mediating with reference to patterns of overt responses,

It is evoked by a variety of stimulus patterns as a result of previous learning,

Attitude is drive producing, and

Attitude towards an object is important for the individual as it describes, evaluates and advocates action.

Thus, attitude is not an immediate observable variable, but a latent one. It has been confirmed by several researchers like, Sherif and Sherif (1956), Newcombe *et al* (1965), Campbell (1950), Kretch and Crutchfield (1948) that attitudes are relatively stable and enduring sets formed by past experience. This stability comes through (a) interrelatedness of the attitudes, (b) reinforcement in the learning of attitude and an active resistance to change when confronted with actual thwarting of motives.

Attitudes are not innate but are the results of the amount of direct experience an individual has had with the attitude object. In addition, attitude reactions are evaluative and affective and give rise to motivation. Motives interact with the situation and determine the outer behaviour of an organism. An attitude does not refer to any specific response, but is an abstraction of a large number of responses of an individual. The attitudes are aroused by some drive state which is reflected in some goal orientation of the frustrated or satisfied individual.

2.1.1 *Components of Attitude*

Virtually all theorists agree that an attitude is not a basic irreducible element within the personality but represents a cluster or syndrome of certain interrelated elements. These elements are basically beliefs or cognitions.

The content of a belief may describe an object or situation as true or false; evaluate it as good or bad; or advocate a certain course of action as desirable or undesirable, or to do all these three together. All beliefs are predispositions to action; and an attitude is thus a set of inter-related predispositions to action organised around an object or situation.

Each belief within the larger whole of those beliefs is conceived to have three components, viz., cognitive, affective and conative. Cognitive component refers to the individual's knowledge of the attitude with varying degree of certitude about what is true or false, desirable or undesirable. Affective or feeling component is central to the attitude, because under suitable conditions the belief is capable of arousing feeling of varying intensity around the object of belief or other objects taking a positive or negative position with respect to the object of belief. It is also this emotional loading which gives attitude their insistent, stirred up, motivating character. Behavioural component includes all the behavioural readiness associated with the attitude. If an individual holds a favourable attitude towards a given object he will be disposed to support the object, act favourably towards it. Thus, if one has a favourable attitude towards information one will have a tendency to seek it out either through frequent use of bibliographic sources of the non-bibliographic ones.

However, these components are not uniformly organised in the same degree in all the individuals. They vary in their ambivalence, intensity and other characteristics that have been identified by the theorists.

Attitude is conventionally conceptualised as a single bipolar attribute with 'positive' and 'negative' or 'favourable' and 'unfavourable' directions or sides, meaning thereby that it would not be found simultaneously at both ends of the dimension, though like 'love-hate relationships' in common parlour, a unified structure and compromised position of positive and negative thoughts and feelings would be possible. A variety of such positional combinations along the continuum from extreme positive to extreme negative positions lead to the concept of a 'neutral attitude' falling in the middle range. The presence of both 'favourable' and 'unfavourable' elements relating to the different features of the same total object in the composite attitude is its ambivalence. Intensity of attitude refers to the strength of feeling.

2.1.2 *Characteristics of Attitude*

Kretch and Crutchfield (1948) group the characteristics of attitude into four categories viz., those referring to the nature of the objects involved; referring to the nature of cognitive structure; referring to the strength and importance of the attitude; and referring to the characteristics of verifiability.

Attitudes differ in kind and content, they are, in fact, as varied in kind as the objects of one's psychological world. As far as the structure of the attitude is concerned, they differ in precision like some of the perceptions are clear, explicit, highly differentiated and others are vague and poorly structured. Not only attitudes vary in their clarity and degree of detail and differentiation within the single belief structure, but they differ in their specificity, i.e. in the sense of being isolated, non-generalised or not connected with other beliefs and attitudes. Although all attitudes have functional utility for the individual, they do not have equal significance. Accordingly strength of the attitude changes from person to person regarding the same object.

2.1.3 *Determinants of Attitude*

Attitudes of an individual on various objects and situations differ in their magnitude because of many reasons. An extensive array of attitude determinants have been explored. Yet a comprehensive attitude theory explaining all such determinants have not been accepted by the researchers in the field. From well over thirty distinct theoretical formulations some significant ones have been identified by the reviewers. All these have in common the view that attitudes can be represented as an evaluative disposition falling somewhere on pro-and-anti continuum. They differ, however, in the extent to which supplementary features are integral to the hypothetical construct. Ostrom (1984) summarises these theories as follows:

The undifferentiated view defines attitude as being nothing more or less than an evaluative disposition i.e., past experience, information and influences, reinforcements and motivational pressures – all contribute to the attitude at the same time they occur. The resulting attitude is the cumulative accretion of those past events. Frequent direct contact with the object and the environment that programme for the person as to what stimuli he receives, what response possibilities are available, and what rewards and punishments are administered to him are the other important determinants of attitude towards the object.

The second category of theories view attitude as the set of beliefs the person holds about the attitude object. In this case the basic elements of an attitude are the individual beliefs or cognitions. The evaluative disposition is but one of the several attributes that characterise the attitude. The evaluative disposition is the result of all those beliefs that are salient at the time the observed response is initiated. According to this view there is no single 'true' evaluative disposition, but only an average that emerges over a variety of responses.

A third point of view refers to the set of motivational forces operating on the person that are relevant to the attitude object. The basic elements consist of the values, needs, drives, motives and personality disposition of the person. Typically this set contains only the more enduring rather than situationally determined motivational dispositions. This view is sometimes referred to as functional approach since attitudes are seen as functionally satisfying the person's more basic motivational needs. While many attitudes are predominant in the service of a single type of motivational process, some may also serve more than one function.

2.1.4 *Attitude Functions*

A wide variety of attitude relevant functions has been identified (Katz, 1960). Attitude can serve as an instrumentality function, in which they are used to obtain rewards and avoid punishments. Perception of the past and present utility of the object by the individual leads to the formation of attitudes. Attitudes can serve as a knowledge function, helping one to deal effectively with the complex and over-whelming flow of information encountered in life. The most important aspect of this function is that it serves the need for cognitive organization and brings consistency and clarity in one's belief system. Attitudes can serve as value maintenance function. An individual derives satisfaction from expressing attitudes appropriate to his personal values and to his concept of himself. Attitudes also provide ego defence, in which the person protects himself from acknowledging the basic truth about himself.

The evaluative characteristics of attitude operates in the service of these motives; positive attitudes emerge only if basic motivational needs are satisfied. Attitude towards information may also be viewed in terms of the functions it serves. It particularly relates to the utility one perceives of the information acquisition activity and the rewards that can be enjoyed in its acquisition.

Thus, attitudes develop through situation and experiences involving the psychological objects concerned that serve to construct various images and concepts, feelings and emotions and behaviour patterns, physical and social contacts and interactions result in the establishment of cognitive structures, conscious and involuntary adjustments and reaction tendencies.

The relevant belief, feelings and response tendencies packed up in an individual constitute his attitude towards a particular object. As the individual acquires more and more stable attitudes his improvisations, fresh examinations and interpretations decrease. His actions and reactions tend to became stereotyped, predictable and consistent.

The group affiliation of the individual play a vital role in the formation of his attitudes. Members of the groups with which the individual affiliates himself and the non-membership groups to which he aspires to belong are important in shaping his attitudes. But the individual does not passively absorb the prevailing or dominant attitudes in the various groups to which he is affiliated. Attitudes develop selectively in the process of need satisfaction. The individual will pick and choose from among the attitudes offered to him those which are want satisfying and those which are more or less consistent with his cognitive structure and affective constellation.

It has been observed, that most researchers in the area of attitude theory are content with the unelaborate assertion that an attitude will have a directive influence on the observed response. However, there have been efforts to explain how attitudes affect behaviour.

2.1.5 *Attitude and Behaviour*

The presence of action tendency and the conceptualisation of motivational and drive producing element in the attitude has made the social scientists to consistently assume that attitudes could be used to explain human action. Most of the theorists have agreed that attitude is drive producing and it is anticipatory and mediating with reference to patterns of overt responses.

Kretch and Crutchfield (1948) feel that behaviour is a function not only of the immediately present stimuli and their momentary perceptions, but of more enduring dispositions. It is therefore more profitable and more realistic to work with a higher order of psychological unit. There are the enduring organizations of perceptual, motivational and emotional factors known as attitudes.

It is traditionally assumed that attitudes and behaviours are closely related in natural settings. The most fertile ground for evidence suggesting consistent relation is found in studies using the "known group method" for validating attitude scales, wherein groups which are known to have extreme attitude also show an extreme attitude score and it results in the behaviour.

From time to time, however, investigators tried to test the assumption that attitudes serve as behavioural predispositions. The first of these studies was Lapiere's (1934) investigation of social prejudice. Contradictory findings of the study raised doubts about the assumption of the strong relation between attitude and behaviour.

Despite these findings, theorists such as Katz and Stotland (1959) conceptualised attitudes in the framework of triology of cognition, affection and conation. By the late 1950s multi-component view of attitude was adopted almost universally and attitudes were viewed as complex system comprising the person's belief about the object, his feelings towards the object and his action tendencies with respect to the object. Given this inclusive view of attitudes as encompassing all the personal experiences with respect to the object, it would be difficult to assume anything other than a strong relationship between attitude and behaviour. Actually attitude behaviour problem received little attention. Most of the investigators simply worked on the assumption that attitudes explain and predict behaviour, and devoted much of their efforts to descriptive attitude surveys.

Schuman and Johnson (1976) state that the correct descriptive summary of the past literature on attitude behaviour relations is that in most cases investigated attitude and behaviour are related to the extent that ranges from small to moderate in degree. So the answer to the question whether attitudes are related to behaviour can range from 'no', 'not at all' to 'yes, nearly perfectly', depending on the act studied or features linked to. In their review of attitude-behaviour relations Schuman and Johnson (1976) conclude that attitude behaviour studies yield positive results, the correlations that do occur are large enough to indicate that important causal forces are involved, whatever one's model of causal forces may be. However, they are rarely large enough to suggest that attitude responses can serve as substitute for behavioural measures. Attitudes always produce pressures to behave consistently with them but external factors and extraneous considerations can cause people to behave inconsistently with their attitudes (Freedman *et al.*, 1970).

In the wake of such results (Fishbein and Ajzen 1972, 1975) have put forth a new area of study, wherein behaviour intentions are measured instead of attitude for predicting the behaviour. However, the attitude-behaviour relations have been further probed into by many recent studies.

Several factors have been postulated to affect the magnitude of the relation between attitude and behaviour measures. For example, it has been suggested that persons are less likely to behave consistently with their attitudes if situational factors constrain their performance of the behaviour (Warner and Defleur, 1969) or if they believe they are unable to perform the behaviour implied by their attitudes (McArthur *et al.*, 1969).

Rokeach (1968) observes that a preferential response toward an attitude object cannot occur in a vacuum. It must necessarily be elicited within the context of some situation about which we also have attitudes. How a person will behave with respect to an object in a situation will therefore depend on the one hand on particular beliefs or predisposition activated by the attitude object and on the other hand by the belief or predisposition activated by the situation. This reliance on 'other factors' to explain observed attitude behaviour inconsistency is commonly known as 'other variables approach'. According to this view, attitude is only one of the number of factors that influence behaviour and other variables must also be taken into account. Among such other variables are: conflicting attitudes, competing motives, verbal, intellectual and social attitudes, individual differences such as personality characteristics, normative prescriptions of proper behaviour, alternative behaviour available and expected or actual consequences of the behaviour (Fishbein and Ajzen, 1980; Wicker, 1971).

These situational variables are also observed by Snyder and Kendzierski (1982) to include the dictates of peer group pressure, reference group norms, role requirements, incentives and sanctions. At times these situational influences may prompt actions that contradict one's attitudes. This study also finds support to attitude-behaviour relations when one believes that his attitude has important implications.

Regan and Fazio (1977), Fazio and Zanna (1981) examine the attitude-behaviour relations in the context of attitude formation. They have found that attitudes derived from prior behavioural experiences are relatively consistent rather than being ephemeral, than do attitudes based on indirect non-behavioural information. Further, it is noted that an individual whose attitude is based on direct behavioural experience with the object may hold that attitude with greater certainty than an individual whose attitude is formed on the basis of indirect experience. The more certain an individual is of his attitude toward some object, the more likely it is that this attitude will guide later behaviour towards the object (Sample and Warland, 1973). So also, it is found that a clear and well defined attitude may, in turn, influence later behaviour to a greater degree than an unfocussed attitude (Sherif *et al.*, 1973), Miller and Grush (1986) have also noted the individual differences in the attitude-behaviour relations, wherein the individuals who are both aware of their own attitudes and unconcerned with the opinions of others would display the given correspondence.

Fazio and Zanna (1981) opine that in general the research suggests a relatively optimistic view of the relationship between attitude and behaviour. Fishbein and Ajzen (1974) and Weigel and Newman

(1976) have also noted that general attitudes are more predictive to general behaviour patterns across multiple acts.

The present study primarily aims at knowing the relative magnitude of the attitude of social scientists towards information and its relation with the information source use behaviour. This exploratory research adopts attitude measuring technique that is traditionally used. The assumption of attitude-behaviour link in the information use context is supported by the study of Summers *et al* (1983), wherein the attitude has been revealed to be a predictor of information use showing a positive and significant relations. The study also takes into consideration the relations of various personnel and psychological factors with ATI and the relations of ATI and other factors with the information source use.

Thus, with this understanding of the attitude concept. The present study adopted following operational definition:

> Attitude is a relatively stable predisposition or readiness to react in a specific way to an object, idea or situation. Attitudes are complex products of learning, experience, situational and emotional processes and include our enduring preferences and prejudices. Attitudes have a positive influence on the related behaviour.

2.1.6 *Attitude Measurement*

The measurement of attitude has generally proceeded as a kind of quasi-psychological problem. It is assumed that attitudes are latent hypothetical variables that cannot be measured directly but can only be inferred from observations of a subject's responses to a selected set of graded statements (Defleur and Westie, 1963).

The purpose of the attitude scale is to assign an individual to a position somewhere between the opposite extremes of favouring or opposing something. This position may be defined with reference to one dimension or more. A few of such single dimension methods attempted are: measuring social distance (Bogardas, 1925) method of equal appearing intervals (Thurstone and Chave, 1929) and methods which take into account range, consistency and intensity of attitude response (Likert, 1967) and deterministic model which hypothesises that each dichotomous item has a perfect biserial correlation with the trait (Guttman, 1944).

Campbell (1950) has distinguished four types of instruments to measure attitudes:

Non-disguised - structured: the classic attitude tests of Thurstone, Likert, Guttman etc.;

Non-disguised-non-structured: including the free response interview and questionnaire approaches, the biographical and essay studies;

Disguised-non-structured: the typical projective techniques such as thematic apperception test (TAT), Şentence completion, etc;

Disguised structured techniques i.e., the tests which approximate the objective testing of attitudes like information tests, estimation of group opinions and social norms, etc.

Most often used techniques of attitude measurement are the non-disguised structured methods. Attitude literature shows that direct tests uniformly have much higher reliability coefficient than indirect tests.

The structured attitude scales are the combinations of many items measuring the evaluation towards the same object in order to obtain a reliable score. A statement or an item in the attitude scale is anything said about the psychological object (Edward, 1969). The individual reacts verbally with expression of approval or disapproval, agreement or disagreement to the items in the scale. The scale provide a quantitative measure of the individuals relative position along a unidimensional attitude continuum.

Generally an attitude scale is based on three important assumptions namely,

(i) The scale deals with a controversial question.
(ii) An individual's feelings and insights with regard to the question will determine his response to the various statements that are made pro-and-con,
(iii) The statements can scale the degree to which they favour or oppose the question under consideration.

Many criteria have been spelt out for scale construction (Edwards, 1969; Kretch and Crutchfield, 1948). These can be summed up as follows: the items must be psychologically related to the belief or attitude being measured, that they must discriminate sharply among people, that they must discriminate all parts of the dimensions and that they must be sufficiently numerous that random and accidental imperfections in the items and in the testing are cancelled out.

For satisfying these assumptions a scale used has to be carefully tested for validity and reliability. It should measure what it purports to measure (validity) and should yield consistent results when applied under the same conditions (reliability). The more commonly used scales can be grouped under different headings namely:

Scales in which scale values of the items and other characteristics are largely determined by a panel of judges. Under this comes Thurstone's technique,

Scales based on item analysis also called as summated rating techniques. This technique was first introduced by Rensis Likert, and

Scales constructed in accordance with the scale analysis techniques devised by Louis Guttman and his co-workers.

2.1.6.1 *Thurstone's Technique*: Thurstone's method of equal appearing interval is one of the most important and useful contributions to attitude scale construction. This scale is devised to represent the attitude of a group on a specified issue. A series of statements can be made to serve as the markers on a base line for measurement of attitudes. Each of these statements represent a specified degree of acceptance or rejection of a belief. It was Thurstone's rationale that specified degree of acceptance or rejection could be equally spaced through out the entire range of the attitude continuum. The theory is that if a person will indicate which of the statements he will accept and which he will reject, we can locate him at a definite position in the continuum.

Various limitations have been observed in the application of Thurstone scale (Edward and Kenney, 1946). Most important of them is that, the method does not necessarily yield intervals which appear equal to the judges. Scale values have also been found to be affected by attitudes of the judges. The work involved in constructing a Thurstone scale led investigators to look for simpler procedures. In 1932 Rensis Likert Proposed a method of summated rating which has been widely adopted thereafter.

2.1.6.2 *Likert Method*: The basic assumptions in the method of summated ratings are that each statement in the scale covers the entire attitude continuum, and the individual items are monotonically related to the underlying trait and that a summation of item scores is approximately linearly related to the trait. The final score has to be viewed as a kind of average estimate which we get from the application of a number of yard-sticks, each one extending the whole length of the continuum. Like Thurstone method, the Likert scaling procedure also results in a single score that represents the degree to which a person is favourable or unfavourable with respect to the attitude object.

2.1.6.3 *Guttman Scale*: Guttman scale or cumulative scale is strictly not a method for constructing attitude scale. It is a procedure for evaluating sets of statements to determine whether they meet the requirement of a particular type of scale. The prime objective of this method is to determine whether or not the attitude in question is scalable i.e., if sufficiently large proportion of the population is measured, they respond to the scale items in a consistent way. The criteria of consistency is that endorsement of a given item is accompanied by endorsement of all other items that are less extreme and rejection of all items that are more extreme. Though this is desirable for ideal situation, it has been observed in adoption to be not necessarily perfect. To add to this, Guttman technique is adoptable only where the hierarchy of feelings are definitely traceable. This may not be the case with all objects of attitude. It has been observed by Stouffer *et al* (1950) that perfect scales are not found in Guttman technique.

2.1.6.4 *Scaling Technique used in the Present Study*: For the purposes of the present study Likert method of scale construction is adopted because of the various advantages and improvements that are found in this method. Some of the advantages are listed below:

The final selection of items does not depend on the subjective assessment of the judges, but on the criteria of internal consistency.

Reliability of Likert method is also found to be higher. Ferguson (1941) has shown that the reliability of the same scale administered to the same set of subjects scored by Thurstone method was 0.88 (corrected). The same explanation was originally offered by Murphy and Likert (1937).

Likert method takes into consideration internal consistency of the items.

In this method each statement is a scale in itself. The final score of the attitude is the average estimate which we get from the application of number of yard-sticks, each one extending the whole length of the continuum.

In addition to these, Likert scale is also relatively easier to construct.

Tittle and Hill (1967) in their attitude study involving evaluation of conditions and measurement techniques using four measurement techniques observes that the Likert scale is the best predictor and exhibits the greatest reliability, whereas the Thurstone's scale is the least reliable. They conclude that in cases where the two types of scales are of equal length one can expect the Likert scale to exhibit higher reliability.

Shukla (1972) has also shown through his study that Likert scale leads all other scales as an attitude measurement technique and is followed by the Thurstone scale, social judgement, ego-involvement approach and Guttman scalogram analysis. He feels that the superiority of the Likert scale may be due to the fact that it facilitates more and better dispersion for discrimination. In respect of construct validity also, the Likert scale tops and the social judgement, ego-involvement approach, Guttman scale and Thurstone scale follow in the descending order. It is also stated that response to understandability to these scaling methods indicate Likert scale to be the easiest to understand. So also in the case of 'ease of filling', the respondents put Likert's scale on the top.

2.2 Information

A debate over the meaning of the term 'information' has been underway almost from the time that information science became a recognised area of study. Despite many attempts made to define the word in a way which is satisfactory to those who wish to use the term in a technical and professional sense, no general consensus has been reached (Pratt, 1980). In the context of the users studies research, the word information is used to denote a physical entity or phenomena (as in the case of questions relating to the number of books read in a given period), the channels of communication through which messages are transferred (as we speak of incidence of oral versus written information) or the factual data empirically determined and presented in a document or transmitted orally.

Information, however, has been defined to be inclusive of many different notions. Schrader (1983) rightly expresses that the proliferation of notion of information in the writings of information science staggers the mind. Reviewing a wide body of literature on definitional aspect of information he lists 134 variant notions information is taken to be synonymous with. These notions vary from 'discoveries', 'wisdom', 'raw data', 'processed data', 'a chemical process', 'a physical process' etc., to 'knowledge in communicable form', scientific, technical and artistic knowledge', 'the written or spoken surrogate of knowledge', 'a collection of facts or other data especially as derived from the processing of data' and such others.

These varied notions point to the observation often made by the information scientists that information is an amorphous concept less susceptible for a precise definition. Knowingly or unknowingly, intentionally or unintentionally all of us at most of the time of our life and work are concerned with information – its generation, recording, processing, repackaging, transfer, receiving, use and application. This is particularly so in the context of academic activities or scientific research.

Shera (1972) notes that information in the sense librarians use it is a 'fact'. It is a stimulus we receive through our senses. It may be an isolated fact or a whole cluster of facts.

Bringing to the focus communication aspect of the information, Viswanathan (1976) expresses that a highly sophisticated method of communication is the act of reading the recorded information in the form of printed books and allied graphic documents.

It has been often expressed that information becomes more meaningful when it is transferred or communicated. Particularly in the context of science, Garvey (1979) observes that communicability becomes a salient feature of a scientific product. The purpose of scientific communication is its use.

Thus, information is essentially the facts, opinions – knowledge, that are communicated. This communication can be either through recorded – printed or otherwise – or unrecorded sources. Recorded sources are also classified into primary (books, journals, theses etc.), secondary (abstracts, indexes and other surrogate sources), and tertiary sources (encyclopaedia, handbooks etc.), based on the information content of the source.

In the context of this study information is considered to be synonymous with the scientific knowledge irrespective of its manifestation. In terms of the manifestations 'information' includes oral and written, documentary and non-documentary, statistical, graphic, bibliographic and other forms from formal and informal sources.

2.3 Motivation

In a general sense motivation is the process of initiating, sustaining and directing physiological or psychological phenomena that stimulates, maintains and directs behaviour (Goldenson, 1984).

Motivation refers to certain properties of action which are found to be different in nature. These actions and drives are often described as guided, directed, goal oriented, persistent or purposive. Such a characterisation may describe its occurrence in a short sequence or over extended periods of time or may describe facets of choice, performance or decision. This selective directed character of actions and the drives associated with it is the critical property which has led to the postulation of a motivational process. It is the condition responsible for variation in the intensity, quality and direction of the ongoing behaviour.

Thus, motivation is conceived as a disposition to strive for a certain kind of satisfaction; as a capacity for satisfaction in the attainment of certain class of incentives (Atkinson, 1964). Several categories of motives recognised such as power, achievement, affiliation etc., are really classes of incentives which produce the same kind of experience of satisfaction.

Motivation is thought of as some kind of internal force which arouses, regulates and sustains all our important actions. It is 'an energizing condition of the organism' that serves to direct the organism towards a goal or goals of certain class (Stanford, 1969).

More technical definitions given by social scientists suggest that motivation is a psychological process that causes the arousal, direction and persistence of behaviour (Atkinson, 1964; Campbell *et al.*, 1970; Huse and Bowditch, 1977; Kast and Rosezweig, 1979; Korman, 1974; Luthans, 1977); many others, like Vroom (1964) add a voluntary component or goal directed emphasis to such a definition.

Motivation process points to the task to be performed as a important intervening link between effort or choice behaviour and the outcomes desired by the individual. People have intentions about what they will do in the face of certain task requirements. These intentions have an influence on the choice they make among task contents and the efforts they extend towards specific performance goals within tasks (Locke 1976).

Locke (1968) and also, Locke *et al* (1970) express that the most immediate motivational determinant of effort or choice is the individual's goal or intentions *vis-a-vis* some task. By implication, such a conscious intention or goal is defined as a goal the individual has consciously decided to pursue. These intentions give behaviour a direction and perform the energizing function. It is also largely agreed upon that, accomplishment of such goals leads to need satisfaction. With such a drive other stimuli – ideas, objects, that are connected with its satisfaction also become more attractive and sought out for further contact.

2.3.1 *Intrinsic and Extrinsic Motivating Factors*

The terms extrinsic and intrinsic motivating factors are used in motivation literature. Campbell and Pritchard (1976) define intrinsic factors as those directly relating to the actual performance of the job and extrinsic factors as those related to the environment in which the job is being performed.

Intrinsic motivation refers to a situation where an individual takes up a particular activity as it provides him with an opportunity to improve his self image to achieve something, to contribute to his personal growth and development, to actualise his potentialities and bring out his inherent abilities. It is the degree to which a person is motivated to perform well because of some subjective rewards of feeling that he expects to receive or experience as a result of performing well (Lawler, 1969). These factors are particularly salient to scientists as they are concerned about higher order needs (Hall and Lawler, 1969).

Extrinsic factors refer to a situation where an individual chooses a job because it has a better pay, working conditions, supervision, human relations etc. Thus, extrinsic factors are those relating to the environment in which the job is being performed (Campbell and Pritchard, 1976). In the context of the organizational behaviour or scientists both the factors are found to have an important influence on performance.

Thus, motivation is a psychological process, that causes the arousal, direction and persistence of behaviour. It is expressed in terms of intentions the individual sets for attainment. As these intentions are consciously expressed individuals could be expected to pursue them (Locke, 1968). Motivating factors may be both intrinsic and extrinsic. Action tendencies created by the strength of motivation would also have an influence on all the related aspects of the goals in question.

2.3.2 *Measurement of Motivation*

Motivations are measured through direct and indirect methods. Direct methods include use of questionnaires, rating scales etc. In these methods respondents are usually asked to agree or disagree with the scale items focusing on aspects of work related activities or indicate the importance they attach to various factors concerning the focus of the study. Indirect or projective measures, on the other hand, try to tap the strength of the motive through such methods as story completion, sentence completion, TAT, etc.

Direct methods are simple to administer and are not prone to be biased in interpretation. Allport (1953), referring to the measurement opines that normal subjects will tell by the direct method precisely what they tell by the projective method. You may therefore take this motivational statements at their face value, for even if you probe you will not find any thing substantially different.

2.3.3 *Motivation Studies Relating to Organizational Scientists*

Motivation is very likely to express itself as a desire for job mastery and professional growth. Among other professions academic jobs – including research and teaching in organizations – provide for such a facility, where intense application of mastery of the specialised fields and various mental capabilities come into operation.

It has been recognised that scientific or academic performance, in terms of effective research and teaching activities, unlike many other kinds of work, cannot be enforced. Rather it must come as a product of enthusiasm that an individual feels towards his work. A key factor, then, in accounting for the quality of work of an academician is his degree of motivation to advance knowledge – the main goal of an academic institution. Cole and Cole (1973) have described this aspect as a 'sacred spark'. They argue that scientists involve in research not because they are rewarded by they have an inner compulsion to do so. This compulsion is likely to result in greater involvement of the individuals in the activities relating to the object of focus which in the present context is effective information source use for better performance in research and teaching activities.

The positive relation between the strength of motivation and quality of performance has been confirmed in a number of systematic studies (Pelz and Andrews, 1962). Research findings dealing with variations in motivation caused by conditions in the organizational work environment point to the strong relations of many factors such as differential reward system in research organizations, organizational *vs* professional loyalties, leadership styles, relations with colleagues, research facilities and other conditions, particularly freedom to research.

Glaser (1965) in his study of organisational scientists observes that a scientist, especially in training and also throughout his career, is constantly reminded by his colleagues that it is his job to advance knowledge. He internalises the goal and becomes 'institutionally motivated' to achieve it.

In the study of scientists in organizations, Pelz and Andrews (1966) have based their motivation measure on a previous study by Davis (1956) wherein he has located one cluster of job factors suggesting the motivation of an individual to a career in his scientific field (i.e., the scientists rated as important the chance to contribute to science, to use his knowledge and skills and to have freedom to carry out this own ideas) which was called science orientation. A second cluster of items suggested motivation towards a career within his organization (the individual placed importance on advancing to a more responsible and important job etc.) which was called institutional orientation. Pelz and Andrews (1966) extending these aspects have identified three types of motives, viz. (1) source of origin of problem, (2) style of approach and (3) professional orientation or direction. It was observed that professional orientation was consistently positive in their relationship to various performance measures. As to the sources of origin of problem 'own ideas' showed a strong and consistent positive trend. Style of approach (e.g. I prefer to map out broad features of important new areas; I prefer to probe deeply and thoroughly in selected areas, even though narrow etc.) do not show a consistent relationship with the performance.

These findings are also supported by Helmreich *et al* (1978) who have found out a significant relation between work and competitiveness in their study of 103 Ph.D. scientists and engineers. This study explored the relations of performance and achievement motivation using a three component measure including work orientation, mastery needs and competitiveness.

Andrews (1979) in a six country study involving more than 1200 respondents with ten different subject specialisations including social sciences has found out a similar trend of motivation and performance relations. The study confirms that relations between motivation and performance tend to be positive. Motivation tends to be most highly related to ratings of R&D effectiveness and so does output of published/written products. Although the relations are not strong, they are remarkably general and occur in different types of units.

Miller (1980) in his study relating to professors teaching management has examined the managerial and professional aspects of motivation. He concludes that professional factors motivate the professors more than the hierarchic ones.

Thus, the strength of motivation for higher achievement shows consistently positive relations with the performance of the scientists in different work settings. Motivation may be intrinsic, in which an individual is motivated to perform well because of some subjective rewards of feeling that he experiences, or it may be extrinsic wherein the conducive external environmental factors give the direction for a better performance. Both these factors facilitate in the goal specific actions. In addition, strength of motivation, as it has been observed earlier, may also have its influence on the other related factors concerning the aims and intentions of the individual. As Locke (1968) observes that with the drive for satisfaction of the expressed intentions other stimuli ideas, objects that are connected with the satisfaction also become more attractive and sought out. This function of motivation supports the point of view that higher strength of motivation for scientific work performance may also be taken as an important contributing factor in the ATI. As information generation and dissemination is the major focus of such research and teaching activities it could be logically expected that motivation has a positive relation with the ATI and also an important factor facilitating attitude-behaviour relations.

2.4 Job Satisfaction

Job satisfaction, according to Hoppock (1935), to whom the credit of bringing the term into currency goes, is any combination of psychological, physiological and environmental circumstances that causes a person to say truthfully – I am satisfied on my job.

Drever (1964) defines job satisfaction as an end state of feeling accompanying the attainment by an impulse of its objective. The resultant feeling of satisfaction depends on the need strength and the opportunity that environment provides for the attainment of appropriate incentive.

Job satisfaction results from the perception that one's job fulfils or allows the fulfilment of one's important job values (Locke, 1976). He also observes that although there are individual differences, there are also many broad similarities in what people want from their jobs. In the realm of work itself most people want something which is significant, instead of success or a sense of accomplishment, progress, growth, responsibility, autonomy, role clarity, role congruence etc.

With respect to pay, people want fairness. So also with promotions, congenial co-workers are preferred who share similar values and who facilitate work accomplishment. Employees like supervisors who are considerate, honest, fair, competent, who recognise and reward good performance, etc.

Thus, job satisfaction is an emotional response to a value judgement by an individual worker. If his job values are perceived as being fulfilled he will experience the pleasurable emotion of satisfaction.

Job satisfaction is governed to a large extent by the individuals perceptions. Individuals work to satisfy these needs and expect their work life to fulfil these needs. The imagined judgement of how well the job life is satisfying the various needs or job values account for the degree of job satisfaction.

Job satisfaction studies are carried out mostly in individual work settings. These studies try to associate feeling of satisfaction with their performance. However, the relationship of job satisfaction to performance is a highly complex one. From many studies conducted with this focus it appears that job satisfaction is a measure of adequacy of the rewards given by employees for the completion of a task and naturally these rewards must commensurate with the quality of performance.

It has been observed that most individuals value jobs which allow them to control their own work place and methods, to exercise their skills and abilities and to learn new things (Vroom, 1964). The opportunity to use one's own judgement, to use one's own mind are the important factors. Jobs which are mentally challenging provide a greater sense of achievement than those which are routine and undemanding. Further, individuals may also aim for different levels of performance. What leaves a person extremely happy might leave another highly dissatisfied. Thus, job satisfaction is a pleasurable or positive emotional state resulting from appraisal of one's job and job experiences (Locke, 1976).

2.4.1 *Measurement of Job Satisfaction*

Job satisfaction measures can give the extent to which an individual is attracted to his occupation and its associated activities, as well as the extent to which he is attracted by his employing organization.

Satisfaction is usually measured by means of interviews or questionnaires in which respondents are asked to state the degree to which they are satisfied or dissatisfied with various aspects of their work. The degree to which a person is satisfied with his job is inferred from the response to questions concerning how he feels about the job (Wanous and Lawler, 1972). Typically dimensions such as nature of work, promotion, recognition, benefits, working conditions, pay, co-workers are studied in these surveys. Overall satisfaction is the sum of all these factors.

Some theories have argued that an individual's affective reaction depends upon the discrepancy between what his environment offers and what he expects (McClelland *et al.*, 1953) Locke (1976), commenting on the studies relating expectancies to satisfaction, states that these have failed to control adequately the effect of values (goals, desires aspirations) or to separate them from the expectancy effects. The reaction one experiences in response to an unexpected event or outcome is a surprise, whether the surprise is pleasant or unpleasant depends upon whether the deviation from expectancy is in a direction one values. Evans (1969) view this measure as theoretically meaningless for high expectancy and high satisfaction and low expectancy and low satisfaction are treated as equal though it is not found to be so in multi-trait, multi-method matrix.

2.4.2 *Satisfaction Studies Relating to Organizational Scientists*

Though satisfaction measures are used widely in industrial settings its usefulness has been found in the studies relating to scientific organizations also. Hulin and Blood (1968) observe, that as a group scientists are not alienated from middle class work norms. It is also stated by Hall and Lawler (1969) that job design factors are particularly salient to scientists and that they are concerned about the higher order needs. Though scientific creativity springs from the individual it is nourished by the environment. Satisfaction refers to such nourishment provided within the organization (Rajan and Subramanian, 1969). Glaser (1964) notes that two basic organizational rewards for a scientist's professional recognition which provide the core of an organizational career are: advancement in position and provision of favourable research conditions.

Job satisfaction studies, though not many, could also be traced in the context of scientists in the organization. Glaser (1964) in his study observes that favourable research conditions are a reward for the professional recognition of all the scientists. However, there are significant variations in the distribution of research conditions for recognition as one advances in organizational career. Linked with each organizational position as a person advances is a somewhat different constellation of working conditions that are provided as organizational rewards for past achievement. These conditions are the resources upon which further and perhaps higher quality achievement is based in order to gain more recognition and further advancement. McCurry and Edwards (1972) have analysed nine job characteristics in this context. They are personal and professional self-development, effective support service, funding of research on one's interest, peer recognition, facilitative working condition, supervision, attending colloquia etc., facilities for promotion and also an adequate salary. This study reveals that the greatest importance is given by the scientists to personal achievement and a secondary one to the recognition.

Arwey and Dewhirst (1979) in their study on scientists' job satisfaction and performance have concluded that diversity of interests in a general and job specific occupational areas are linearly and positively related to intrinsic satisfaction.

McCurrey and Edwards (1973) in their study on biological scientists have found that three meaningful and independent performance dimensions underlie a large part of role related variations in the performance measures.

Misshauk (1970) has also found out a significant relationship between job satisfaction and performance in R and D organizations.

Rajan and Subramanian (1969) express that job incentives have a positive role to play in the research process. Incentives or satisfying factors are needed to attract talent to secure and sustain a higher level of effort. Four important factors which govern these incentives, authors opine, are: provision of psychological security, recognition, opportunity for self-expression and provision of facilities to widen the perimeter of one's job.

In another extensive investigation involving scientists in six countries (Stolte-Heiskanen, 1979) it has been observed that among other externally determined resources, satisfaction with human resources (colleagues/supervisors etc.) seem to have the most important single effect on performance.

Anand and Sohal (1982) in their study of job satisfaction of scientists opine that satisfaction is the effect of a number of factors within the organization's interpersonal relations of superiors and subordinates, and also individual's own needs, aspiration and motivations.

Pioneering work in correlating job satisfaction and performance of scientists is reported by Pelz and Andrews (1966). They report that feeling of satisfaction can be expected to associate with willingness to work among the workers. This study reports that many research papers are turned out by the scientists who are satisfied on the job. But high satisfaction does not correlate with high performance in terms of research of greater scientific value as well as greater usefulness to the organization. However, the authors feel that job satisfaction is an important variable to be considered in the performance of the scientists. It is logical that a dissatisfied scientist has less to give to his job and his willingness to do and indulge in various job related activities would be less, except when satisfaction is extraneous to the job content. Thus, satisfaction within the organizational context as perceived by the researchers has been found to be related to their performance.

Job satisfaction can be studied to know how it contributes to other attitudes or actions. As is noted a positive appraisal may result in repeating the act and show interest in the related activities. Locke (1976) recognises that action tendencies going with relative satisfaction is affected by one's values, beliefs and method of thinking which has a close knit relation with one's emotional state. It would strengthen the feeling towards objects and actions relating to that mental state.

As satisfaction implies need fulfilment such a state of mind can be expected to exert a strong influence not only on their performance but various other related aspects. This could be particularly so in the context of ATI and also use of information sources. This argument gains its strength from the importance placed on the information sources in the research and related activities by the scientists themselves as an important contributing factor in performance. A positive state of mind concerning the organizational facilities can be expected to bring in greater readiness for information use for academic work and also facilitate ATI and source use relations.

2.5 Dedication to Job

Concept of dedication to job was first used in the study by Pelz and Andrews (1966). It is taken to be a summation of obligation, interest, challenge, and involvement in the assigned work. Dedicating overlaps with commitment to job. It is also designed in terms of one's loyalty, identification and involvement in the work of the organization. It is seen as a binding force on individuals to carry out and adhere to organizational philosophy and policies.

Dedication to job is an extension of concept of job involvement. Though motivation and job satisfaction seem to be related to dedication, studies generally support the view that in research on job attitudes it is important to distinguish between satisfaction, involvement and intrinsic motivation. That a sense of involvement in a work should not be confused with either satisfaction with work or with a belief that specific rewards will follow from a job well done (Lawler and Hall, 1970). This observation has also been confirmed in the study of R and D units by Shanthamani (1982), which states that it is possible for some people to be highly involved and not happy and others to be happy but not involved in their research job. Lee's (1971) empirical study has recognised that a scientist's identification with the organization is an important factor in understanding their work behaviour. This study analysed the determinants and correlates of scientist's organizational identification. It concluded that differences in personal and job variables correlate with high or low identification.

Locke (1976) also views that job involvement or morale though is related to, but is distinguishable from job satisfaction. Both involvement and satisfaction refer to positive emotional states which may be experienced by employees. Involvement or dedication is future oriented while satisfaction is present or past oriented. Involvement in addition has a group referent.

Dedication is a desire to continue in and willingness to strive for the goals of a particular group or organization. It is to take the job seriously or being mentally preoccupied with the job. It is the degree to which an individual identified psychologically with his work or the importance of work in his total self image (Vitales, 1953; Lodhal and Kejner, 1965). Dedication may be viewed as the summation of involvement, feeling a sense of obligation to organizational goals, taking interest in the assigned jobs and also concentrating on the jobs.

To understand this concept we may visualise a totally dedicated worker. For such a person his job would be the most important and interesting thing in his life. His thoughts would revolve around his work and nearly all times he would be preoccupied with analysing and solving any of the problem concerning his work. His programmes and actions would centre around his work role. This is noticeable in the items recommended by Lodahl and Kejner (1965) as a measure of involvement: "The major satisfaction in my life comes from my job", "The most important things that happen to me involves my job", "I am very much involved personally in my job" and so on. A highly dedicated worker would seek to satisfy his needs from the reward he obtains from his job. It is a sense of personal satisfaction and self-fulfilment in doing his work well. Many researchers have emphasised dedication as a personal characteristic. It is considered as the outcome of work values acquired by the individual. Kornhauser (1962) has presented arguments and findings suggesting that one of the best ways to increase the productivity of professionals in research organizations is to provide them with jobs demanding more involvement.

In a particular organizational context an academician may have to function in a given work role and his performance depends on the dedication he has for the assigned jobs. A total overlap of individual needs and job provisions is a rare phenomenon. So comes the necessity for need adjusted role in the academic organizations. Dedication corresponds to such an adjustment. In general dedication is caused by personal characteristics. It is more a function of a person than that of a job (Lodhal and Kejner, 1965). It is an individual difference factor that a person takes from job to job and is akin to characteristic interaction by the individual with his job.

2.5.1 *Dedication Studies Relating to Organizational Scientists*

Pelz and Andrews (1966) incorporated in their study a set of five items that they used to measure dedication. The items asked scientists to indicate their feeling of involvement and identification with their work, and to say how challenging, important and interesting they found it. Using data from more than 1300 scientists they found that these items showed significant positive relationships to both ratings of performance and actual output of scientific products among scientists of widely different types. The relations were consistent and positive.

In the context of the present study a cue has been taken from the findings of the above cited study and also a few others in which job involvement has been considered. It is expected that dedication has a positive relationship with ATI. In addition, dedication is expected to facilitate ATI and information source use behaviour relations.

2.6 Aspiration

The concept of level of aspiration was introduced into experimental psychology by Hoppe (in Gardner, 1940). He conceived the level of aspiration as a technique for studying psychological factors which operate in the production of feelings of success and failure. He defined the level of aspiration as a person's goals or claims on his own future achievement.

Level of aspiration designates goal seeking behaviour of the type where behaviour operates under cognitive influence. Understanding of aspiration is recognised to be of importance by the behavioural scientists since individuals have notions of diversity regarding their future status and believe that by their selection and decision they can materially affect the role they will acquire and discharge. (Bealer and Kuvlesky, 1968).

Aspiration denotes an estimation by the subject with regard to his future achievement. It is a projected level of achievement and an individual's conception of future prospects. Aspiration, Haller (1968) views, correlated with attainment, as people adjust their level of aspiration so that they are not totally out of line with the prospects of attaining them. In this attempt, real or imagined, to enact a level of aspiration people learn something about their chance of success and failure. That is, there is probably a real but imperfect feedback of attainment on aspiration. So much so, level of aspiration, as set by the individual is affected by considerations of self-preservation. In addition, it is likely that expectations of future performance will be affected by a desire to do well.

Haller (1968) opines that the level of attainment or action is a non-linear accelerating function of level of aspiration and also the facilities offered by the environment of the aspirant. To some extent people adjust their aspiration to that they are not totally out of line with the prospects of attaining them.

Referring to the level of aspiration Hoppe views that the subject always undertakes the task with certain demands which can change in the course of the activity. The totality of this constantly shifting, now indefinite, now precise expectations, goal settings or demands in connection with one's own future performance, we shall call the level of aspiration.

Gardner (1940) defines level of aspiration as a quantitative indication which an individual makes concerning his future performance in an activity. This study adopted the more specific definition given by Longman dictionary of psychology and psychiatry (Goldson, 1984). Level of aspiration is the standard used by the individual in setting his significant goals. The level of performance to which he aspires. The aspiration level is an important component of the persons self-image and may reflect a reasonable evaluation of himself.

Level of aspiration is not specific to each situation but it is more or less a 'general trait' in the person. The term high or low level aspiration is used to indicate relative level of goal satisfaction.

Factors which determine one's level of aspiration include past achievements, interests, abilities, personal needs and group standards (Stacey and De martino, 1965). These are classed as situational, reference group and personality factors.

Situational factors in the context of the research and teaching jobs include academic environment, attractiveness of the task to the individuals and his ego involvement for attaining the goal. Most important of the reference group factors is achievement of the peer group. Added to these are social and personality factors in the individuals such as need for achievement, competitiveness, ambition, prudence, courage to face reality, ability to dismiss failure etc.

Real or ideal aspiration has often been a question of debate. Lewin (1936) distinguished between these two types the 'real' aspiration being what the person thinks he might really be able to attain and the 'ideal' what he hoped to attain if all went well.

Raising expectations alone will not give a feeling of success but if followed by achievements if may lead to further effort and success. Further more, a hopelessly high or a needlessly low goal of endeavour tends to reduce both interests and achievements. It has also been found that a succession of interesting goals, each of which is slightly more ambitious than the preceding one, but is possible for achievement after it comes into operation is more effective than a single distant higher goal that can be achieved only in a relatively remote future and after a long endeavour.

The general findings noted above in the context of level of aspiration can be expected to have their implications in research and teaching job environment as well (Jhansi Rani, 1985). Aspirations, whenever realistically set have to match with the factors which facilitate performance. Higher goal achievement by academicians in the 'ladder of academic performance' necessitates frequent use of the sources of information in order to keep up to date with research findings and it may also bring in a favourable ATI among those who aspire for higher goals. This higher goal achievement need not correlate with hierarchic positions as it corresponds to research contributions and peer group recognition.

A favourable attitude is particularly important in the context, as academic/scientific performance is often measured in terms of original contribution in the field of specialisation – equating it almost with information generation and dissemination activity. So it can be logically expected that realistic aspiration for higher goal achievement would be related to favourable attitude towards information. It can also be expected to enthuse the aspirers for the use of information sources frequently and more effectively to correspond their attitudinal favourability.

2.7 Personal Attributes

Attitudes are learned phenomena and are organised through interactions with the object itself in addition to various other factors exerting their influence. So it can be logically expected that personal factors have a direct or indirect impact on the attitudes relating to various objects, ideas or situations. It is particularly so in case of attitudes towards information. Important among the personal variables which affect ATI are professional/academic experience, educational attainment and the position in the hierarchy.

2.7.1 *Professional Experience*

User studies conducted so far do not reveal a general pattern and a definite trend in information source use correlating with personal variables. However, some of the user studies have examined the relations of personal variables in detail which needs consideration here. INFROSS, for instance, has concluded that the experienced researchers tend to use fewer libraries and their source use would be lesser than the new entrants to the profession. Garvey (1971), in his study on social and physical scientists, has also revealed that book and journal use generally comes down with increasing experience. Similar observations have also been made by Meadows (1974). Commenting that some orientation towards literature usage is essential for a successful scientist, he qualifies, referring to Clark (1957), that there are difficulties in trying to generalise further on these lines. For example, some surveys suggest that older scientists make less use of journals than younger ones. Many reasons might be adduced for this, ranging from lesser hours of reading time senior scientists have to the greater ease with which they acquire information through informal channels. It may also be due to longer standing of a scientist in the concerned research area and consequent lesser need for retrospective information. However, need for current research information do not vary with increasing experience and also experienced researchers' greater accessibility to informal sources of information more often be expected to result in relatively greater information use. So also ATI may be expected to become favourable with the increasing experience. As has been observed earlier, longer association with the attitude object viz., information sources and the continuous need for their use in the work environment would facilitate a favourable ATI. Summers *et al* (1983) in a study measuring users affective response to educational information have found out a strong positive relationship between years of experience and attitude towards information. Thus, it can be expected that ATI may strengthen with the increase in the experience due to information generation activities in which researches are continuously engaged in. So also need for current information as opposed to retrospective studies may show a trend of increase with the experience. Survey of educational practitioners conducted by Summers *et al* (1983a) has shown that the use of journals tend to increase as a function of increasing professional experience.

2.7.2 *Education*

Educational proficiency may also have a say in the ATI and also on information source use. Summers *et al* (1983) have in their study concluded that education is a predictor of ATI, i.e., higher the education level more favourable the attitude. Education level in this study (Summers *et al*) ranged from high school to Ph.D. However, in the present context respondents invariably possessed a master's degree in one of the disciplines of social sciences and in addition a sizable proportion also have M.Phil., and Ph.D. degree. Performance studies of scientists have uniformly observed a distinction between Ph.D's and non-Ph.D's. Pelz and Andrews in their study have reported that Ph.D's differed from non-Ph.D's in their motivations and the quality and quantity of their output. They further express "we are convinced that doctoral scientists are distinct unto themselves – whether by selection or by training – and should be analysed separately" (1966, p. 3). Based on the general understanding of the course content and requirements, it is generally noticeable that Ph.D's tend to have narrower specialisation and in depth understanding of the narrower focus of a discipline. This higher level of attainment is not only a result of intensive use of information sources but also results in a favourable ATI later in their career.

2.7.3 *Position*

Position in the academic hierarchy is another variable of importance. Summers *et al* (1983) in their study on educational practitioners have revealed that position is a predictor of ATI i.e., higher the position more favourable is the attitude. In the present study four positions were discernible namely, (1) Research Associate/Assistant, (2) Lecturer/Assistant Director, (3) Reader/Deputy Director and (4) Professor/Director. Though the designation used varies in many of these organizations, requirements such as minimum academic experience, professional attainment are broadly agreed upon. As promotion into higher position is the most important reward that can be got in any job, it can be expected that academicians as well would put forth the efforts for achieving this through research contributions and the like. In addition, for those in the higher positions responsibilities would be more, demanding capacity for research guidance etc. It is logical to guess that ATI and the need for information from various sources use would be higher as the position enhances.

3

RESEARCH DESIGN AND METHODOLOGY

The previous chapter has introduced different variables, dependent and independent, considered in the study. Within this framework the research was carried on to:

- measure the ATI of the social scientists;
- know the extent of information source use of the social scientists;
- examine the extent to which ATI is related to overt behaviour in terms of information source use;
- study the nature of relationship of ATI with selected personal and psychological attributes, and also the job environment with which the social scientists are affiliated, taken individually and in meaningful combinations;
- understand the effect of variations in the level of personal, psychological attributes and the job environment on the ATI and source use relations. The research also examined the constraints experienced in the information source use.

The study was designed as an *ex post facto* research, as the respondents were those who have been working in various university departments of social sciences and also in social science research institutions. The following sections deal with the response population, the procedures used for empirical measurement of the variables, and also statistical analysis adopted for the study.

3.1 Respondents of the Study

Respondents of the study consisted of social scientists affiliated to various social science research and training institutions and the university post-graduate social science departments in the twin cities of Hyderabad-Secunderabad. Eleven such organizations were identified for the purpose of collecting data from the professional staff engaged in research and teaching/training focusing on one or more of the social science disciplines. Operationally social sciences were defined to include the following disciplines: Economics, Political Science, Public Administration, Anthropology, Sociology, Social Work, Communication, Education and Applied Statistics.

The study drew the respondents from the following institutions:

1. National Institute of Rural Development
2. Administrative Staff College of India
3. National Institute of Nutrition
4. National Institute of Small Industries Extension and Training
5. Tribal Research Institute
6. Institute of Public Enterprises
7. Centre for Economic and Social Studies
8. National Academy of Agricultural Research Management
9. Osmania University
10. University of Hyderabad
11. Andhra Pradesh Agricultural University.

3.2 Development of the Questionnaire

3.2.1 *Construction of the ATI Scale*

As the ready-made scale for measuring the attitude towards information was not available, an attempt was made to construct the scale and examine its reliability and validity with the help of a preliminary or pilot survey, prior to the final data collection.

ATI of the social scientists was conceived to be their predisposition for the use of information. To know the relative intensity of the same preliminary scale items were constructed based on the survey of the published literature concerning the nuances of the social science knowledge growth and social scientists as the users of information, to ascertain the possible issues that could matter in the information use. Based on this survey five areas were noted under which the items could be broadly classified and the reasons for relative variations in the information use could possibly be attributed to. These five areas were: *Value* (an enduring belief or a disposition to acquire new information and holding it to be of importance in the normal course of life); *Utility* (valid benefits that can be derived from the acquisition and use of the information); *Motivation* (acquired drive to perform competitively by realising the best one is capable of with the acquisition and use of information in the academic context); *Constraints* (perceived, situational and personal hindrances in the process of information acquisition); *Sources* (media through which information is stored and disseminated).

Scale items focusing on these areas were formulated based on the already published literature, opinions of experts and the investigator's own experience with the information users. Suitability of these items were thoroughly discussed and a final list of 110 items were made. These items invariably centred on the affective and conative aspects of the information seeking activity. Prior to conducting a pilot survey the listing of the proposed attitudinal statements were referred to twelve judges with high academic standing and specialisation in different disciplines of social sciences. Rating by the judges on a three-point scale (relevant, not relevant, neutral) was sought to know the item relevance and the content validity. Based on the opinion of the judges several items in the scale were edited and focus was sharpened eliminating the observed ambiguity of the item structure. The first version-including items revised and edited – of the scale was again referred to the judges. This exercise assured a consensus among the experts and 97 items were found to be of common acceptance.* These items were used in the pilot survey for ascertaining the reliability and validity of the scale. On these items five answer categories – strongly agree, agree, undecided, disagree, strongly disagree – were adopted to elicit the response. The preliminary scale used for the pilot survey consisted of 68 negatively keyed and 29 positively keyed items.

3.2.2 *Pilot Survey*

Suitability, homogeneity and reliability of the 97 items were tested for ascertaining the utility of the ATI scale on a sub-sample of the study universe. An equal number of respondents from universities and research and training institutions (25 each) were selected for eliciting their response on the scale items. In addition, a balanced representation from different positions in the academic hierarchy was also sought in both the study environments. As the researcher could es-

---

* See Appendix C

tablish a personal rapport with the respondents, all of the them returned the questionnaire duly filled-in.

The pilot study data were scored for positive and negative items, i.e., reversing the scoring pattern for the negatively keyed items. Three statistical tests were used for the item selection as indicated by McIver and Carmines (1981). The individual score of 97 items were summed up and as a first measure the item scores were correlated using product moment correlation, to find out to what extent the individual item scores correlate with the total score. This gave an indication as to whether each item is more or less uniformly contributing to the total score. Further, as a second measure corrected correlation was computed wherein the contribution of the *i*th item was eliminated from the total score to correct the bias introduced to the total by the item being correlated. In addition to these the respondents were divided into high and low groups based on the quartile one and three values taking their total attitude score (the middle group was not considered for this analysis). Critical ratios (*t* ratio) were worked out for each statement to establish the discriminatory power of the item between high and low groups. The final selection of the items was based on the combination of all the three techniques of item selection. Those items which were statistically significant at .01 level were included in the final scale. Wherever there was discrepancy in these three measures the item was deleted from consideration. In all 38 items could be retained for the final scale.

Split-half reliability was worked out for the selected 38 items by splitting the scale into two halves *A* and *B*, one half consisting of all the odd numbered items and the other even numbered ones. Correlation between these two halves was 0.77 ($P < .01$). Spearman-Brown formula was used to assess the reliability coefficient based on the correlation of two halves. Estimate of reliability for 38 items scale was 0.87. It is significant at 0.01 level indicating the satisfactory reliability of the scale.

Further, the known-group method was used to assess the tentative validity of the scale. Twenty social scientists, ten each from university and research and training institutions, who fell in the two extremes as to their extent of information source use, academic participation etc. (ascertained with the help of heads of the faculty), were requested to respond to the 38 items. It was found that avid information seekers consistently scored higher than the other half who were known to be relatively unfavourably inclined to the information use.

The final scale used in the survey had 38 items, including eight positively keyed and 30 negatively keyed ones. The scale had a score range of 0-38-76-114-152, where higher score indicated better or favourable ATI.

3.3 Information Source Use

Information use behaviour studies have over the decades elicited the response on frequency of the source use through questionnaires. Though interview method and structured observations have been used in some of the studies, by far the most frequently used technique is the questionnaire method. Paisley (1965) speaks of questionnaire as a compromise technique expedient to use when the sample is widely spread.

Initial discussion with the researchers and the post-graduate teachers gave a clue that as many as 15 different information sources are used in varied measures by the social scientists. These sources could be broadly grouped as bibliographic and non-bibliographic ones. The bibliographic sources can be further divided into primary sources, including journals/periodicals, books/research reports, theses/dissertations, government publications, maps and newspapers; and secondary sources comprising of abstracting/indexing sources, citations in books and periodicals, published bibliographies, and the library in-house service mostly rendered in the form of documentation lists/reading lists prepared by the library staff. Non-bibliographic sources of information found to be of general use were primary data collected in the field surveys, consulting experts in different subject disciplines, attending seminars/workshops, discussion with colleagues and the use of mass media like radio, television etc.

As to the measure of frequency of use of these sources in social scientists' current academic work, several ways were initially thought of. The frequently used answer categories such as 'sometimes', 'often' etc., was found to create response bias despite the definitions that could be given to these terms. Accessing the library everyday was not found to make a person more intense user of sources, compared to the others who visit the library once in every two or three days. Library visits seemed to vary with the relative position in the hierarchy and also share of other academic duties, assistance available etc. Initial discussions also revealed that in many cases a systematic pattern in either library visits or source consultation is not followed, as they often tended to reply that they consult journals or experts, for instance, whenever they want, which may be every day in a certain stage of research and not so frequently in other stages.

As the respondents were spread over several organisations observation of the source use was not found feasible. Count of the book/journal borrowings could be made only in one organisation, where the issue records were maintained in a loan register. Such a measure even when feasible would not have given correct data, as the respondents did not invariably borrow books from the libraries but referred them within the premises and also to a certain extent were found to depend on their own personal collection. So also the initial try out of the actual number of hours spent on reading and information gathering activities was found to yield very rough approximation. Because of these limitations, it was decided to treat the data relating to information use qualitatively. For eliciting the response as to the extent of use of sources, a numerical scale with ten points (0-9) was used, with a prior intention of collapsing the scale into four units – 'not used' (0), 'rarely used' (1-3), 'moderately used' (4-6) and 'frequently used' (7-9). The two extreme points of the scale were defined as 'not used' and 'often used'. Collapsing the use categories (apart from those who have not used) in three units was found to accommodate the response variations due to various other factors. Absence of the commonly used adjectives as answer categories also facilitated in avoiding response bias to a large extent. This method has also been adopted by the INFROSS Study for ascertaining the source use.

The pilot survey which included 15 sources and elicited the response in the above said method indicated that 12 of these 15 sources were commonly used by majority of the respondents. The two sources: mass media (Radio, TV etc.) and newspapers were not found to be of use in their current academic activities by most of the respondents, in particular the mass media were not used by any one. Use of maps were found to be more or less confined to the geographers, though a few exceptions were noticeable, respondents with subject specialisation in economics, psychology, anthropology, public administration, communications, commented about its non-relevance in their research and teaching activities. As a result, the final questionnaire included twelve sources: four of them non-bibliographic and the others bibliographic. Among the bibliographic sources were four primary sources, namely, periodicals, books/research reports, government publications, theses/dissertations. Secondary sources included abstracting and indexing sources, book reviews, published bibliographies and library in-house services. Consulting with experts, discussions with colleagues, attending workshops and seminars and also primary survey data were the non-bibliographic sources.

3.4 Motivation

The measure of motivation consisted of response to the scale items as to the importance attached to the professional and status factors concerning the work. The items focusing on academic work aspects included: opportunity to keep up with the new developments, publish research findings, freedom in selecting research projects, to work on difficult problems, and also to make full use of the learned skills and knowledge. The items also focused on the status issues such as importance attached to promotion, salary, professional reputation etc.

These items were earlier used by Davis (1956) in his study on researchers in National Institute of Health, U.S.A. These items also formed part of motivation measure in the study of organisational scientists by Pelz and Andrews (1966), wherein these items were intended to measure professional and status orientation. In their study five response categories were adopted which ranged from slight/none (importance) to utmost (importance). However, in the present context ratings of importance on these items were taken on a five point scale – extremely important (5), quite important (4), I can't say (3), somewhat important (2), not very important (1). Higher score represented stronger motivation.

To know the reliability of the scale in the context of the study, the split-half method was adopted based on the responses in the pilot survey. The correlation of total of odd and even items showed a coefficient of 0.59. The reliability coefficient obtained using Spearman – Brown formula was 0.74 ($P < .01$).

3.5 Job Satisfaction

Job satisfaction was measured through a scale of 15 items. This scale was earlier used by Pelz and Andrews (1966) for measuring job satisfaction in their study of scientists in organisations and by Vollmer (1969) for measuring the job attitudes of scientists in research laboratories. The scale included items covering areas such as facilities for use of skills and knowledge, autonomy, recognition for work, facilities for professional participation and publishing research. Satisfaction on factors such as salary, promotional opportunities were also enquired. Special care was taken so that the items in the scale suit the specific context in which it is applied. A few items that were included in the study of Pelz and Andrews (1966) were deleted in the present context. These items are: to advance in administrative authority and status, to work under chiefs of high technical competence (another item focusing on the technical competence of the colleagues was found sufficient). To associate with top executives in the organisation, to work on problems of value to the nation's well being. As per the opinion of the judges these items were either a repetition or not appropriate in our context. The five response categories used by Pelz and Andrews (1966) ranged from slight/none to complete satisfaction. However, in the present context it was found convenient to use – "yes, definitely" (5) "Yes, I think so" (4), "I can't say" (3), "No, I don't think so" (2), "No, definitely not" (1). These response categories are used by Vollmer (1964) in his study. The score range of the scale was 15-30-45-60-75 where higher score indicated higher satisfaction.

Pelz and Andrews (1966) have explored several ways of scoring these items as satisfaction measure. A correlation of the provision and desire of all the job factors was found and also discrepancy of the two were ascertained as a clue to the satisfaction. However, in the present study satisfaction was scored separately from the desire (motivation). A clue to this was also taken from the observation of Pelz and Andrews, on the scoring, wherein they opine ". . . satisfaction (as we have scored it) is unrealistic as a key to understanding scientific achievement. It is likely to correlate meaningfully only if the strength of desire is unrelated to performance although provision is related and this is a dubious assumption. It would be wiser for the investigator to measure the two components separately and not one in relation with the other" (1966, p. 128).

Reliability of the 15 items used in the scale was established from the pilot survey data. Product moment correlation of the two halves of the scale, one consisting of odd and the other even numbered items in the scale, worked out to be 0.62 ($P < .01$). Reliability coefficient as per Spearman – Brown formula was 0.77.

3.6 Dedication

Dedication is considered to be the summation of sense of involvement, obligation, interests and challenge one feels in their research and teaching jobs. Accordingly four items were framed to elicit the responses on these aspects. Similar items were used by Pelz and Andrews (1966) in their study in addition to one on identification with the work. However, this item was felt to be same as involvement by the judges and so was not included in the scale. A change in the response categories was also made in the present study. In the study quoted earlier six point scale was used on four items and five-point scale for the item dealing with the challenge. In the present context a five-point scale was adopted uniformly. The items and response categories read as follows:

- To what extent do you feel obliged in supporting the goals of your organisation? [strong (5), moderate (4), slight (2), and no obligation (1), the response, "I can't say" (3) was placed in neutral category].
- How interesting do you find your present research/teaching work? [very interesting (5), interesting enough (4), somewhat interesting (2), hardly interesting (1), I can't say (3)].
- Some individuals are completely involved in their research and teaching work, absorbed by it day and night, for others this work is simply one of the several interests. How involved are you in your work? [completely involved (5), involved (4), somewhat involved (2), not much involved (1), I can't say (3)].
- How challenging do you find your present work in the sense of demanding concentration, intelligence etc. [very challenging (5), challenging (4), somewhat challenging (2), not at all challenging (1), I can't say (3)].

The items were scored as indicated in the brackets against the response categories above. Higher scores indicated higher dedication.

The reliability test worked out on the pilot survey data revealed a high reliability coefficient based on the Spearman-Brown formula (0.86 $P < .01$) and also high correlation of the total scores of odd and even numbered items (0.76 $P < .01$).

3.7 Aspiration

In the earlier studies the level of aspiration has been measured through questionnaire technique (Muthayya, 1971) as well as through projective techniques (Pareek and Chattopadhyay, 1965). But the most popular technique is the measurement through cantril's pictorial self-anchoring ladder scale (Kilpatrick and Cantril, 1960). The same has been used in the present study. The original scale provides anchoring points from 0 to 10 for the self ratings with reference to the past, present and future. In the present context it was limited to the present and future. The two anchoring points and the rungs in between were defined as follows:

> Here is a ladder with ten rungs. The lowest rung (0) can possibly indicate the place a person graduates into when he takes up an academic job after his studies. The highest rung (10) can indicate the best one can possibly achieve in the academic life, like making substantial original contributions in the field of specialisation, propounding a new theory etc., which guarantees international reputation. The remaining rungs falling in between represent increasing level of academic attainment. Imagine your academic career as one representing the different rungs in the ladder and indicate – where you would place yourself at the present moment of time and three years hence.

The response in the pilot survey indicated the feasibility of such a measure.

The relative high and low aspirers were designated based on the discrepancy of actual future and present positions and also by grouping the respondents as high (7 and above), low (0-3), and middle (4-6) in the two time dimensions, and their relative progression from one group to another.

3.8 Personal Attributes

Personal data from the respondents were also collected as they formed part of the study. These included educational level, professional experience, position in the hierarchy, age and sex of the respondents.

3.8.1 *Experience*

The data regarding total professional experience were collected in intervals of five years. The data were treated analogous to career phases (Slocum and Cron, 1985). Accordingly initial phase (experience below five years i.e., recent entrants into academic position), middle phase (experience ranging from 6 to 15 years i.e., those who have stabilised in the academic profession) and later phase (those with 16 years of experience and above i.e., those with relatively longer professional standing) were adopted.

3.8.2 *Education*

The respondents for the study had three levels of educational attainment such as Master of Arts, Master of Philosophy or Ph.D. degree, in one of the social science disciplines. Respondents were asked to check their highest degree and indicate their subject area of study, such as political science, sociology etc.

3.8.3 *Position*

Four professional positions were generally discernible in all the organisations. These were in accordance with the UGC norms, though the title associated with the positions vary. In the universities the designations used are – (1) Research Assistant, (2) Lecturer/Assistant Professor, (3) Reader/Associate Professor and (4) Professor. In research organisations these positions are designated as (1) Research Associate/Assistant, (2) Assistant Director/Research Officer/Faculty member, (3) Deputy Director/Senior Faculty and (4) Director of the Faculty. These positions overlap considerably in the pay structure, job duties and academic responsibilities. With this understanding, provision was made in the questionnaire for checking the appropriate position title of the respondent. These four positions were retained for the analysis.

3.9 **Professional Activities and other Information Use Data**

Questions were also included to elicit data on the current research and teaching activities, library service use and constraints in the use of information sources.

Respondents were asked to mention the percentage of time spent on teaching, research and administrative activities as a part of their job. The respondents were instructed to round off the figures to the nearest ten per cent. For those engaged in research activities information was collected as to whether such activities were undertaken individually or in group. In case it is group or team research, the respondents were requested to check their status such as project directors or associates. Data were also collected on the number of projects the respondents were engaged in and the number of researchers in the group.

3.10 Constraints in Information Use

Nine constraints in the information seeking process were identified. These constraints included both situational and personal ones. Situational constraints include problem of locating suitable sources, qualified help and procedures adopted in libraries. Personal constraints were that of finding time, getting information quickly, getting up to date material, understanding research reports, problem of languages and knowing how to use abstracts/indexes etc. Provision was also made to specify any other constraint the respondents encountered. Four answer categories (no problem, a little difficulty, considerable difficulty, extreme difficulty) were given to indicate the degree of problem faced by the respondents. These responses were scored 4 to 1, higher score indicating lesser constraints. Similar items were also used by Summers *et al* (1983a) to measure the constraints in information seeking behaviour of the educational practitioners.

Data were also elicited on the respondents need for current information and ways of keeping up to date, and also different library services used in the past three months duration.

3.11 Final Survey and the Characteristics of the Respondents

A complete list of research and teaching personnel specialising in one of the selected social science disciplines was taken from all the eleven identified organisations for data collection. A total of 310 potential respondents occupying different positions in the professional hierarchy was spotted. As the study intended to cover the total universe of population all the potential respondents were contacted individually by the researcher and after explaining the purpose of data collection the final questionnaire was given to them for filling it at their leisure. In all 262 valid and complete responses were collected. Non-response included those who were away for a long time after the first contact and also those who returned the questionnaire incompletely filled in. Accessibility of the respondents was one of the advantages which helped the researcher in ensuring a relatively higher response rate. In all 84.5 per cent of the potential respondents returned the questionnaire duly filled in which was found to be satisfactory.

The study population consisted of social scientists from University Social Science Departments and Research and Training Institutions. In all three universities and eight research and training institutions were selected for the purposes of data collection. 103 (39.31%) respondents were from one of the three Universities and 159 (60.69%) from Research and Training Institutions. A small proportion (14.12% – N-37) of the response population were women.

Age

Respondents were observed in all the age groups ranging from 20 – 25 to 56 – 60 (Table 3.1). Mean age for the study population was 39.51 years. Those with university affiliation were relatively older with mean age of 42.52 years and it is 37.56 years for Research and Training Institutions.

TABLE 3.1: Age-wise Distribution of Respondents

Age Group	Research and Training Institutions	Universities	Total
20 - 25	3	—	3
26 - 30	30	11	41
31 - 35	44	15	59
36 - 40	30	13	43
41 - 45	18	22	40
46 - 50	21	23	44
51 - 55	13	14	27
56 - 60	—	5	5
	159	103	262

Education

All the respondents had a masters degree in one of the social science disciplines. In addition 33 of them possessed an M.Phil degree and 123 a Ph.D. degree (Table 3.2).

TABLE 3.2: Education-wise Distribution of Respondents

Education	M.A.	M.Phil	Ph.D.	Total
Research and Training Institutions	81	22	56	159
Universities	25	11	67	103
Total	106	33	123	262

A greater proportion of the respondents from the Universities (N-67 – 65.05%) possessed a Ph.D. degree as opposed to 35.22% (N-56) from the Research and Training Institutes. M.A. degree holders formed 50.94% (N-81) of the study population from Research Institutes where as 24.27% were with a similar degree from universities.

Subject Specialisation of the Respondents

Respondents of the study specialised in one of the social science disciplines. Social sciences were defined to include disciplines such as sociology, social work, anthropology, psychology, economics, regional geography, political science, public administration, education including extension education and communication. Applied statisticians in the research institutes were also formed the part of the study population as they were found to work strictly in the social research context. Table 3.3 gives the subject specialisation of the respondents from universities and research and training institutes.

Experience

Experience-wise distribution of respondents are presented in Table 3.4. Mean professional experience for the study population works out to be 12.79 years. Average experience is slightly on the lesser side (11.05 years) for Research and Training Institutions and for the universities it is 15.47 years. This trend of longer experience among the university respondents is also a reflection of higher mean age found among them.

TABLE 3.3: Subject Specialisation of the Respondents

Environment	Subject Area							
	Psychology	Economics	Extension Education and Communication	Geography	Sociology/ social work/ Anthropology	Political Science/ Public Administration	Statistics	Total
Research and Training Institutions	14	50	18	7	40	17	13	159
Universities	8	20	20	8	11	28	—	103
Total	22	70	38	15	51	45	13	262

TABLE 3.4: Experience-wise Distribution of the Respondents

Experience	Research and Training Institutions	University Departments	Total
1 - 5	42	16	58
6 - 10	44	21	65
11 - 15	32	7	39
16 - 20	22	25	47
21 - 25	13	22	35
26 - 30	5	11	16
31 - 35	1	1	2
Total	159	103	262

Position

Respondents were holding one of the four positions, though designation given by the different institutions varied. Understandably there were lesser number of them (N-34) in the highest position in the hierarchy i.e., professor or director of the faculty. In the other three positions the distribution was more or less equal. However, a larger majority of the Research Assistants/Associates were from Research and Training Institutions.

TABLE 3.5: Position-wise Distribution of the Respondents

Position	Research and Training Institutes	Universities	Total
Research Associates/Assistants	70	6	76
Assistant Director/Lecturers/ Assistant Professors	38	41	79
Deputy Directors/Readers/ Associate Professors	40	33	73
Professors/Directors	19	15	34
Total	159	103	262

Research and Teaching

The main overlapping interest of the social scientists with different institutional affiliations was the research and teaching/training activities in their respective field of specialisation. The study population as a whole spent approximately 55 per cent of their working time on research and research guidance activities and 30 per cent of the work time on teaching/training work. The remaining part in administrative duties. The average teaching and research time varies from universities to Research and Training Institutions. Average teaching time was considerably less in Research and Training Institutions (18.62%) as opposed to universities (46.89%). In addition, as many as 38.99 per cent in the research institutions do not have regular teaching work. So also the time spent on research activities tend to dominate (67.23%) in the Research and Training Institutions, which works out to be an average of 37.77 per cent in university departments (Table 3.6).

A small proportion of the respondents (5.73% – N-15) did not involve in research (Table 3.7). Of the remaining, 125 (47.71%) were conducting research individually, in some cases in addition to the group involvement (19.47% – N-51) and the rest in group of 2 to 5 members. Group research was more prevalent in Research and Training Institutions as 80.50 per cent (N-128) were in one of such a team.

TABLE 3.6: Distribution of Work Time in Research/Teaching Activities

	0%	10%	20%	30%	40%	50%	60%	70%	80%	90%	100%	Total	(Percentage)
Universities													
Teaching	7	2	10	20	9	16	10	19	3	2	5	103	(46.89)
Research/Research Guidance	10	6	16	14	17	19	8	8	4	0	1	103	(37.77)
Administrative Work	28	31	24	10	6	1	2	0	1	0	0	103	(15.34)
Research and Training Institutions													
Teaching	62	19	28	20	12	6	7	2	1	1	1	159	(18.62)
Research/Research Guidance	5	1	5	6	6	19	30	23	23	14	27	159	(67.23)
Administrative Work	55	40	40	8	6	7	1	0	2	0	0	159	(14.15)

TABLE 3.7: Details of the Research Activity

	Individually	In group	Individually and in Group	Not conducting Research	Total
Research and Training Institutions	26	93	35	5	159
Universities	48	29	16	10	103

The following section presents the description of statistical techniques used for the analysis of the data.

3.12 Statistical Methods used for the Analysis

The effect of criterion variable ATI on the information source use i.e., attitude-behaviour relations was examined applying Kurskal and Goodman's Gamma statistic. To know the effect of psychological attributes such as job satisfaction, motivation, dedication, level of aspiration and personal attributes including professional experience and position in the hierarchy on ATI Analysis of Variance (ANOVA) statistic was used. Critical ratios (*t* ratios) were computed in the case of education and environment as the response population was categorised into two distinct groups on these variables. For examining whether the effect of personal and psychological attributes on ATI is same in both the job environments, and also to find out whether the effect of psychological attributes is same for respondents showing variations in their personal attributes two-way analysis of variance was computed. To find out the nature of ATI and information source use relations in case of varying psychological and personal attributes Goodman and Kurskal's Gamma statistic was extended. Partial or conditional contingency tables of ATI and information source use was made taking at a time one of the personal or psychological attributes into consideration. For detailed examination of the differences in ATI among the sub-groups (high, moderate, low etc.) *t* ratios were computed. In cases of bivariate classification of ATI, Duncan's multiple range test for unequal number of group size was used at 5 per cent confidence limit. Pearson's product-moment correlation was computed to examine the relations of each of the item in job satisfaction, motivation and dedication scales with that of ATI.

On variables such as job satisfaction, motivation, dedication and ATI (for ATI and source use analysis) respondents were classified into high, moderate and low groups based on the quartile one and three cut off point. In the case of level of aspiration, goal discrepancy scores were used, in addition to the groupings – high, middle and low based on the arbitrary cut off points in the ladder scale. These groupings, however do not mean low or high in absolute sense. Lowness is interpreted to mean that a respondent within that score ranks low on a given variable relative to the other respondents on the same variable.

As to the personal attributes, four hierarchical positions were treated as it is and two groups – Ph.D's and non-Ph.D's – were made based on the respondents educational attainment. Professional experience was treated analogous to career phases (Slocum and Cron, 1985). Accordingly initial phase (experience below 5 years i.e. recent entrants into the academic positions) middle phase (experience ranging from 6 to 15 years – i.e., those who have stabilised in the academic profession) and later phase (those with 16 years of above i.e., those who have relatively longer professional standing) were adopted for the analysis.

Goodman and Kurskal's Gamma, a proportional reduction of error (PRE) measure, has been considered more versatile and informative when order is implied in the variables. PRE measures examine our ability to predict the individual scores for one or the other of the attributes in bivariate distribution. Like all PRE measures, Gamma compares two methods of prediction. The first method is based on randomly predicting all untied pairs of score to be either in agreement or disagreement. The second method predicts all tied pairs to be of the same type whether there is agreement or disagreement is determined by the direction of the bivariate distribution.

Beyond having ordinal level of measurement the requirements for an inference test with gamma are that the sample size should not be too small. The exact minimum is debated to be ranging from 10 to 200 and depends on the existence of the tied pairs in the sample (Lutz, 1984). In the present study 30 observations were taken as a minimum for assuming a normal z sampling distribution. The z transformation formula was used to determine the statistical significance of the gamma value. As the research so far points to the positive relations of attitude and behaviour in varied fields of study, the Gamma statistics was used as a one tailed test.

Gamma values were calculated by using the formula –

formula $$G = \frac{n_s - n_r}{n_s + n_r}$$

z transformation is worked out by using the formula

formula $$z = (G - \mu)\sqrt{\frac{n_s + n_r}{n(1 - G^2)}}$$

where

G = Gamma value

n_s = number of pairs ranked in the same direction

n_r = number of pairs ranked in the opposite direction

n = number of observations

The technique of ANOVA was used for the analysis as it is found to be more sensitive, precise, sophisticated and sound than the technique of correlation for determining relationship in casual comparative studies. Hence the ANOVA with F test for significance of differences arising from and within the variables considered and also from interactions between them was selected to verify the hypotheses. The concern here was with the effect of different levels of predictor variables on the criterion variable.

F ratios in the one way ANOVA are computed by using the formula

Sum of Square Total (SST) = $$\sum_{j=1}^{k} \sum_{i=1}^{W} Y_{ij}^2 - \frac{Y^2}{N}$$

Sum of Square Among Samples (SSA) = $$\sum_{j=1}^{k} \frac{1}{n} Y_j^2 - \frac{1}{N} Y^2$$

Sum of Square within Samples (SSW) = SST – SSA

Mean Square Among Samples (MSA) = $$\frac{\text{SSA}}{\text{Degrees of Freedom Among Samples}}$$

Mean Squares within Samples (MSW) = $$\frac{\text{SSW}}{\text{Degrees of Freedom within samples}}$$

F = $$\frac{\text{MSA}}{\text{MSW}}$$

where

Y = Grand total of all measures

Y_{ij} = *i*th measure in the *j*th sample

n = number of observations within the sub-samples

N = Total observations

As to the individual and combined effects of two or more variables, whenever they are quantified researchers no doubt make use of partial correlation technique in order to rule out the effect of one or more variables in relation to the other variable. In the context perhaps the observation of Lindquist (1968) is appropriate. Cautioning about the use of partial correlation in the psychological studies, he opines that none of the score is a pure or perfect valid measure, even aside from chance errors in measurement of the ability implied in the title of the test, but it partially is a measure of many irrelevant factors which may or may not influence the scores on the other tests as well. So also he feels we are rarely able to provide a very meaningful and exact description of what each test is intended to measure, to say nothing of what is actually measures.

The method of Multiple Analysis of Variance and analysis of covariance is profitably employed with reference to any concomitant variable, whether or not it may be measured at the beginning of the experiment in order to determine how the criterion means would have differed if a concomitant variable had been held constant. In the present study it may be suspected, for instance, that education level could interfere with the job satisfaction. It is therefore desirable to know which education group would have resulted in more favourable ATI when the job satisfaction is equated in each education group. By this method the difference in mean scores on the criterion tests are so adjusted to eliminate the effect of the other variable. It could be thus determined whether or not the mean differences in ATI is significant when, for instance, education is held constant and when it is not. The adjusted sums of squares are regarded by the statisticians as better estimates of the treatment effect than the unadjusted means. Because in this technique one of the sources of experimental errors get removed by the adjustment. In the case of bivariate classification several techniques have been devised which are capable of correcting disproportionality and adjusting the main effects the simplest and the most expeditious of these methods is that reported by Paterson (1946). According to this method the border means of the double classification are successively adjusted until they equal the general mean. The adjustment terms are then used to compute the adjusted sum of squares for one or both main effects (Wert, 1954). In addition to the two main effects two-way ANOVA also reveals whether an interaction exists between the two variables. An interaction exists when the effect of the combined action of the variables is different from that which would be predicted by the individual effects. It is based on the difference among the cell means beyond that which is predicted by the individual effects of the two variables. Significant interaction means that the effect of one of the factors on the dependent variable is not the same at all the levels of the other factor. Though one way ANOVA need not be presented when two way design has been worked out, for the purpose of clarity both the analysis are presented in the report.

The *t* statistic is considered to be appropriate measure whenever two sample means have to be compared. The formula used for computing *t* ratios was

formula $$\frac{\bar{x}_1 - \bar{x}_2}{\sqrt{\frac{(n_1-1)s_1^2 + (n_2-1)s_2^2}{n_1+n_2-2} \times \frac{1}{n_1} + \frac{1}{n_2}}}$$

where

$\bar{x}_1$ and $\bar{x}_2$ stands for mean of two sample groups
n_1 and n_2 number of observations in two groups
s_1 and s_2 standard deviations of the mean scores for the two groups.

For finding out the significance of aspiration of the respondents the present and future dimensions formula used was

formula $$t = \frac{\bar{d}}{\sqrt{s^2/(n-1)}}$$

where

$\bar{d}$ is the mean of the differences between the two aspiration scores.

Duncan's Range Test (DRT) is a multiple comparison test used when there are more treatment groups. In Duncan's test for an equal number of replications the difference between any two ranked means is significant if the difference exceeds a shortest significant range. The shortest significant range is designated by R_p and is obtained by multiplying the standard error of a mean, $s_{\bar{x}}$ by a given value, z_p, n_2, obtained from a table of significant studentised ranges which Duncan has tabled for both the five per cent and one per cent test. In Duncan's terminology n_2 is the degree of freedom of the error mean square and $p = 1, 2 \ldots t$ is the number of means concerned.

In the case of unequal number of replications the formula used for computing the test value is:

formula $$\bar{x}_B - \bar{x}_C > \sqrt{\frac{1}{2}\left(\frac{1}{n_B}+\frac{1}{n_C}\right)s^2 z} \;.\; n_2$$

where

$\bar{x}_B$ and $\bar{x}_C$ are the mean scores for two groups
n_2 = degrees of freedom
n = number of observations
s^2 = standard error of the mean

For group means based on unequal numbers a table of factors $R_p^1 = s_2 p, n_2$, where s^2 is the mean square of error, should be set up, in each individual case. Duncan's test is identical to a t test if there are only two means (Kramer 1956).

And lastly the statistical formula used for computing the product moment correlation:

formula $$\gamma = \frac{1}{N} \cdot \frac{\Sigma XY - \bar{x} \cdot \bar{y}}{\sigma x \cdot \sigma y}$$

where

N = number of observations
$\bar{x}$ and $\bar{y}$ = mean of X and Y variables
σx and σy = standard deviation of the X and Y variables

The next chapter presents the analysis of the data collected for the study and interpretations of the same using the above stated statistical techniques.

4

RESULTS AND DISCUSSIONS

4.1 Attitude towards Information

Attitude towards information (ATI) was measured with a 38-item attitude scale covering various aspects of information-seeking behaviour of social scientists. Items in the scale elicited the evaluative opinion of the respondents on the statements on a five-point scale. Answer categories ranged from 'strongly agree' to 'strongly disagree'. The degree of agreement indirectly reflected the intensity of their ATI. The scale consisted of 6 positively directed items and 32 negatively directed ones. While a positively directed item was scored in an order from 0 to 4, a negatively directed item was scored in the

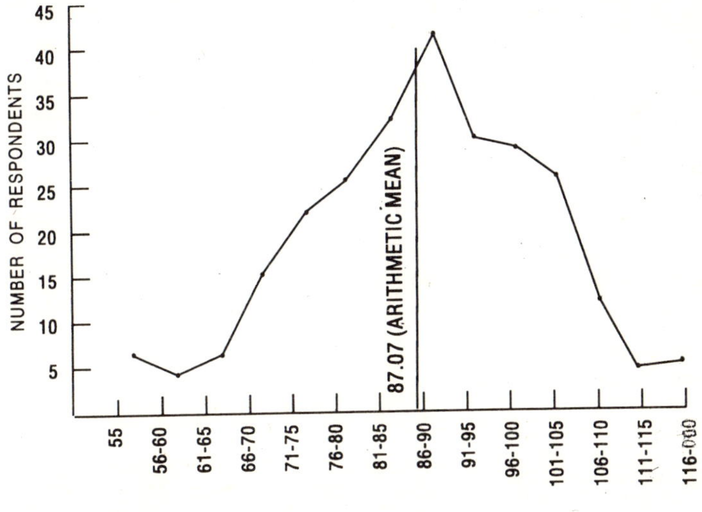

FIG. 4.1: Distribution of Respondents on ATI Scores

reverse order from 4 to 0 so that higher total score on ATI for a respondent represented a more favourable ATI. Total ATI score range for 38 items was 0–152 and the observed range was from 45 to 137. The distribution (Fig. 4.1) showed skewness of –0.43 and had a Kurtosis –0.33.

The mean ATI score for the respondents was 87.07. Judging from the theoretical mid point of the scale – which is 78 – the observed mean score suggests a trend of favourable ATI. However, favourableness borders around neutrality as the mean score is slightly above the neutral point. For the respondents as a whole, it suggests that the degree of favourableness is not as definite as could be expected from the academicians at this level.

Items used in the ATI scale and the distribution of the respondents in different scale points are shown in Table 4.1.

TABLE 4.1: Frequency Distribution of Respondents on ATI Scale Items

(N=262)

Items	SA	A	U	D	SD
Personal experience are always more educative than published information	82 (31.30)	111 (42.37)	24 (09.16)	42 (16.03)	3 (01.14)
Research reports dealing with different cultural context rarely carry worthwhile information for us	13 (04.96)	48 (18.32)	35 (13.36)	125 (47.71)	41 (15.65)
Presentation of information in statistical terms poses difficulties in understanding	18 (06.87)	60 (22.90)	23 (08.78)	120 (45.80)	41 (15.65)
Intellectual curiosity is satisfied mostly through reading	53 (20.23)	137 (52.29)	23 (08.78)	42 (16.03)	7 (02.67)
Factual information rarely gets recorded in the research reports	15 (05.73)	44 (16.79)	33 (12.60)	142 (54.20)	28 (10.68)
It is better to do something else than spend the time in academic reading	6 (02.29)	27 (10.31)	18 (06.87)	126 (48.09)	85 (32.44)

(*Contd.*)

TABLE 4.1 *(Contd.)*

Items	SA	A	U	D	SD
As an individual reads more his understanding of the reality would increase	73 (27.86)	140 (53.44)	21 (08.02)	23 (08.78)	5 (01.90)
Few people have adequate time to go through the required information	15 (05.73)	110 (41.98)	39 (14.89)	86 (32.82)	12 (04.58)
Published information influences the value system of the individuals	20 (07.63)	140 (53.44)	55 (20.99)	42 (16.03)	5 (01.91)
Most research reports are monotonous to read through	12 (04.58)	103 (39.31)	43 (16.41)	97 (37.02)	7 (02.67)
An effective teacher is not always one who updates his information	14 (05.34)	67 (25.57)	27 (10.30)	117 (44.66)	37 (14.12)
Findings in social sciences are usually confirmatory rather than contributory	18 (06.87)	93 (35.50)	30 (11.45)	108 (41.22)	13 (04.96)
In social science research ideas borrowed from other published sources are rarely acknowledged	9 (03.44)	71 (27.10)	45 (17.18)	128 (48.85)	9 (03.44)
After a certain stage most academicians lose their interest in academic reading, for it fetches them nothing	21 (08.02)	73 (27.86)	56 (21.37)	95 (36.26)	17 (06.49)
Research conclusions are rarely different from common man's understanding	16 (06.11)	69 (26.34)	38 (14.50)	120 (45.80	19 (07.25)
Peer group appreciation is mostly ensured to those who are well read in their respective discipline	26 (09.92)	163 (62.21)	46 (17.56)	25 (09.54)	2 (00.76)
Elaborate procedures in libraries more often restricts their use	24 (09.16)	124 47.33)	36 (13.74)	71 (27.10)	7 (02.67)

TABLE 4.1 *(Contd.)*

Items	SA	A	U	D	SD
In most cases it is extraneous factors and not extensive reading which ensures academic reputation	22 (08.40)	72 (27.48)	59 (22.52)	95 (36.26)	14 (05.34)
Information acquisition fosters scientific attitude among people	30 (11.45)	176 (67.18)	36 (13.74)	17 (06.49)	3 (01.15)
Most people do not abide by the copyright laws	12 (04.58)	114 (43.51)	93 (35.50)	40 (15.27)	3 (01.15)
Social research reports are often fabricated	5 (01.91)	49 (18.70)	75 (28.63)	117 (44.66)	16 (06.11)
Information updating is not essential for success in teaching jobs these days	11 (04.20)	46 (17.56)	17 (06.49)	141 (53.82)	47 (17.94)
Published information is useful only for research purposes and is rarely of significance in practical life	13 (04.96)	63 (24.05)	22 (08.40)	141 (53.82)	23 (08.78)
The nature of many academic jobs does not demand regular information seeking	8 (03.05)	75 (28.63)	25 (09.54)	130 (49.62)	24 (09.16)
Available information on many social research topics is so confusing that it is better not to take notice of many of them	5 (01.91)	25 (09.54)	47 (17.94)	158 (60.31)	27 (10.31)
Social scientists need not necessarily look through all the available information in their areas of specialisation	4 (01.53)	38 (14.50)	14 (05.34)	160 (61.07)	46 (17.56)
Many of the literature guides are so confusing that they seem to scare the users away	7 (02.67)	77 (29.39)	81 (30.92)	91 (34.73)	6 (02.29)
Computer information retrieval would only prove uneconomical investment in our situation	7 (02.67)	411 (15.65)	60 (22.90)	125 (47.71)	29 (11.07)

(Contd.)

TABLE 4.1 *(Concld.)*

Items	SA	A	U	D	SD
However much one aspires it is often other factors and not wide reading which help in the academic jobs	25 (09.54)	76 (29.01)	64 (24.43)	83 (31.68)	14 (05.34)
Even if most of the current research reports are overlooked it hardly matters in academic jobs these days	12 (04.58)	71 (27.10)	48 (19.32)	115 (43.89)	16 (06.11)
Published reviews of researches are often based on personal likes and dislikes.	11 (04.20)	90 (34.35)	65 (24.81)	90 (34.35)	6 (02.29)
Information updating is not always an important criterion for decision-making in matters relating to academic work	8 (03.05)	64 (24.43)	38 (14.50)	138 (52.67)	14 (05.34)
Voracious readers are rarely innovative in their jobs	8 (03.05)	54 (20.61)	77 (29.39)	105 (40.08)	18 (06.87)
There is nothing of practical value in acquiring published information	3 (01.15)	21 (08.02)	33 (12.60)	177 (67.56)	28 (10.69)
Social research is often duplicated due to the absence of information about the research already done	20 (07.63)	140 (53.44)	42 (16.03)	50 (19.08)	10 (03.82)
New job opportunities are rarely available to those who are widely read in their respective disciplines	18 (06.87)	85 (32.44)	54 (20.61)	89 (33.97)	16 (06.11)
Many research reports arrive at wide generalisation on the basis of inadequate data	25 (09.54)	149 (56.87)	50 (19.08)	35 (13.36)	3 (01.15)
Cultural richness of a country is mostly reflected in the information base (in terms of libraries, archives) it has	63 (24.05)	140 (53.44)	19 (07.25)	33 (12.59)	7 (02.67)

SA : Strongly Agree
A : Agree
U : Undecided
D : Disagree
SD : Strongly Disagree

TABLE 4.2: Distribution of Respondents on ATI Scores

ATI scores	Frequency
< 55	7
56 - 60	5
61 - 65	7
66 - 70	15
71 - 75	22
76 - 80	25
81 - 85	32
86 - 90	41
91 - 95	30
96 - 100	29
101 - 105	24
106 - 110	14
111 - 115	5
116 >	6
	262

4.2 Information Source Use

Importance of the information sources available either in bibliographic form or otherwise for research and teaching activities needs no emphasis. In the introductory chapter the need for information use *vis-a-vis* research and teaching has been discussed. Though largely the link between information source use and performance is treated as axiomatic, studies have also shown that research and teaching performance is closely related to information use and also up dating of information in one's field of specialisation from both bibliographic and non-bibliographic sources. Need for consultation of different sources of information is particularly important in social sciences as the knowledge structure in these disciplines is non-accumulative one and accommodates for different schools of thought on the same issues (Brittain, 1979).

Information for research and teaching has to be gathered either from the published sources or through informal sources such as discussion with colleagues, consulting experts in the field etc. In addition, for survey type research carried out in the social sciences, primary survey data also forms an important component.

With this understanding a list of 15 sources of information was included in the questionnaire designed for pilot survey. These included periodicals, books/research reports, theses/dissertations, government publications, maps, newspapers, references in books and periodicals, book reviews, abstracting/indexing sources, library inhouse services, primary data/field survey data, discussion with colleagues, consulting experts, workshops and seminars and audio-visual materials. It was observed that social scientists generally made use of twelve of these sources in different degrees in their academic activities. Of the three sources which were not in general use were maps — more often used only by geographers, newspapers — used by those with political science specialisation. Audio-visual sources were found to be generally of very sparse use for all the subject specialities.

Data about the extent of use of these 12 sources in their current research and teaching activities were collected on a numerical scale with ten points (0-9). As it was intended in the survey design, the scale was collapsed into four categories viz., not used (0), rarely used (1-3), moderately used (4-6) and frequently used (7-9). Rating scale of a similar type has been earlier adopted in the INFROSS study.

4.2.1 *Distribution of Respondents in the Information Source-use Categories*

A glance at Table 4.3 shows that the respondents fall in the use categories. Books and periodicals are the most used sources of information and abstracting and indexing sources are the least used ones.

4.2.1.1 *Primary Sources*: Four primary sources formed part of the final list of information sources. They included books/research reports, periodicals, theses/dissertations, and government publications.

Periodicals: Periodicals carry large body of current research publications and one of the most important sources of information for academic work. Distribution of the respondents on four use categories reveal that only a negligible proportion (0.76%) have not made use of this source, 12.22 per cent have used it rarely, 39.69 per cent moderately and nearly half (47.33%) have made use of this source frequently. Mean use ratings for this source works out to be 2.34 which is greater than the scale mid point of 1.50. Periodicals stand second as to the frequency of source use by the social scientists.

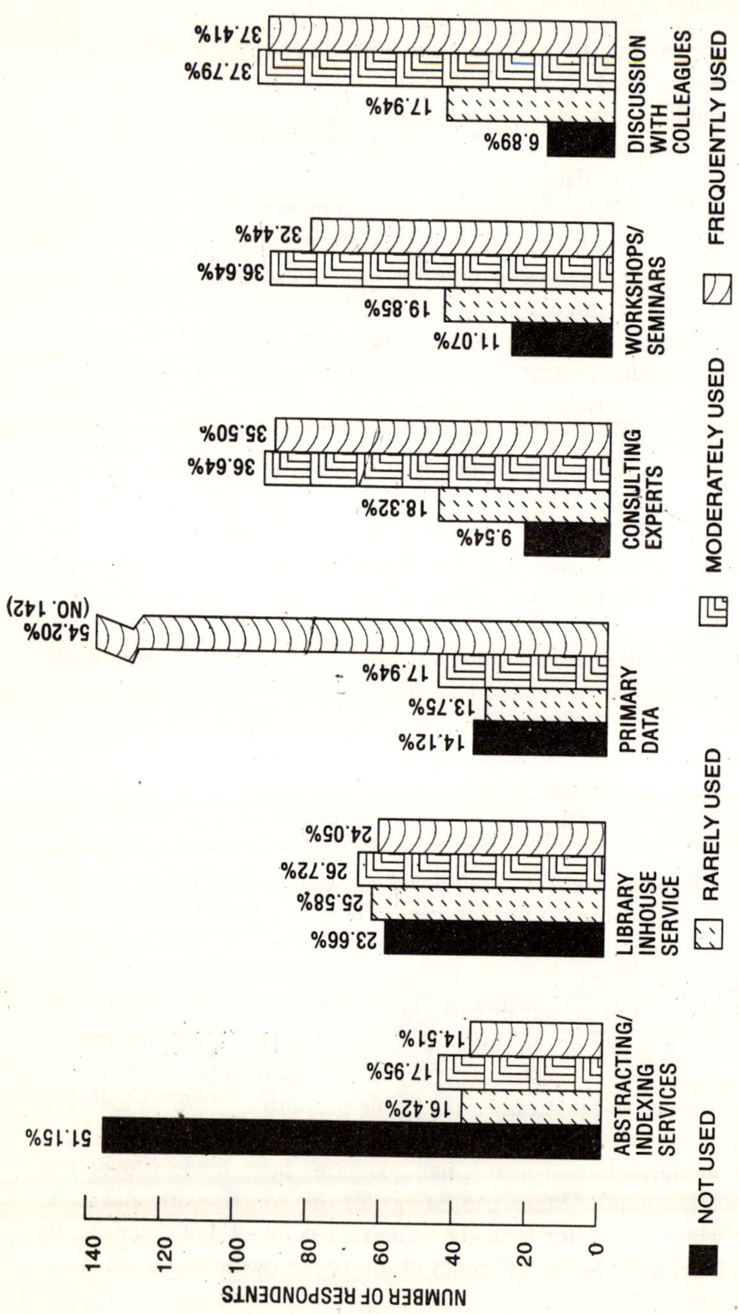

FIG. 4.2: Distribution of Respondents in Information Source Use Categories

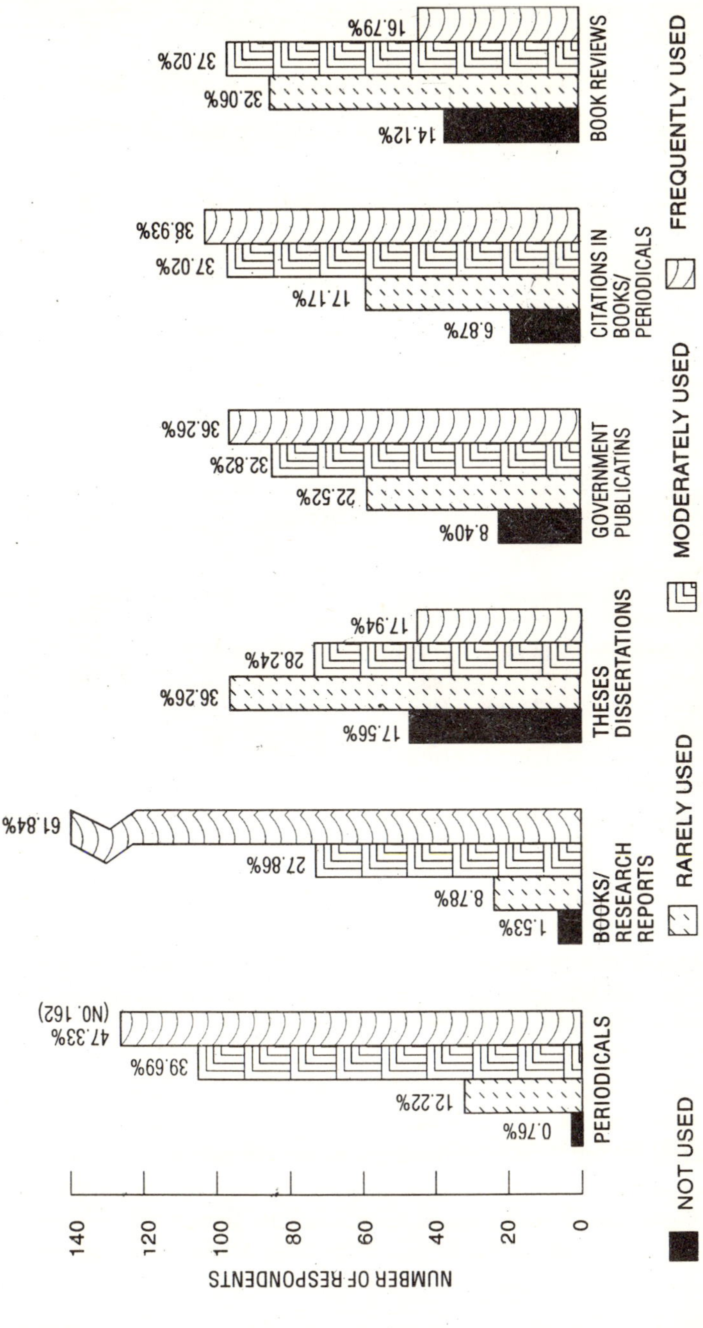

GRAPH 2 : DISTRIBUTION OF RESPONDENTS IN INFORMATION SOURCE USE CATEGORIES

TABLE 4.3: Distribution of Respondents in Information Source Use Categories (N = 262)

	Not at all	Rarely	Moderately	Frequently	Mean rankings
Periodicals	2 (0.76)	32 (12.22)	104 (39.69)	124 (47.33)	2.34 (2)
Books	4 (1.53)	23 (8.78)	73 (27.86)	162 (61.84)	2.50 (1)
Theses/Dissertations	46 (17.56)	95 (36.26)	74 (28.24)	47 (17.94)	1.47 (11)
Government Publications	22 (8.40)	59 (22.52)	86 (32.82)	95 (36.26)	1.97 (7)
Citations in books and periodicals	18 (6.87)	45 (17.17)	97 (37.02)	102 (38.93)	2.08 (4)
Book Review	37 (14.12)	84 (32.06)	97 (37.02)	44 (16.79)	1.57 (9)
Abstracting and indexing sources	134 (51.15)	43 (16.42)	47 (17.95)	38 (14.51)	0.96 (12)
Library inhouse services	62 (23.66)	67 (25.58)	70 (26.72)	63 (24.05)	1.51 (10)
Primary data/ Survey data	37 (14.12)	36 (13.75)	47 (17.94)	142 (54.2)	2.12 (3)
Consulting Experts	25 (9.54)	48 (18.32)	96 (36.64)	93 (35.5)	1.98 (6)
Workshops/ Seminars	29 (11.07)	52 (19.85)	96 (36.64)	85 (32.44)	1.91 (8)
Discussion with colleagues	18 (6.89)	47 (17.94)	99 (37.79)	98 (37.41)	2.06 (5)

Books/Research Reports: Books are the most used source of information by the social scientists. Only four respondents have not used this source as against 61.84 per cent who have made frequent use. Mean use rating for the population is 2.50 and it ranks first in the order of importance among the twelve sources.

Theses/Dissertations: Theses and dissertations are the unpublished sources. They form the research work carried on for academic degrees awarded by the universities. These are useful sources of information as they generally contain a scholarly review of the relevant literature. Though original findings are often subsequently published in the appropriate journals, theses will still have their value in yielding full details of methods and procedures used together with most extensive data. In the present study 17.56 per cent report not to have made use of this source. 36.26 per cent have used it rarely, 28.24 per cent moderately and only 17.94 per cent have frequently used in the course of their research and teaching activities. Among the four primary sources this is the least used one.

Government Publications: Government publications include various reference sources brought out by the Central and State Governments of India and also by the governments of other countries. These publications largely consist of reports of committees and commissions appointed by the government, various statistical sources such as census, year books, annual reports etc., and also rules and procedures laid down for operationalisation of the social welfare and development programmes launched by the government bodies. Use of these sources has become all important in the context of the focus of social research on the socio-economic development aspects of the country. 8.4 per cent of the respondents report to have not used this source and 22.52 per cent have rarely used and more or less equal proportion of respondents fall in moderate and frequent use categories.

4.2.1.2 *Secondary Sources*: With the exponential growth of primary sources of information many specialised sources focusing on particular needs of researchers have emerged. These sources, often referred to as surrogate or secondary sources, perform the function of guiding the readers to original primary sources or provide them a gist of information contained in original sources. These sources include, reviews of research, abstracts and indexes, book reviews, library inhouse services such as documentation lists, digests, etc. In addition, it has also been observed that social scientists resort to citations and references quoted in journal articles and books in the process of their literature search. Data regarding the frequency of use of four such sources were elicited in the present study. They included use of references/citations in books and periodicals, book reviews, abstracting and indexing sources and library inhouse services.

Citations in Books and Periodicals: As knowledge structure in social sciences is non-accumulative, varied arguments and findings in studies find their support through related studies which share their school of thought. Comprehensive listings of the older studies are relatively few. Hence, references in books and periodicals are frequently used by the social scientists as a secondary source of information leading to the supportive studies. INFROSS study has reported that among the secondary sources social scientists rely more on the references gathered through citation than the organised sources. (Line *et al*, 1971, p. 62). In the present study also it has been found that references in books and periodicals are the most frequently used secondary source. 38.93 per cent report to have made frequent use, 37.02 per cent moderate use and only 6.87 per cent have not used this source. This source ranks fourth among the twelve sources and is much above the other organised sources such abstracts, published bibliographies, etc.

Book Reviews: Book reviews are the sources through which researchers become aware of the publications of new books, their contents and also the critical evaluation of the research presented in the books. Book reviews normally form part of the periodicals. Reviews at times also appear in the form of a separate journal in itself focusing on some specific discipline. This source is either rarely or moderately used by 32.06 per cent and 37.02 per cent respectively and only 16.79 per cent report to have made use of this source frequently. Mean use score of this source is 1.57 and ranks ninth among the twelve sources.

Abstracting and Indexing Sources: Abstracts and indexing journals are the organised secondary sources. These sources which focus on specific disciplines provide summaries of the research studies published in the journals and other primary sources. These are brought out by the professional bodies and aim at currency and comprehensiveness. In the present study more than one half of the respondents (51.15%) have reported not to have used these sources. More or less equal proportion of the respondents fall in the three use categories. The mean use score for population is 0.96 and this source ranks last. The relative non-use of this source cannot be attributed to the inaccessibility. It has been noted by the investigator that all the important Indian and international abstracting and indexing journals commercially available are subscribed to in the libraries of both research institutes and universities from where the respondents are drawn. Similar observations are also made in earlier studies with the focus on social scientists conducted by Wood and Bower (1969) and Line et al (1971). It seems that there is no great eagerness among the social scientists to make use of these services regularly. Brittain (1970) commenting on this finding observes that may be these tools are in some way inadequate for the requirement of the users, or the tools are not known to the users, or users have no tradition of instruction in the use of these bibliographic tools or a combination of these three. Non-use or less frequent use of abstracting services is one of the important lacuna in the information use of the social scientists which is also shared by the respondents of this study.

Reading Lists prepared by the Libraries: Most of the libraries catering to the researchers also provide documentation services like compiling bibliographies, documentation lists, digests and the like. These services aim to keep their clientele up to date with the literature availability in the library and also to make them aware of trends in the research, facilitate in the literature search etc. It is found that in all the four use categories the respondents more or less show an equal distribution. This source ranks low (tenth) in its usefulness for the response population as a whole.

4.2.1.3 *Non-bibliographic Sources*: It has been acknowledged that various non-bibliographic sources including discussion with colleagues, consulting experts in the field and workshops and seminars are also relied upon by the academicians and have an important role in information acquisition process. These sources, because of the information transfer at person to person level, carry with them various advantages that are not possible in the bibliographic sources. In addition, Menzel (1967) has noted several advantages in this form of communication viz., (1) promptness of information return; (2) selective switching i.e. information is adopted to a particular recipient; (3) screening, evaluation and synthesis of the information is carried out by one's colleagues; (4) methodological aspects of the research can be considered in great detail and (5) instantaneous feedback from recipient to purveyor occurs. Data were collected from the respondents as to the frequency of use of these sources in their current academic activities.

Consulting Experts: Prevalence of interdisciplinary research and also high degree of specialisation within the disciplines have brought in the need for consulting experts in all disciplines. Only 9.54 per cent have not consulted experts as opposed to 35.5 per cent who have consulted them frequently and 36.64 per cent who have made moderate use of this source. Mean score for the use of this source is 1.98 per cent. It may be noted that though almost a half of the respondents possessed Ph.D. degree frequency of use of this source is fairly higher compared to some of the bibliographic sources.

Participating in Workshops/Seminars: Workshops and seminars organised for exchange of views on particular topic are often attended by academicians and the discussions and lectures in these sessions serve as a valuable source of information. As is observed in the case of consulting experts, roughly one-tenth (11.07%) report to have not made use of this source as opposed to 36.64 per cent who have used this source moderately and 32.44 per cent frequently. As per the mean ratings, this source ranks eighth in the decreasing order of importance.

Discussion with Colleagues: Discussion with colleagues as opposed to consulting experts is frequently resorted to by the researchers. Pelz and Andrews (1966) and also Parker *et al* (1968) have revealed that the highly productive scientists involve in frequent communication with their colleagues. The dependence on this source seems to be more compared to the other two non-bibliographic sources. Only 6.89 per cent report to have not discussed their research with their colleagues as opposed to 37.79 per cent and 37.41 per cent who have done this moderately and frequently in that order.

Primary Data or Survey Data: It was observed by the investigator that a vast majority of the respondents use the primary data collected through surveys in the research and training process. The response in the present context also seems to confirm this observation as this source ranks only next to books and periodicals in dependence of the social scientists for their research/teaching. These surveys are not necessarily the ones conducted by themselves for a particular research but may be those conducted by fellow professionals for other purposes. These surveys provide data which may not be available in other bibliographic sources. 54.2 per cent of the respondents have made frequent use of this source and 17.94 per cent moderate use. 14.12 per cent have reported non-use of the primary data. The rest have found it to be of rare use.

Thus, it may be inferred from the discussion that all the sources of information are made use of by the respondents. Most used source based on the mean ranking is books followed by periodicals and primary data collected in surveys etc. Among the secondary sources, citations in periodicals and books are the most frequently resorted source which rank fourth. Non-bibliographic sources such as discussion with colleagues and consulting experts rank fifth and sixth. Government publications rank seventh followed by participation in workshops, seminars etc., book reviews, library inhouse services, theses/dissertations and abstracting sources are the less often used sources which rank in the same order after government publications.

In general the pattern of the source use largely confirms the earlier findings of INFROSS study which has revealed that books and periodicals are the most used among the primary sources. Use pattern of secondary sources which made the investigators of INFROSS study comment on the 'haphazard use' of the information sources by social scientists also seem to hold good in this study. Social scientists show a preference to the citations in the periodicals, etc., as opposed to the systematically indexed sources such as abstracts and other documentation services.

4.3 ATI and Information Source Use

One of the important assumptions of this investigation is that favourable ATI leads to frequent use of information sources or ATI and information source use have positive and significant relations. The analysis thus explores the latent aspect of the information use i.e. ATI and its relations with the manifest use behaviour. Attitude, as it has been observed, is a predisposition to action relating to the object of focus. Multicomponent view of the attitude, conceptualised by many of the contemporary attitude researchers, holds that attitude towards a psychological object consists of cognitive, affective and conative components towards the object. The relationship of attitudes to overt behaviour has been an area of persistent interest to the researchers.

A preferential response towards an object cannot occur in a vacuum. Within a given situation how a person will behave in relation to the object depends on the particular beliefs and predispositions activated by the attitude towards the object (Rockeach, 1968). Schuman and Johnson (1976) in their review of the attitude-behaviour link state that in most cases studies yield positive results. The correlations that do occur are large enough to indicate that important causal forces are involved. Attitudes exert pressure to behave consistently, but external forces and extraneous considerations can cause people to behave inconsistently with their attitude. That is, consistent overt behaviour under the influence of attitudes one has cultivated may be disturbed by the external forces. In the area of information use research Summers *et al* (1983) have through a study of attitudes of educational practitioners confirmed that ATI is powerful construct and shows a strong causal relation with the information source use.

In the present study the relation of the ATI with that of information source use is examined by applying Goodman and Kurskal's Gamma statistic. Both the variables are ordered categories. ATI groups are low, moderate and high based on the quartile cut off points $q_1 = 77$ and $q_3 = 98$ and the four information use categories are: not used, rarely used, moderately used, and frequently used.

4.3.1 *Primary Sources*

The distribution of respondents in the four use — categories for the primary sources is given in Table 4.4 a-d. The Goodman and Kurskal's Gamma statistic worked out for the observed distribution shows a significant positive association for three of the four sources, viz., books and research reports, periodicals, and theses/dissertations. In other words, more frequent use of these three primary sources tends to occur jointly with more favourable ATI. Strength of association is, however, moderate and significant in case of periodicals and books explaining 32.8 per cent and 33.5 per cent of the differences in their use. In the case of theses, the association is weak, nonetheless significant at five per cent confidence limit. The differences of 22.2 per cent in the use of this source is explained by ATI. Use of Government publications does not show significant association with the ATI. It may be further noted from the distribution table that 61.19% (N=41) of those in the high ATI group use periodicals frequently as compared to 46.15% (N=60) in moderate and 34.85 % (N=23) in low group. Proportion of respondents using periodicals rarely and moderately tend to decrease from low to high group.

So also in the case of books and research reports — 79.10%(N=53) of those in high ATI group use them frequently compared to 58.91%(N=76) and 50.00% (N=33) in moderate and low group respectively. As observed for periodicals the proportion of respondents in rare and moderate use categories tend to decrease as they move from low to high group.

A trend similar to that of books and periodical use — though less pronounced — is observable in the use of theses and dissertations. Of those in high group 28.36%(N=19) use this source frequently, as opposed to 15.50%(N=20) and 12.12%(N=19) in moderate and low group respectively.

4.3.2 *Secondary Sources*

Tables 4.4e-h present the distribution of social scientists and Gamma values as to the use of four secondary sources viz., references in books and periodicals, book reviews, abstracts and library inhouse service. Gamma values reveal that three of those sources show a significant positive association. The exception for this trend being the frequency of use of library in-house services. The possible reasons for this trend could be non-availability of regular documentation services in some of the university libraries and also scholars' dependence on themselves for literature search etc.

The strength of association in case of use of of book reviews (G: 0.293 $P < .01$) and abstracts (G: 0.321 $P < .01$) is moderate explaining 29.3 per cent and 32.1 per cent respectively the differences in the frequency of their use. As to the dependence on citation in books and periodicals the association is weak but positive and significant, and 23.3 per cent of the difference in the frequency of use is explained by the ATI.

Further examination of the distribution shows that 50.75%(N=34) of those in the high group report the use of citations in books and periodicals frequently compared to 36.43%(N=47) and 31.82%(N=21) in the moderate and low group respectively. This trend is more pronounced in the case of book reviews 31.34%(N=21) in high group use this frequently compared to 13.95%(N=18) and 7.58%(N=5) in moderate and low group respectively) and abstracts 22.39%(N=15) in high group use this frequently compared to 12.40%(N=16) and 10.60%(N=7) in moderate and low group respectively.

4.3.3 *Non-bibliographic Sources*

Tables 4.4 i-l give the distribution of respondents in high, moderate and low ATI groups as to the frequency of use of sources viz., primary data, consulting experts in the discipline, discussions with colleagues and attending workshops and seminars. Excepting for primary data other three sources show significant positive association in their frequency of use with ATI. The association of all the three sources with ATI is moderate and explains 26.3 per cent of the difference in the case of consulting experts, 29.3 per cent in the case of workshops and seminars and 26.2 per cent for discussions with colleagues.

As was observed with respect to primary and secondary sources the proportion of respondents who use these sources frequently tends to increase from low to high ATI group i.e., 47.76%(N=32) of those in high group consult experts frequently as opposed to 36.43%(N=47) and 21.21%(N=14) in moderate and low group respectively. So also 50.75%(N=34) of those in high group find the use of workshops and seminars and 27.91%(N=36) and 22.73%(N=15) in moderate and low groups. An overlapping trend is noticeable as to the source discussion with colleagues. Nearly 50% (N=33) with high ATI resort to discussions frequently and find it useful in their current research as opposed to 34.11%(N=44) and 31.82%(N=21) in moderate and low ATI groups respectively.

Use of primary data in the current research and teaching activities do not show a significant association with ATI. The nature of research being carried out and also in many cases inevitability of this source may have influenced this trend.

Thus, the data establishes positive and consistently significant relations of the source use and the ATI. However, association in most of the cases range from weak to moderate. In the order of strength of relations of source use and ATI, books stand first followed by periodicals, abstracting and indexing sources, use of book reviews, workshops and seminars, and discussion with colleagues, all of which show moderate association, citation in books and periodicals and the use of theses and dissertations tend to associate weakly but significantly with ATI. The explanation for the three sources for which significant relations fail to appear may be found in the nature of the source and its availability.

TABLE 4.4: Frequency Distribution and the Gamma Values for ATI and the Information Source Use

(N = 262)

ATI	Use Frequency			
	Not at all	Rarely	Moderately	Frequently
1	2	3	4	5
Primary Sources				
a *Periodicals*				
Low	0	15	28	23
Moderate	2	15	52	60
High	0	2	24	41
	G: 0.328		Z: 2.458**	

(Contd.)

TABLE 4.4. *(Contd.)*

1	2	3	4	5
b *Books and Research Reports*				
Low	1	10	22	33
Moderate	1	11	41	76
High	2	2	10	53
	G: 0.338		Z: 2.389**	
c *Theses and Dissertations*				
Low	12	27	19	8
Moderate	31	44	34	20
High	3	24	21	19
	G: 0.222		Z: 1.764*	
d *Government Publications*				
Low	6	17	24	19
Moderate	12	29	35	53
High	4	13	27	23
	G: 0.084		Z: 0.640	
Secondary Sources				
e *Citations*				
Low	6	16	23	21
Moderate	11	20	51	47
High	1	9	23	34
	G: 0.233		Z: 1.793*	
f *Book Reviews*				
Low	9	28	24	5
Moderate	25	39	47	18
High	3	17	26	21
	G: 0.293		Z: 2.355**	
g *Abstracting and Indexing Sources*				
Low	43	10	6	7
Moderate	68	24	21	16
High	23	9	20	15
	G: 0.321		Z: 2.516**	
h *Library inhouse services*				
Low	18	22	15	11
Moderate	31	30	36	32
High	13	15	19	20
	G: 0.163		Z: 1.300	

(Contd.)

TABLE 4.4. *(Concld.)*

1	2	3	4	5
Non-bibliographic Sources				
i *Primary data*				
Low	8	16	12	30
Moderate	24	11	20	74
High	5	9	15	38
	G: 0.130		Z: 0.956	
j *Consulting Experts*				
Low	7	15	30	14
Moderate	17	23	42	47
High	1	10	24	32
	G: 0.263		Z: 2.007*	
k *Attending Workshops and Seminars*				
Low	8	18	25	15
Moderate	20	23	50	36
High	1	11	21	34
	G: 0.293		Z: 2.351**	
l *Discussion with Colleagues*				
Low	4	22	19	21
Moderate	11	21	53	44
High	3	4	27	33
	G: 0.262		Z: 2.039*	

* Significance $p < .05$
** Significance $p < .01$

4.4 Institutional Affiliation (Environment)

4.4.1 *Institutional Affiliation (Environment) and ATI*

The respondents for the study were drawn from several social science research and teaching institutions. It was within the focus of the study to know whether ATI differs among respondents with different institutional affiliations. For the purposes of the statistical comparison two different environments or affiliations were recognised viz., Research and Training Institutions and University Departments. Research and teaching is carried on in both the environments and considerable overlap in level of specialisation, facilities for research etc., are noticeable in both the environments. Teaching work tends to dominate in the Universities, whereas more time is spent on research related work in the Research and Training Institutes. However, recognising the possible deviations in the nature of work *t* ratio was computed on the ATI mean scores of the respondents from University departments and Research and Training Institutions (Table 4.5). The resulting value is not significant indicating that there remains no difference between the respondents from these environments as far as ATI is concerned.

TABLE 4.5: *t* Ratio comparing the ATI Scores for Respondents from Universities and Research and Training Institutions

Environment	N	Mean	SD	*t* ratio
Universities	103	86.81	14.58	0.22 (NS)
Research and Training Institutions	159	87.23	15.44	

4.4.2 *ATI and Information Source use Relationship vis-a-vis Environments*

It has been noted in the discussions relating to attitude and behaviour relations that overt behaviour under the influence of the attitudinal disposition one has towards the object may get affected by the external or situational factors. The following analysis examines how far the job environments affect the observed relations of ATI and the use of information sources. That is, whether the observed relations are different in the two work settings implying that the observed zero-order relations are partial or conditional to the affiliation. Nine sources of information which have shown positive and significant zero-order ATI and information source use relations are retained for this analysis.

For the purpose of analysis the partial tables were made by dividing the respondents based on their institutional affiliation. Table 4.6 a-i give the frequency distribution and Gamma values for the ATI and source use.

TABLE 4.6: Frequency Distribution and Gamma Values for ATI and Information Source Use Relations for Universities and Research and Training Institutions

	Use Frequency							
	Research and Training Institutions (N = 159)				Universities (N = 103)			
ATI	Not at all	Rarely	Moderately	Frequently	Not at all	Rarely	Moderately	Frequently
1	2	3	4	5	6	7	8	9
a *Periodicals*								
Low	0	11	15	14	0	4	13	9
Moderate	1	12	30	35	1	3	22	25
High	0	1	15	25	0	1	9	16
	G: 0.340		Z: 2.020*		G: 0.314		Z: 1.435	
b *Books and Research Reports*								
Low	1	8	11	20	0	2	11	13
Moderate	1	8	25	44	0	3	16	32
High	0	2	6	33	2	0	4	20
	G: 0.374		Z: 2.116*		G: 0.287		Z: 1.225	
c *Theses/Dissertations*								
Low	9	19	7	5	3	8	12	3
Moderate	19	29	22	8	12	15	12	12
High	3	18	11	9	0	6	10	10
	G: 0.217		Z: 1.326		G: 0.252		Z: 1.274	
d *Citation in Books and Periodicals*								
Low	4	11	13	12	2	5	10	9
Moderate	4	13	27	34	7	7	24	13
High	0	7	16	18	1	2	7	16
	G: 0.211		Z: 1.258		G: 0.260		Z: 1.272	

(Contd.)

TABLE 4.6 *(Concld.)*

1	2	3	4	5	6	7	8	9
e *Book Reviews*								
Low	6	18	15	1	3	10	9	4
Moderate	15	21	30	12	10	18	17	6
High	2	14	13	12	1	3	13	9
	G: 0.280		Z: 1.746*		G: 0.310		Z: 1.579	
f *Abstracting and Indexing Sources*								
Low	28	6	3	3	15	4	3	4
Moderate	37	14	13	13	31	10	8	3
High	12	7	12	11	11	2	8	4
	G: 0.417		Z: 2.699*		G: 0.159		Z: 0.729	
g *Consulting Experts*								
Low	4	7	18	11	3	8	12	3
Moderate	4	11	29	34	13	12	13	13
High	1	9	16	15	0	1	8	17
	G: 0.095		Z: 0.537		G: 0.452		Z: 2.499*	
h *Attending Workshops and Seminars*								
Low	5	10	14	11	3	8	11	4
Moderate	14	16	26	22	6	7	24	14
High	1	11	14	15	0	0	7	19
	G: 0.118		Z: 0.715		G: 0.604		Z: 3.617*	
i *Discussion with Colleagues*								
Low	3	15	7	15	1	7	12	6
Moderate	3	10	33	31	8	11	20	13
High	2	4	17	19	1	0	10	14
	G: 0.206		Z: 1.235		G: 0.326		Z: 1.631	

* Significance : P < .05
** Significance : P < .01
(One tailed tests)

The results of the analysis reveal that Gamma values for two of the three primary sources viz., periodicals (G: 0.34 $P < .05$) and books (G: 0.374 $P < .05$) tend to be statistically significant and positive for the respondents from Research and Training Institutions. In both the cases, however, the explained association or relations are moderate. As to the respondents with University affiliation, neither of the Gamma value tends to be significant. Nonetheless, the Gamma values are not very low compared to the ones observed in zero-order relations for the source periodicals and comes within the range of 10 per cent level of significance. As far as the frequency of use of theses/dissertations, both the groups show non-significant results. The strength of first order relation is nonetheless more for those with the University affiliation than what is observed for the study population.

Among the secondary sources as well significant attitude-behaviour relations are noticeable for those with Research and Training Institutions affiliation with respect to their frequency of use of book reviews (G: 0.280 $P < .05$) and abstracting sources (G: 0.417 $P < .05$). For the university social scientists on the other hand the attitude-behaviour relations tend to be statistically non-significant. However, it is noteworthy that strength of association is relatively more for university social scientists compared with the other group and the Gamma value also nears five per cent level of significance. Neither group tends to show a positive and significant relation as to the use of citations in books and periodicals as a literature search tool going along with their strength of ATI. Derived values are either nearing or more than what is observed for the study population as such.

Entirely different trend is noticeable with respect to the use of non-bibliographic sources viz., consulting experts, attending workshops and seminars, and discussion with colleagues. In all the three cases those with university affiliation show statistically significant and positive attitude-behaviour relations. Gamma value for the source, workshops/seminars (G. 0.604 $P < .01$) indicate a strong attitude-behaviour relations and on the other two sources viz., consulting experts (G. 0.452 $P < .05$) and discussion with colleagues (G. 0.326 $P < .05$), the strength of the relations is moderate. For none of these three sources the relation with ATI tends to be statistically significant for those with Research and Training Institutions affiliation.

It can be inferred from the analysis that ATI and information source use relations are to a certain extent conditional to the respondents' institutional affiliation. As far as the bibliographic sources are concerned significant trend is noticeable for those with Research and Training Institutions affiliation. That is, those who are more favourable to information use also make more frequent use of four of the six bibliographic sources that have shown significant zero-order relations. On the contrary attitude-behaviour relations are statistically significant on non-bibliographic sources for those with university affiliation. Possible explanation for this trend can be found in the nature of job duties dominating in the two environments. As the teaching work is more for the university respondents and the courses taught more often remain same for the individual teacher, need for retrospective information is considerably less. As to the research activities, in majority of the cases university teachers involve in research guidance for masters and doctoral students, who inturn make intense bibliographic information source use. In Research and Training Institutions on the contrary research work dominates and calls for the knowledge of current research reported in the bibliographic sources. However, it is not to rule out the importance of the non-bibliographic sources and attitude-behaviour relations as to these sources. It is noteworthy that in both the environments ATI and information source use relations are positive implying that attitude-behaviour relations tend towards the expected direction irrespective of their institutional affiliations.

4.5 Education

4.5.1 *Education and ATI*

Educational attainment is expected to be one of the main determinants of the ATI. As attitude is a learned phenomenon, higher educational attainment could be logically expected to bring in greater awareness of the utility and importance of information and also information source use. Summers *et al* (1983) have through their study of ATI on educational practitioners concluded that higher education, in terms of high school, Bachelors, Master's and Doctoral Degree, would lead to more favourable attitude. In the present study all the 262 respondents invariably possessed a masters degree in one of the social science disciplines, for this is the minimum prescribed qualification for research and teaching jobs. Among them 123 were also found to be with Doctoral Degree, while among the remaining 139 non-Ph.D's, 33 had M.Phil. degree and 106 just Master's degree. As among the 139, who did not possess Ph.D. degree, 81 respondents were in various stages of their Ph.D. pursuit (Doctoral Scholars) while 58 had no such pursuits. Hence, while relating educational level with information use behaviour, two analyses have been carried out viz., comparison of Ph.D. Degree holders *vs* non-Ph.D's and the other between Doctoral Scholars and those who are not Doctoral Scholars. The results of these two analyses are presented below.

4.5.2 *ATI-Ph.D's.* vs *non-Ph.D's.*

Mean ATI scores for the two groups show a trend wherein Ph.D's tend to score higher than the non-Ph.D's. The computed *t* ratio (6.14; $P < .01$) reveals that those who have higher educational attainment, Ph.D. in the present context, tend to be significantly more favourable compared with the non-Ph.D's.

TABLE 4.7: Mean, S.D. of ATI and *t* Ratio for Ph.D's. and non-Ph.D's.

	N	Mean	S.D.	*t*
Ph.D's	123	92.76	15.12	6.14 P < .01
Non-Ph.D's.	139	82.02	12.86	

Relative intense use of information by the Ph.D. holders during their research and later in their academic jobs could be expected to have influenced them and consequently they are generally found to possess more favourable ATI.

4.5.3 *ATI-Doctoral Scholars* vs *non-Doctoral Scholars*

It was observed in the pilot survey that many of the respondents who were not Ph.D. holders, were then in pursuit of that educational attainment. In the final survey data on this aspect were collected. It could be observed that among the 139 non-Ph.D's, 81 reported to be in various stages of their Ph.D. work and the others, not in any such pursuit. The analyses explored whether this categorisation shows any distinct trend in their ATI.

TABLE 4.8: Mean, S.D. and *t* Ratio for Doctoral Scholars vs Non-doctoral Scholars

	N	Mean	S.D.	*t*
Doctoral Scholars	81	83.30	15.37	1.18 (NS)
Non-Doctoral Scholars	58	80.24	14.56	

The mean ATI score for those who are working for Ph.D. tends to be higher than those who are not in any such pursuit. However, computed *t* ratio does not reveal a significant difference between the two groups. It may be noted that Ph.D. is considered to be a prerequisite for promotions to higher positions. This requirement has made many non-Ph.D's to register for this degree. Many of the respondents who have reported to be working towards attainment of this qualification were found to be either in very initial stages of their work or had not made any progress despite considerable time lapse. This probably has off set the trend for those who have a higher involvement in their doctoral studies and consequently make intense use of information sources and also possess a favourable ATI. It is also possible that those who have not been working for their Ph.D. may have already put in more years of academic experience and have risen to higher academic positions which may have made them more favourably disposed to information use. However, it may be noted that neither of the group possess a mean score which is higher than the mean score for the response population.

Thus, the analysis confirms the assumption that higher educational attainment has a positive effect on the ATI. Further investigation of this trend reveals that those who have at present registered for Ph.D. Degree do not seem to differ from those who are not in such a pursuit.

4.5.4 *ATI*-vis-a-vis *Education and Environment*

This section examines the individual and interaction effects of Environment and Education on ATI. The analysis specifically probes into the individual effect of the two independent variables when the possible overlapping effect of each other is controlled statistically. The interaction effect specifies the influence of combination of two variables over and above the individual effects. That is whether the trend of relations of education and ATI is same in both the job environments

The mean ATI scores, in the bivariate classification of respondents into Ph.D's and non-Ph.D's within their respective institutional affiliation show a trend of increasing favourability to information use among the Ph.D's. (Table 4.9). In addition to this both the education groups from the Research and Training Institutions tend to score higher than their counterparts in the university departments.

TABLE 4.9: (a) Mean, S.D. (b) ANOVA Summary and (c) D.R.T. Results for ATI *vis-a-vis* Environment X Education

(a)

Environment	Education	
	Non-Ph.D's (N = 139)	Ph.D's (N = 123)
Universities	N 35 75.77 13.51	N 68 92.49 11.42
Research and Training Institutions	N 104 84.13 15.05	N 55 93.11 14.45

(b)

Source	S.S.	D.F.	M.S.	F
Education	8515.607	1	8515.61	43.70 P < .01
Environment	996.20	1	996.20	5.11 P < .05
Education X Environment	840.01	1	843.01	4.33 P < .05
Error	50277.88	258	194.88	

(c)

Standard error (S.e.) 13.96

N	55	68	104	35
Mean Score	93.11	92.49	84.13	75.77

Duncan's Range Test (D.R.T.)

Mean ATI scores underlined in (c) do not differ significantly at P < .05.

Two way ANOVA reveals a significant main effect of education on the ATI. To add to this, job environment i.e. being in University or Research and Training Institutions also result in a significant *F* ratio, indicating that environment also has a significant bearing on ATI when the effect of the other variable is statistically controlled. At the initial looks this may seem to be a deviation from the hitherto noted trend of ATI for the respondents in two different job environments. However, it may be observed in the present context the two-way classification separates the education level of the respondents in their respective affiliation. The sums of square for environment in the context is corrected or adjusted so that effect of educational attainment which was possibly clouding the differences in the social scientists' ATI is now statistically corrected. Thus, the job environment has significant bearing on the respondents readiness to use information. In addition, analysis also reveals that the interaction of the education and the environment has a significant influence on the ATI, over and above the two main effects. In other words the effect of each variable on ATI is different over the levels of other variables.

Further analysis of the four groups were made to understand the nature of differences in the ATI. It can be noted that Ph.D's in both the job environments tend to possess more favourable ATI than the non-Ph.D's. However, significant variations in ATI is not noticeable among the Ph.D's working in University departments or Research and Training Institutions. This trend does not seem to hold good as far as the non-Ph.D's are concerned. Non-Ph.D's with the Research and Training Institution affiliation tend to have a significantly more favourable ATI compared to their counterparts in the universities. Ph.D's irrespective of their affiliation generally are more favourable and express a greater readiness to use information. As to the non-Ph.D's institutional affiliation seem to matter as far as their ATI is concerned. The possible explanation to this trend is in the nature of job duties for non-Ph.D's in the two job environments. Though the non-Ph.D's in Research and Training Institutions do not have the advantage of higher educational attainment, their collaboration in the research activities may have induced them to be more receptive and ready to use information. On the other hand non-Ph.D's with university affiliation, who are lesser in proportion, do not show a similar trend probably because of lesser involvement in research and information generation activities as opposed to teaching.

Thus, it can be inferred that higher educational attainment has a positive effect on the ATI in both the environments. Because of their greater exposure and involvement in the research activities, non-Ph.D's in Research and Training Institutions tend to be more favourable than their counterparts in the university departments. In addition, a general trend of those with Research and Training Institution affiliation tending to posses more favourable ATI is revealed by the analysis, when the effect of the education is statistically controlled.

4.5.5 *ATI and Information Source use vis-a-vis Education*

Educational attainment, it has been observed, bears a significant relation with the ATI. In this context it is examined as to whether the zero-order relation that occur between attitude and behaviour varies because of the differing educational attainment of the social scientists. In other words, whether the attitude-behaviour relations are conditional to the level of education.

For the purpose of analysis eighteen contingency tables were prepared to know the nature and strength of relations between ATI and source use. Nine of these refer to Ph.D's and the other nine to non-Ph.D's.* Table 4.10 a-i gives the frequency distribution and the Gamma values for the two education groups.

TABLE 4.10: Frequency Distribution and Gamma Values for ATI and Information Source use for Ph.D's and non-Ph.D's.

	Use Frequency							
	Non-Ph.D's (N = 139)				Ph.D's (N = 123)			
ATI	Not at all	Rarely	Moderately	Frequently	Not at all	Rarely	Moderately	Frequently
1	2	3	4	5	6	7	8	9
a *Periodicals*								
Low	0	12	22	15	0	3	6	8
Moderate	1	8	31	33	1	7	21	27
High	0	2	5	10	0	0	19	31
	G: 0.303		Z: 1.616		G: 0.282		Z: 1.362	

(Contd.)

* Discussion confines only to those sources which bear significant zero-order relation. First order ATI and source use relations for other three sources have consistently shown non-significant results.

TABLE 4.10 *Contd.)*

1	2	3	4	5	6	7	8	9
b *Books and Research Reports*								
Low	0	8	16	25	1	2	6	8
Moderate	0	8	22	43	1	3	19	33
High	2	0	4	11	0	2	6	42
	G: 0.145		Z: 0.709		G: 0.496		Z: 2.489**	
c *Theses and Dissertations*								
Low	9	19	16	5	3	8	3	3
Moderate	20	24	16	13	11	20	18	7
High	2	8	5	2	1	16	16	17
	G: -0.006		Z: -0.033		G: 0.380		Z: 2.149*	
d *Citation in Books and Periodicals*								
Low	5	11	16	17	1	5	7	44
Moderate	7	11	29	26	4	9	22	21
High	0	3	6	8	1	6	17	26
	G: 0.137		Z: 0.733		G: 0.307		Z: 1.615	
c *Book Reviews*								
Low	8	24	12	5	1	4	12	0
Moderate	18	22	24	9	7	17	23	9
High	1	7	5	4	2	10	21	17
	G: 0.139		Z: 0.759		G: 0.315		Z: 1.676*	
f *Abstracting and Indexing Sources*								
Low	32	8	4	5	11	2	2	2
Moderate	39	14	12	8	29	10	9	8
High	8	2	3	4	15	7	17	11
	G: 0.224		Z: 1.152		G: 0.357		Z: 1.964*	
g *Consulting Experts*								
Low	6	7	22	14	1	8	8	0
Moderate	8	12	23	30	9	11	19	17
High	1	0	6	10	0	10	18	22
	G: 0.240		Z: 1.304		G: 0.408		Z: 2.316*	
h *Attending Workshops and Seminars*								
Low	5	13	17	14	3	5	8	1
Moderate	16	16	23	18	4	7	27	18
High	1	5	6	5	0	6	15	29
	G: -0.047		Z: -0.257		G: 0.524		Z: 3.125**	

(Contd.)

TABLE 4.10 *Contd.)*

1	2	3	4	5	6	7	8	9
i *Discussion with Colleagues*								
Low	3	15	14	17	1	7	5	4
Moderate	6	9	29	29	5	12	24	15
High	1	0	6	10	2	4	21	23
	G: 0.258		Z: 1.409		G: 0.369		Z: 2.025*	

* Significance : $P < .05$ ** Significance : $P < .01$
(one tailed tests)

The results show that for seven of the nine sources a significant positive association with ATI is noticeable for the Ph.D's. As far as the non-Ph.D's are concerned, ATI – information source use relations are consistently low and non-significant. Among the primary sources Ph.D's tend to use books (G. 0.496 $P < .01$) and theses/dissertations (G. 0.380 $P < .05$) more frequently when they show relatively greater readiness for the information use. In both the cases association is moderate, but positive and significant. Though positive attitude-behaviour association is noticeable for non-Ph.D's as well, for two of the three primary sources, viz., books and periodicals neither of them has a significant Gamma value. However, it may be noted that on both the sources the association is in the vicinity of five per cent level of significance. As to the use of periodicals neither of the education group shows statistically significant association with the ATI implying that to a certain extent the educational level explains off the observed zero-order association.

A trend similar to one observed earlier is discernible in the use of secondary sources of information. Gamma values indicate a greater strength of attitude-behaviour relations as far as book reviews (G. 0.315 $P < .05$) and abstracting/indexing sources (G. 0.357 $P < .05$) are concerned. For non-Ph.D's on the other hand though the Gamma values are positive they are not statistically significant. Again, for one of the secondary sources viz., citation in books and periodicals neither group shows a statistically significant first order relation.

Consistently positive and statistically significant attitude-behaviour relations are found to be present for Ph.D's as to the frequency of use of all the three non-bibliographic sources. The associations for consulting experts (G. 0.408 $P < .05$) workshops/seminars (G. 0.524 $P < .01$) and discussion with colleagues (G. 0.369 $P < .05$)

with ATI are moderate but relatively greater in strength than the observed values in the zero-order relations. The trend of non-significant ATI and source use relations has repeated for the non-Ph.D's even on these three sources. Gamma value is also negative, though not statistically significant, for workshops/seminars as a source of information which may be due to lack of opportunity for attending and making use of such sources.

Thus, for none of the information sources significant ATI and source use relation is noticeable among the non-Ph.D's. In contrast to this on seven of the sources the strength of association for Ph.D's tend to increase from what was observed for the total population. It can be inferred from the analysis that ATI and source use relations are to a certain extent conditional to the educational attainment of the social scientists. The probability of favourable ATI resulting in more frequent use of various sources is greater and also statistically significant among Ph.D's as opposed to non-Ph.D's. Attainment of higher specialisation and also greater awareness of the information sources seems to be the possible reasons for this trend. Non-Ph.D's, in addition, are often found in greater proportion in the lower positions of the hierarchy, wherein due to nature of the job assignments, the opportunities for the intense use of the information sources are also observed to be relatively less.

4.6 Experience

4.6.1 *Experience and ATI*

The total academic experience gained after completing the basic academic requirements is taken to be another important variable which could determine the favourability to ATI. It has been observed that experience with the attitude object could in itself have an influence on the person's evaluation of the object. Summers *et al* (1983) have established a strong relationship between experience and ATI wherein ATI has shown a progressive trend with the experience.

In the present study the respondents are categorised based on their total academic experience into three distinct classes or career phases. They are: those who have less than five years of experience, six to fifteen years, and sixteen years or more. The respondents in these three categories had a total experience ranging from one to thirty years. Keeping in view the distinct phases of academic career it is observed that in the initial phase of one's career, which is expected to extend to five years, social scientists are exposed to various academic job duties. In this stage they are often taken as assistants in research work and the teaching work dominates in the universities. They are usually allowed to adjust within the institutional framework, learning responsibilities and duties as an academician. In the second phase, social scientists are given due importance in terms of giving them project responsibilities, research guidance work etc. This is the phase wherein they more often publish research articles and also having put in the required years of experience can aspire to move higher up in the hierarchy. This is the middle phase of the career. After fifteen years of academic experience one can be expected to have a good grounding in the job requirements. They can also be expected to be in higher positions and consequently share greater responsibilities both in research and teaching. This experience range could be termed as later phase.

Along with these three phases of career it could be expected that ATI shows an upward trend as one moves from the initial phase to later phase in the career.

TABLE 4.11: (a) Mean, S.D. (b) ANOVA Summary and (c) *t* Ratios for ATI *vis-a-vis* Experience

(a)

Experience	N	Mean	S.D.
Initial phase	58	80.89	10.84
Middle phase	104	86.65	17.02
Later phase	100	91.07	13.74

(b)

Source	S.S.	D.F.	M.S.	F
Experience	3828.47	2	1914.24	8.88 $P < .01$
Error	55819.42	259	215.52	
Total	59647.89	261		

(c)

Later phase	—	Initial phase	4.83 $P < .01$
Later phase	—	Middle phase	2.04 $P < .05$
Middle phase	—	Initial phase	2.33 $P < .05$

From Table 4.11 it may be noted that ATI mean score tends to increase from initial to later phase in the career. Computed *F* ratio of 8.88 $P < .01$ reveals a positive and significant effect of years of professional experience on the ATI. Pairwise comparisons of the groups indicate that significant difference in the ATI appear for respondents in later and middle phase, later and initial phase and also middle and initial phase.

Thus, it could be inferred that professional experience of the social science researchers and teachers generally leads to a favourable ATI. Further ATI shows a gradual progression in three different phases of the academic career and significant difference in favourability is noticeable in relatively more experienced groups.

4.6.2 *ATI* vis-a-vis *Experience and Environment*

Academic experience broadly classified into three different phases of the career has revealed a significant effect on the ATI. Readiness to use information tends to increase as the social scientists move from initial to later phase. The data were further examined to know the possible deviations in the effect of experience on ATI in the two different job environments and also the possible variation in the main effect.

In Table 4.12, giving a bivariate distribution of ATI based on environment and experience, a trend similar to one observed for the response population as a whole tends to hold good. That is, for the respondents from University departments and Research and Training Institutions ATI mean scores show a progressive trend with the increasing experience. Two way ANOVA confirms the main effect of the experience. Significant differences, however, do not appear between the two job environments. That is, when the individual effect of experience and job environment is examined, eliminating in each case the effect of the other variable and thus adjusting the sums of squares, the significance level of main effects on ATI do not change from what has been observed in one way ANOVA. Thus, experience bears a significant main effect whereas environment does not. As the magnitude of the ATI shows a similar trend of increase in both the cases interaction effect of experience and the environment is not significant. That is, there is no significant variation in the effect of experience on ATI in the two environments.

Multiple comparisons of the six different groups reveal that social scientists in the later phase of their career in Universities and

Research and Training Institutions alike show significantly favourable ATI compared with those in the initial phase of their career. Respondents in their middle phase, i.e. with academic experience ranging from five to fifteen years, do not show significant differences in their ATI from the other two groups. Thus, the trend indicates a gradual increase in the favourability to information use. Magnitude of the ATI does not show significant variation for the social scientists in the two environments as long as they are within the same phase of the career.

It can be inferred from the analysis that increasing years of academic experience leads to more favourable ATI in both the environments. Being in a particular job environment in itself does not show any effect on the ATI. The joint effect, i.e., being in a given phase of the career in a particular job environment, over and above the individual effects, is not noticeable.

TABLE 4.12: (a) Mean, S.D. (b) ANOVA Summary and (c) D.R.T. Results for ATI *vis-a-vis* Experience X Environment

(a)

	Experience		
Environment	Initial	Middle	Later
Universities	N 16 79.44 12.33	N 37 85.70 15.22	N 50 89.98 13.63
Research & Training Institutions	N 42 81.45 10.16	N 67 87.18 17.91	N 50 92.16 13.77

(b)

Source	S.S.	D.F.	M.S.	F
Experience	4028.62	2	2014.31	9.27 P < .01
Environment	211.54	1	211.54	0.97 NS
Experience X Environment	6.26	2	3.13	0.01 NS
Error	55601.62	256	217.19	

(c)

S.e. 14.74

N	50	50	67	37	42	16
Mean Score	92.16	89.98	87.18	85.70	81.45	79.44

Mean scores underlined do not differ significantly at P < .05.

4.6.3 *ATI and Information Source Use* vis-a-vis *Experience*

In the present analysis it has been examined as to whether ATI and source use relations are conditional to the respondents' career phase. This analysis takes its strength from the observations made in earlier studies relating to information use. It has been noted in the INFROSS study that the more experienced social scientists tend to use libraries less frequently. Garvey *et al* (1979) have observed that the books and journals are less frequently used by the more experienced social scientists. The reasons attributed for this trend is that with longer standing in the profession one is often acquainted with the basic information required for the job functioning. However, as longer association with the attitude object, i.e. information, is expected to result in favourable disposition it is examined here as to whether being in different phases of the career in itself brings in variation in the strength of ATI and source use relations.

Tables 4.13 a-i give the frequency distribution and the Gamma values showing ATI and source use relations for the respondents in the three phases of their career. Analysis reveals that respondents make frequent use of two of the three primary sources. Books/research reports (G. 0.47 $P < .05$) and periodicals (G. 456 $P < .05$) show positive and significant association with the ATI for those in the middle phase of the career. Statistically significant attitude-behaviour relation is not noticeable for those in the initial and later phases of the career. However, Gamma values are positive for all the three groups. As far the use of theses and dissertations, none of the three groups show a significant relation. It may be noted that the magnitude of the Gamma value for the use of theses is slightly greater than that of zero-order relations for those in middle and later phases of the career. Nonetheless, the results are not statistically significant.

The trend observed for primary sources does not hold good as far as the use of secondary sources are concerned. Statistically significant and positive association between ATI and source use is found among those in the later phase of the career. The strength of the association for citations (G. 0.359 $P < .05$), book review (G. 0.338 $P < 0.5$) and abstracts (G. 0.418 $P < .05$) are moderate but significant. That is, favourable ATI jointly occurring with frequent source use is to the tune of 35.9 per cent for citations, 33.8 per cent for book reviews and 41.8 per cent as to the use of abstracting and indexing services. For those in initial and middle phases secondary source use does not tend to be in accordance with their ATI.

TABLE 4.13: Frequency Distribution and Gamma Values for ATI and Source Use for Experience Groupings

Experience	Use Frequency											
	Initial N 58				Middle N 104				Later N 100			
ATI	Not at all	Rarely	Modera-tely	Frequen-tly	Not at all	Rarely	Modera-tely	Frequen-tly	Not at all	Rarely	Modera-tely	Frequen-tly
1	2	3	4	5	6	7	8	9	10	11	12	13
a *Periodicals*												
Low	0	8	5	6	0	6	18	8	0	1	5	9
Moderate	2	5	11	18	0	4	21	19	0	6	20	23
High	0	0	0	3	0	1	9	18	0	1	15	20
	G: 0.446		Z: 1.568		G: 0.456		Z: 2.321*		G: 0.060		Z: 0.248	
b *Books and Research Reports*												
Low	0	4	5	10	1	5	11	15	0	1	6	8
Moderate	1	4	9	22	0	5	16	23	0	2	16	31
High	0	0	0	3	0	0	4	24	2	2	6	26
	G: 0.284		Z: 0.845		G: 0.470		Z: 2.318*		G: 0.169		Z: 0.873	
c *Theses and Dissertations*												
Low	4	6	7	2	7	13	8	4	1	8	4	2
Moderate	10	10	8	8	11	17	9	7	10	17	17	5
High	0	1	2	0	1	9	10	8	2	14	9	11
	G: 0.046		Z: 0.152		G: 0.279		Z: 1.451		G: 0.231		Z: 1.108	

Contd.

TABLE 4.13 (*Contd.*)

1	2	3	4	5	6	7	8	9	10	11	12	13
d *Citations in Journals and Books*												
Low	2	2	7	8	3	9	8	12	1	5	8	1
Moderate	4	7	16	11	3	7	18	16	4	6	17	20
High	0	0	1	2	0	4	11	13	1	5	11	19
	G: -0.049		Z: -0.159		G: 0.151		Z: 0.715		G: 0.359		Z: 1.726*	
e *Books Reviews*												
Low	4	6	6	3	4	16	10	2	1	6	8	0
Moderate	8	12	11	5	9	13	17	5	8	14	19	8
High	0	0	1	2	2	8	11	7	1	9	14	12
	G: 0.147		Z: 0.490		G: 0.269		Z: 1.372		G: 0.338		Z: 1.658*	
f *Abstracting and Indexing Journals*												
Low	11	5	1	2	22	4	2	4	10	1	3	1
Moderate	24	4	2	6	23	11	8	2	21	9	11	8
High	1	1	0	1	13	4	9	2	9	4	11	12
	G: 0.042		Z: 0.123		G: 0.233		Z: 1.106		G: 0.418		Z: 2.157*	

Contd.

TABLE 4.13 *(Contd.)*

1	2	3	4	5	6	7	8	9	10	11	12	13
g *Consulting Experts*												
Low	2	3	7	7	4	6	15	7	1	6	8	0
Moderate	6	5	12	13	5	8	13	18	6	10	17	16
High	0	0	1	2	0	3	14	11	1	7	9	19
	G: 0.061		Z: 0.195		G: 0.249		Z: 1.245		G: 0.404		Z: 2.066*	
h *Attending Workshops and Seminars*												
Low	2	6	6	5	4	9	11	8	2	3	8	2
Moderate	10	7	8	11	6	9	19	10	4	7	23	15
High	1	0	0	2	0	5	10	13	0	6	11	19
	G: -0.031		Z: -0.103		G: 0.276		Z: 1.413		G: 0.379		Z: 1.865*	
i *Discussion with Colleagues*												
Low	2	6	8	3	2	11	7	12	0	5	4	6
Moderate	5	5	10	16	3	6	20	15	3	10	23	13
High	0	2	1	0	0	0	10	18	3	2	16	15
	G: 0.179		Z: 0.605		G: 0.402		Z: 2.104*		G: 0.164		Z: 0.755	

* Significance $P < .05$ ** Significance $P < .01$ (one tailed tests)

As far as the non-bibliographic sources are concerned, statistically significant positive relations are noticeable for sources such as consulting experts (G. 0.404 $P < .05$) and attending workshops/ seminars (G. 0.379 $P < .05$), for those in the later phase of their career. Though the strength of association is more than what is observed in zero-order relations, they are moderate. As opposed to this, respondents in the middle phase of their career tend to involve in discussions with their colleagues more often (G. 0.402 $P < .05$) when they are favourably inclined to information use. Gamma values for other two groups work out to be non-significant.

It can be inferred from the analysis that ATI and source use in conditional to the respondents in different phases of their career. A definite overall pattern, however, does not emerge as three sources including periodicals, books and discussions show positive and significant association with ATI for those in middle phase. All the secondary sources and two non-bibliographic sources tend to be more often used by those in the later phase, and also possess relatively more favourable attitudinal disposition. It may, however, be concluded that more experienced social scientists gather research information either through non-bibliographic sources or through use of the secondary sources. Availability of research assistance and also relatively lesser need for basic and retrospective information may have affected the attitude-behaviour relation with respect to books and periodicals for those in the later phase, i.e., relatively more experienced group. Attitude-behaviour relations are consistently low and non-significant for those in the initial phase of the career. It may also be noted that only a minor proportion of those in the initial phase fall in the high ATI group. Nature of jobs duties, which is often perceived to be that of a routine type as opposed to academic ones may have contributed for this trend.

Thus, in addition to favourable ATI the chances of favourable ATI resulting in more frequent source use is conditional to the professional experience. More often the relations hold good for those in later phase and also in middle phase of the career. On the contrary such relations do not tend to occur for those in the initial phase of the career.

4.7 **Position**

4.7.1 *Position and ATI*

In the Indian social science academic scene four different positions in the hierarchy could be seen. Though they are variously titled there is a considerable overlap in the pay structure, required formal academic requirements and years of professional experience.

In the population studied 29 per cent of the respondents were in the lowest rung – Research Associates/Assistants, 30.15 per cent were Lecturers/Assistant Directors, 27.86 per cent were readers/ Deputy Director and 12.98 per cent were Professors/Directors. Because of the observed similarities, these four position groups were recognised for the analysis. As there are only a few rungs to go higher up within the existing framework of the academic jobs, it was expected that the process of competition for promotion leads to greater academic participation in terms of bringing improved information content in the lectures, research publication and also participation in professional activities. This could lead social scientists possessing a more favourable ATI as their position in the hierarchy enhances.

TABLE 4.14: (a) Mean, S.D., (b) ANOVA Summary for ATI *vis-a-vis* Position

(a) *Position*	N	Mean	S.D.	
R.As.	76	83.72	16.54	
Lecturers	79	89.62	14.77	
Readers	73	87.74	14.35	
Professors	34	87.15	12.36	
(b) *Source*	S.S.	D.F.	M.S.	F
Position	1397.79	3	465.93	2.06 (NS)
Error	58250.10	258	225.78	
Total	59647.89	261		

It may be observed from Table 4.14 that the mean ATI scores do not show the expected trend of increase with the position. Respondents in position two show a slightly higher mean score than the other position groups. However, computed *F* ratio does not confirm a significant effect of position on the ATI indicating that the attitude of the respondents does not differ with differences in their position. The presence of respondents with varying educational qualifications in the same position group and also variance in the psychological attributes may have a bearing on respondents in the same position groups which would be examined in the succeeding sections.

4.7.2 *ATI* vis-a-vis *Position and Environment*

Having found that being in a particular position in the academic hierarchy does not seem to have any bearing on the ATI, a further analysis, viz., two-way ANOVA was computed to examine the possible variation in the trend of ATI for four position groups in the two job environments.

Table 4.15 presents the mean ATI scores and ANOVA summary for the social scientists' occupying different positions in their job environment. A definite trend of the ATI is again not noticeable. Further, the mean scores tend to overlap for different position, excepting a higher ATI mean score noticeable for those in position two in Research and Training Institutions and a considerably lesser mean score for the Research Assistants in the University departments.

Analysis of the data shows that the individual effects of the position and the environment and also the interaction effect of these two variable over and above the two main effects on ATI are not statistically significant.

TABLE 4.15: (a) Mean, S.D., and (b) ANOVA Summary for ATI vis-a-vis Environment X Position

	Position			
Environment	Research Associates/ Assistants	Lecturers/ Assistant Directors	Readers/ Deputy Directors	Professors/ Directors
(a) Universities	N 6 78.33 12.30	N 38 86.58 15.22	N 40 88.00 15.26	N 19 87.42 10.71
Research and Training Institutions	N 70 84.19 16.77	N 41 92.44 13.75	N 33 87.42 13.15	N 15 86.80 14.17

(b) Source	S.S. (Adj.)	D.F.	M.S.	F
Position	1724.10	3	574.70	2.54 (NS)
Environment	337.70	1	337.70	1.50 (NS)
Position X Environment	538.03	3	179.34	0.79 (NS)
Error	57374.37	254	225.68	

It can be inferred that position in the hierarchy in both the environments does not seem to have a significant bearing on the ATI. Job environments as such also do not show variations in respondents' ATI even when the disproportionality in their distribution on two independent variables is controlled or statistically corrected. So also significant deviations in the ATI mean scores for the respondents in overlapping positions in two different job environments do not exist.

4.7.3 *ATI and Information Source Use* vis-a-vis *Position in the Hierarchy*

This section examines whether the attitude-behaviour relations initially noted are conditional to the respondents' position group. That is, whether attitudinal disposition to information show variations in strength of its association with the information source use behaviour. For the purposes of analysis partial contingency tables were prepared taking their position into consideration. Kurskal and Goodman's Gamma statistic was worked out for each of the position groups on the nine sources of information. Table 4.16 a-i shows the frequency of source use corresponding to the high, moderate and low ATI groups.

An initial look at the results reveal that variation in the attitude-behaviour association is noticeable for different position group. In case of all the three primary sources which have shown significant zero-order relations with ATI, respondents in position two consisting of Lecturers, Research Officers and Assistant Directors tend to show consistently positive and significant relations with the information use. Thus, all the three sources show moderate association. Gamma value for periodicals (G. 0.501 $P < .05$) is on the higher side explaining 50.1 per cent of the difference and for books (G. 0.453 $P < .01$) the probability of favourable ATI and frequent source use jointly occurring is 45.3 per cent. As to the other three positions though Gamma value for books and periodicals is positive in five of the six cases they are not statistically significant. None of the first order relations turn out significant as to the frequency of use of theses and dissertations.

TABLE 4.16: Frequency Distribution and Gamma Values for ATI and Source use *vis-a-vis* Position Groups

	Use Frequency															
Position	Research Associates/Assistant				Lecturers/Assistant Directors				Readers/Deputy Directors				Professors/Directors			
	N=76				N=79				N=73				N 34			
ATI	Not at all	Rarely	Mode-rately	Frequen-tly	Not at all	Rarely	Mode-rately	Frequen-tly	Not at all	Rarely	Mode-rately	Frequen-tly	Not at all	Rarely	Mode-rately	Frequen-tly
1	2	3	4	5	6	7	8	9	10	11	12	13	14	15	16	17
a *Periodicals*																
Low	0	9	10	7	0	4	8	5	0	2	7	6	0	0	3	5
Moderate	1	7	13	16	1	2	14	20	0	4	20	15	0	2	5	9
High	0	1	5	7	0	0	7	18	0	1	8	10	0	0	4	6
	G: 0.329		Z: 1.375		G: 0.501		Z: 2. 214*		G: 0.175		Z: 0.638		G: -0.010		Z: -0.04	
b *Books and Research Reports*																
Low	1	5	8	12	0	3	5	9	0	1	5	9	0	1	4	3
Moderate	1	6	10	20	0	2	12	23	0	3	16	20	0	0	3	13
High	0	0	2	11	0	0	4	21	1	2	2	14	1	0	2	7
	G: 0.369		Z: 1.469		G: 0.453		Z: 3.589**		G: 0.108		Z: 0.380		G: 0.319		Z: 0.798	

Contd.

TABLE 4.16 *(Contd.)*

1	2	3	4	5	6	7	8	9	10	11	12	13	14	15	16	17
c *Theses and Dissertations*																
Low	6	12	5	3	2	6	8	1	3	4	6	2	1	5	0	2
Moderate	11	11	7	8	6	13	12	6	13	13	11	2	1	7	4	4
High	2	5	3	3	0	9	8	8	1	6	9	3	0	4	1	5
	G: 0.129		Z: 0.539		G: 0.260		Z: 1.134		G: 0.174		Z: 0.707		G: 0.380		Z: 1.096	
d *Citations in Journals*																
Low	3	7	10	6	2	5	4	6	0	2	6	7	1	2	3	2
Moderate	3	6	18	10	1	7	15	14	6	5	13	15	1	2	5	8
High	0	3	5	5	0	0	7	18	0	4	8	7	1	2	3	4
	G: 0.212		Z: 0.873		G: 0.517		Z: 2.455**		G: -0.081		Z: -0.313		G: 0.109		Z: 0.302	
e *Books Reviews*																
Low	5	14	6	1	3	6	6	2	1	8	4	2	0	0	8	0
Moderate	10	9	13	5	5	13	13	6	8	12	16	3	2	5	5	4
High	1	6	3	3	0	4	10	11	1	4	10	4	1	3	3	3
	G: 0.224		Z: 1.467		G: 0.462		Z: 2.255*		G: 0.271		Z: 1.107		G: -0.085		Z: -0.246	

Contd.

TABLE 4.16 *(Contd.)*

1	2	3	4	5	6	7	8	9	10	11	12	13	14	15	16	17
f *Abstracting and Indexing Services*																
Low	17	3	3	3	15	2	0	0	7	4	1	3	4	1	2	1
Moderate	22	7	4	4	19	8	6	5	21	7	6	5	6	2	5	3
High	5	2	4	2	6	2	8	8	9	4	3	3	3	1	5	1
	G: 0.225		Z: 0.651		G: 0.666		Z: 3.695**		G: 0.009		Z: 0.035		G: 0.159		Z: 0.444	
g *Consulting Experts*																
Low	4	3	11	8	3	5	9	0	0	5	6	4	0	2	4	2
Moderate	5	6	10	16	4	5	14	14	6	8	13	12	2	4	5	5
High	0	0	7	6	0	4	6	15	0	4	7	8	1	2	4	3
	G: 0.222		Z: 0.910		G: 0.534		Z: 2.685**		G: 0.163		Z: 0.651		G: -0.019		Z: -0.053	
h *Attending Workshops and Seminars*																
Low	5	8	8	5	2	5	9	1	1	4	6	4	0	1	2	5
Moderate	9	8	8	12	6	9	16	6	5	3	17	14	0	3	9	4
High	0	2	6	5	0	6	3	16	1	2	6	10	0	1	6	3
	G: 0.249		Z: 1.078		G: 0.455		Z: 2.227*		G: 0.261		Z: 1.049		G: -0.217		Z: -0.578	
i *Discussion with Colleagues*																
Low	4	9	5	8	0	4	7	6	0	8	4	3	0	1	3	4
Moderate	3	7	10	17	4	2	17	14	3	8	20	8	1	4	6	5
High	0	0	5	8	1	3	13	8	0	0	5	14	2	1	4	3
	G: 0.418		Z: 1.863*		G: -0.002		Z: -0.008		G: 0.631		Z: 3.255**		G: -0.25		Z: -0.709	

* Significance $P < .05$ ** Significance $P < .05$ (one tailed tests)

A trend similar to one observed for primary sources of information holds good with regard to the use of secondary sources also. Frequency of consulting sources such as citation in books and journals (G. 0.517 $P < .01$), book reviews (G. 0.462 $P < .05$) and abstracts (G. 0.666 $P < .01$), show a positive and significant association for those in position two. In addition the probability of more favourable ATI and more frequent source use occurring jointly is to the tune of 66.6 per cent for abstracts, and 51.7 per cent for citations in books and journals, and 46.2 per cent in the case of book reviews. Thus, the association is strong for the abstracts and moderate for the other two sources. As to the other three positions, though the Gamma values showing ATI and source use relations are positive, in none of the cases it is significant.

A slight deviation from the hitherto observed trend is noticeable for the association of non-bibliographic sources and the ATI among the position groups. Those in position two show statistically significant and positive attitude-behaviour relations as to their frequency of resorting to use of sources such as experts in the discipline (G. 0.534 $P < .01$) and also attending workshops and seminars (G. 0.455 $P < .05$). In both the cases the association is moderate, indicating that 53.4 per cent and 45.5 per cent of the use of experts and workshops respectively occur together with more favourable ATI. However, analysis does not confirm statistically significant relation as to the frequency of discussion with colleagues.

In addition to this statistically significant attitude-behaviour relations are also noticeable for those in position one. Probability of more favourable ATI and engaging in discussions with colleagues (G. 0.418 $P < .05$) more frequently occurring together with the ATI is to the tune of 41.8 per cent.

A strong relation between ATI and discussion with colleagues is also noticeable for those in position three. The Gamma value in this case is 0.631 ($P < .01$).

Thus, to a greater extent favourable ATI and more frequent use of information sources is conditional to the respondents position in the hierarchy. More often than not those in position two, because of their due academic initiation and experience and relatively lesser administrative work seem to show a tendency to act positively corresponding to their attitudinal disposition. This trend also holds good for those in the lowest position in one case viz., discussion with colleagues. Possible reason for this trend is that they are relatively new entrants to the academic jobs and would have lesser academic experience needing the guidance from those who have a better standing in the academic field.

Among those in the higher positions, though favourability is noticeable in terms of respondents falling in moderate and high ATI groups the resultant behaviour is not significant. The attitude-behaviour relations for those in the highest position as to the use of certain sources such as discussion with colleagues, attending workshops/seminars and consulting experts is negative though non-significant. Relatively longer standing in the profession, coupled with lesser need for consulting basic sources in their area of specialisation and also research assistance available, whenever it is group research, may have off-set the expected trend of positive attitude-behaviour relations for this group.

ATI in Relation to Psychological Attributes: Information use studies have largely left aside psychological attributes as though they do not have any relation with the information use. Certain exceptions however, could be noted. Mick *et al* (1980) examine a management oriented model for describing information behaviour. That is, variables that can be manipulated by managers. Studies relating to scientific performance on the contrary have examined the relation of these job factors more extensively and have found them to be of importance. Performance is measured in terms of information generation or research output and dissemination activities for which use of various information sources is a prerequisite. Hence, a relatively higher strength of motivation, job satisfaction, dedication to job and higher level of aspirations could be expected to induce a favourable ATI. They are also important situational factors which could in itself affect ATI and information source use relations. The possible influence of these psychological attributes and the situational factors are examined in the following sections.

4.8 Motivation

4.8.1. *Motivation and ATI*

Motivation for performing job duties or work motivation was measured with the help of a 13-item scale. These items include both extrinsic and intrinsic factors of motivation.

The 13 items had a theoretical score range of 13-65. Observed motivation scores for the respondents ranged from 19 to 65. The response group had a mean score of 54.67. Distribution of the respondents on different scale points showed a negative skewness of -0.4 and a kurtosis -1.06.

4.8.1.1 *Correlation of Motivation Scale Items with ATI*: Initially, to examine the relations of items used in the motivation scale with the ATI, product moment correlation was computed. The results show (Table 4.17) that the direction of motivation, elicited in terms of importance attached to professional and status aspects of the job, correlate significantly with the ATI. That is, ATI tends to be more favourable when the importance attached or the achievement intention is higher.

TABLE 4.17: Correlation Coefficients Between Motivation Items and ATI

	Mean	S.D.	*r*	Significance
To make full use of present knowledge	4.53	0.74	0.15	P < .05
Opportunity to keep up to date	4.38	0.98	0.33	P < .01
Opportunity to write and publish	4.35	0.91	0.26	P < .01
A high degree of freedom in selecting research projects	4.15	1.06	0.30	P < .01
Opportunity for promotion	4.14	1.07	0.25	P < .01
Adequate salary	4.26	0.94	0.14	P < .05
To work with colleagues high competence	4.34	0.94	0.16	P < .01
Congenial colleagues	4.17	1.06	0.20	P < .01
Building a professional reputation	4.29	0.95	0.17	P < .01
Working on difficult and challenging problems	3.93	1.05	0.16	P < .01
Freedom in day-to-day activities	4.24	0.93	0.30	P < .01
Attending professional meetings	3.76	1.21	0.16	P < .01
Contributing to broad research knowledge	4.07	1.05	0.23	P < .01
Total motivation score	54.67	7.33	0.19	P < .01

D.f = 260

Among the 13 items opportunity to keep up to date is the most important factor, judging from the magnitude of correlation (r=0.33). This is followed by freedom in selecting the projects and teaching assignments ($r=0.30$), and also freedom in day-to-day activities ($r=0.30$). Importance attached for research and publishing activities ($r=0.26$) and contributing to research knowledge ($r=0.33$) fall in that order, other intrinsic factors such as motivation to build professional reputation ($r=0.17$), work on difficult and challenging problems ($r=0.16$) correlate with ATI at 0.01 level of significance. Wanting to make full use of their knowledge in the job context, which a majority of the respondents express a desire to, correlates at five per cent level of significance ($r=0.15$).

Among the extrinsic factors such as congenial colleagues ($r=0.20$), promotions into the higher rungs ($r=0.25$), to work with colleagues of high competence ($r=0.16$) and salary ($r=0.14$) come in lower end in their magnitude of relations with ATI. Total score of motivation scale items correlate ($r=0.19$) significantly at 1 per cent confidence limit with the ATI confirming the trend of individual items.

4.8.1.2. *Motivation Groups and their Relationship with ATI*: Data were further analysed to examine how the ATI behaves given a level of motivation. For this purpose respondents were categorised into low, moderate and high groups based on the quartile one and three values. The two cut off points were $Q_1=51$ (i.e. 51 and below formed low group) and $Q_3=60$ (i.e. those with scores 60 and above formed high group), respondents falling between these cut off points were designated as moderate group.

Table 4.18 shows a distinct trend of increase in the mean ATI scores from low through high motivation groups. Analysis of variance (F 11.33 $P < .01$) confirms the assumption that motivation has a significant effect on the ATI. Pairwise comparisons also show significant differences among all the three pairs indicating that the differences in the mean ATI scores among the motivation groups are not due to chance factor. Results of analysis of variance confirms the significant correlations noticed in the initial analysis of motivation scale items and ATI scores.

4.8.2 *ATI vis-a-vis Motivation and Environment*

ATI scores of three groups forming high, moderate and low motivation were further divided across the job environment with which the social scientists are affiliated. The analysis intended to examine the individual effects of two independent variables and also the interaction effect of these two variables on ATI.

TABLE 4.18: (a) Mean, S.D., (b) ANOVA Summary and (c) t Ratios for ATI *vis-a-vis* motivation

(a)

	Motivation		
	N	Mean	S.D.
Low	65	81.20	11.82
Moderate	313	86.85	13.37
High	66	93.27	18.40

(b)

Source	S.S.	D.F.	M.S.	F.
Motivation	4798.30	2	2399.15	11.33 $P < .01$
Error	54849.59	259	211.77	
Total	59647.89	261		

(c)

Moderate - low	2.89 $P < .01$
High - low	5.29 $P < .01$
High - moderate	2.79 $P < .01$

It could be noted from Table 4.19 that the mean scores show a progression as the respondents move from low to high groups in both the work settings. the F ratios computed confirm the significant effect of motivation on ATI. The effect of institutional affiliation, as has been observed in the other instances, is not significant. In addition, the results reveal that these two variables together do not account for significant variation in the ATI over and above the two main effects. In other words, the interaction of these variables does not seem to account for significant variation in the ATI. So much so the effect of motivation is largely uniform in the two environments.

Group-wise comparisons indicate that those in high group in University and Research and Training Institutions have a more favourable ATI than the low motivation groups. In addition, significant difference are also noticeable between high and moderate groups for the respondents from Research and Training Institutions. Though a higher mean ATI score is noticeable for moderate group compared to the low one, the differences are not statistically significant. Those with overlapping degree of motivation in two job environments do not seem to possess varying magnitude of ATI.

Thus, it can be concluded that motivation has a positive effect on the ATI in Universities and Research and Training Institutions. Deviation in the ATI mean scores for the individual group in two environments is not present. That is to say, in the present analysis motivation along bears a significant relations with ATI and neither the other independent variable-work environment-nor the combination of the two independent variables account for variance in the attitude intensity.

TABLE 4.19: (a) Mean, S.D., (b) ANOVA Summary and (c) D.R.T. Results for ATI vis-a-vis Environment X Motivation

(a)

Environment	Motivation: Low	Moderate	High
Universities	N 24 80.50 8.67	N 53 86.72 14.68	N 26 92.81 15.93
Research and Training Institutions	N 41 81.61 13.30	N 78 86.94 12.41	N 40 93.58 19.84

(b)

Source	S.S. (Adj.)	D.F.	M.S.	F.
Motivation	4794.59	2	2397.29	11.19 $P < .01$
Environment	7.69	1	7.69	0.04 (NS)
Motivation X Environment	8.91	2	4.46	0.02 (NS)
Error	54833.00	256	214.19	

(c)

S.e.: 14.64

N	40	26	78	53	41	24
Mean score	93.58	92.81	86.94	86.72	81.61	80.50

Means scores underlined do not differ significantly at $P < .05$

Motivation and Personal Attributes: Motivation as an independent variable is found to bear a significant relation with the ATI. Further this trend also holds good in two environments. In this section the analysis was carried out to know the effect of motivation on ATI when the respondents are further divided on the basis of their personal attributes such as education, experience and position. That is whether the effect of motivation on ATI is same for the different sub-classifications of personal attributes. In other words, the analysis examines the possible interaction effect of any given two variables on the ATI and also their individual relations when the possible influence of the other variable is statistically controlled.

4.8.3 *ATI vis-a-vis Motivation and Education*

A general progressive trend of ATI mean scores for Ph.D's and non-Ph.d's alike is noticeable as they move from low to high groups of motivation (Table 4.20).

Two way analysis of variance confirms the significant main effects of motivation and education when disproportionality in the distributions is corrected statistically. However, data do not support the assumptions of possible presence of significant interaction of the education and motivation on ATI. The two independent variables individually account for most of the variation that is present and when they are taken together they do not account for significant variation over and above the individual effects. Non-significant interaction effect also means that the effect of each variable is largely same over the levels of the other variable.

Multiple comparisons of the six groups reveal that Ph.D's who possess high motivation tend to have more favourable ATI and differ significantly from all the other groups. Between Ph.D's and non-Ph.D's significant difference in favour of Ph.D's are observable among moderate and high motivation groups. Ph.D's with low motivation do not differ from non-Ph.D's in the same group.

A distinct and statistically significant difference is discernible among Ph.D's at different levels of motivation, wherein those who fall in low, moderate and high groups tend to possess attitudinal favourability which significantly differs from one another. However, among non-Ph.D's such a difference is absent between low and moderate groups.

Non-Ph.D's who show a high motivation and Ph.D's in moderate motivation group tend to possess overlapping intensity of ATI. It can be inferred that high motivation among non-Ph.D's may tend to act as a compensation in the absence of that higher educational attainment as far as its relation with ATI is concerned.

TABLE 4.20: (a) Mean, S.D., (b) ANOVA Summary and (c) D.R.T. Results for ATI *vis-a-vis* Motivation X Education

(a)

Environment	Motivation		
	Low	Moderate	High
Non-Ph.D's	N 42 79.07 12.47	N 66 81.92 12.26	N 31 86.23 21.55
Ph.D's	N 23 85.02 9.33	N 65 91.90 12.58	N 35 99.51 12.01

(b)

Source	S:S. (Adj.)	D.F.	M.S.	F.
Education	6303.18	1	6303.18	33.48 $P < .01$
Motivation	3570.68	2	1785.34	9.48 $P < .01$
Education X Motivation	697.03	2	348.52	1.85 (NS)
Error	48197.90	256	188.27	

(c)

S.e.: 13.72

N	35	65	31	23	66	42
Mean score	99.51	91.90	86.23	85.02	81.92	79.07

Means scores underlined do not differ significantly at $P < .05$.

Thus, relatively more favourable ATI could be observed among Ph.D's in high motivation group. Low motivation even among Ph.D's would lead to relatively less favourable ATI. So also non-Ph.D's within the high group differ from the non-Ph.D's with low motivation, but show a similarity with Ph.D's in low and moderate groups. The effect of the two variables is additive in nature.

4.8.4 *Motivation and Experience*

The analysis was carried out to examine whether the effect of motivation on ATI differ for social scientists in different career phases i.e., to know the presence of interaction effect of the two independent variables in the design and also the main effects of the variables when the sums of squares are adjusted.

The respondents falling in three different phases of their career (based on their experience) show an increasing trend in their attitudinal favourability to information as they move from low to high motivation groups. So also a trend of increasing ATI mean score is noticeable in all the three groups of motivation for the respondents falling in initial to later phases of their career. (Table 4.21).

Analysis brings out that motivation and experience independently have a significant influence on ATI even when the effect of each variable on the other is controlled and disproportionality corrected statistically. Taken together these variables do not seem to explain the variance in the ATI more than that of individual effects. In other words, the effect of motivation on ATI is more or less same for those in different experience groups and *vice versa*. Thus, the interaction effect of the two variables on ATI is not significant.

Multiple comparisons of the nine cells show that those with high motivation in their middle and later phases of the career possess a more favourable ATI which is significantly different from other groups. In high motivation group, for those in their initial phase, despite an increasing trend of ATI mean scores, significant differences do not appear indicating that motivation has no significant relation with the ATI in that particular context.

Distinct influence of motivation is discernible among those in middle phase of their career. Respondents in different motivation groups show a statistically significant progression from low to moderate and moderate to high. So also in the later phase differences appear between high and low groups.

Within the high and moderate groups those in middle and later phase tend to be more favourable than those in their initial phase. Statistical differences do not appear for those in low group across different phases of their career.

It could be inferred that though motivation generally has a significant effect on the ATI of the social scientists, it is pronounced among those respondents who are in the middle and later phases of their career. The joint effect of motivation and experience is additive on the dependent variable – ATI.

TABLE 4.21: (a) Mean, S.D., (b) ANOVA Summary and (c) D.R.T. Results for ATI *vis-a-vis* Motivation X Experience

(a) Environment	Motivation		
	Low	Moderate	High
Initial phase	N 20 77.05 8.79	N 26 81.96 8.78	N 12 85.00 15.11
Middle phase	N 23 80.61 12.09	N 58 86.41 14.43	N 23 93.30 23.58
Later phase	N 22 85.59 12.42	N 47 90.06 13.23	N 31 96.48 13.51

(b)

Source	S.S. (Adj.)	D.F.	M.S.	F.
Motivation	3881.03	2	1940.52	9.48 $P < .01$
Experience	2911.20	2	1455.60	7.10 $P < .01$
Motivation X Experience	124.19	4	31.05	0.15 (NS)
Error	51814.19	253	204.80	

(c)

S.e. 14.31

N.	31	23	47	58	22	12	26	23	20
Mean ATI	96.48	93.30	90.06	86.41	85.59	85.00	81.96	80.61	77.05

Means scores underlined do not differ significantly at $P < .05$

4.8.5 *ATI vis-a-vis Motivation and Position*

In this bivariate classification of ATI the analysis aims to find out whether the effect of motivation on ATI is uniform for all the position groups, i.e., to examine the interaction effect and also the individual effects of two independent variables in the two way design.

TABLE 4.22: (a) Mean, S.D., (b) Anova Summary and (c) D.R.T. Results for ATI *vis-a-vis* Motivation X Position

	Motivation		
Position	Low	Moderate	High
	N 21	N 32	N 23
Research Associates/	77.14	83.91	89.48
Assistants	12.28	11.99	22.21
	N 21	N 46	N 12
Lecturers/Assistant	83.28	88.48	105.08
Directors	12.46	12.81	14.87
	N 14	N 34	N 25
Readers/ Deputy	84.00	86.12	92.04
Directors	10.14	14.57	15.01
	N 9	N 19	N 6
Professors/	81.44	89.16	89.33
Directors	8.55	13.68	9.84

(b)

Source	S.S. (Adj.)	D.F.	M.S.	F.
Motivation	5245.32	2	2622.66	12.69 $P < .01$
Position	937.97	3	312.66	1.51 (NS)
Motivation X Position	2264.14	6	377.36	1.83(NS)
Error	51660.29	250	206.64	

(c)

S.e. 14.38

N	12	25	23	6	19	46	34	14	32	21	9	21
Mean score	105.08	92.04	89.48	89.33	89.16	88.48	86.12	84.00	83.91	83.28	81.44	77.14

Means scores underlined do not differ significantly at $P < .05$

Table 4.22 shows that within each of the four positions ATI generally shows an increasing trend with low, moderate and higher levels of motivation. Analysis confirms the significant effect of motivation despite the adjustment in the sums of squares carried out to correct the disproportionality in the distribution. However, main effect of the position and the interaction effect of the two variables, position and motivation, are not significant. It implies that there is no significant deviations in the general trend of impact of motivation for different position groups as far as its relation with ATI is concerned.

Multiple comparisons of the groups show that distinctly more favourable ATI can be noticed among the Lecturers/Assistant Directors with high motivation, who tend to differ from all other groups including those in the high group in other positions. Within different position groups one and two show a similarity, wherein both the cases high group tend to possess more favourable ATI compared with the respective low groups. Such a pattern does not appear among those in position three and four where the differences in ATI are not statistically significant despite the progressive mean scores.

Thus, the analysis reveals that extreme groups of motivation in first two positions tend to show the difference in their ATI. Motivation has a distinct influence for those in position two. Respondents in this position would have put more than five years of professional experience and secured for themselves the academic requirements to a large extent. In addition, this is a crucial phase in building up a good academic career and peer group recognition by various academic activities like research publication, attending professional meetings etc. Those who show high motivation for such academic activities also tend to possess more favourable ATI. This tendency is not so pronounced in the other position groups.

4.8.6. *ATI and Information Source Use* vis-a-vis *Motivation*

Motivation, it has been observed, has a significant bearing on the ATI. A general trend signifying this has also been found among respondents in different work environments educational level, experience and position groups. However, these results do not summarily deny a minor portion of the respondents in low and moderate groups possessing a relatively more favourable attitudinal disposition to information. In the present analysis it is examined whether ATI and information source use relations that are observed initially (zero-order relations) vary as a consequence of differing strength of motivation. In other words the analysis probes as to whether the strength of motivation is a facilitating factor which improves the attitude-behaviour relations in the context. Accordingly conditional contingency tables (4.16 a-i) were prepared for ATI and source use categories for three groups of motivation viz., low, moderate and

TABLE 4.23: Frequency Distribution and Gamma Values for ATI and Source use vis-a-vis Motivation Groups

ATI	Motivation											
	Low N 65				Moderate N 131				High N 66			
	Use Frequency				Use Frequency				Use Frequency			
	Not at all	Rarely	Moderately	Frequently	Not at all	Rarely	Moderately	Frequently	Not at all	Rarely	Moderately	Frequently
1	2	3	4	5	6	7	8	9	10	11	12	13
a *Periodicals*												
Low	0	5	7	12	0	5	16	9	0	5	5	2
Moderate	2	3	15	16	0	9	31	30	0	3	6	14
High	0	0	0	5	0	1	14	16	0	1	10	20
		G: 0.199	Z: 0.672			G: 0.265	Z: 1.336			G: 0.482	Z: 1.975*	
b *Books and Research Reports*												
Low	0	6	5	13	0	3	12	15	1	1	5	5
Moderate	0	2	10	24	1	7	26	36	0	2	5	16
High	0	0	1	4	1	1	6	23	1	1	3	26
		G: 0.353	Z: 1.172			G: 0.243	Z: 1.82*			G: 0.487	Z: 1.782*	

Contd.

TABLE 4.23 *Contd.*

1	2	3	4	5	6	7	8	9	10	11	12	13
c *Theses and Dissertations*												
Low	4	11	7	2	7	12	7	4	1	4	5	2
Moderate	9	12	5	10	16	28	21	5	6	4	8	5
High	0	5	0	0	0	19	12	0	3	0	9	19
	G: -0.012			Z: -0.043		G: 0.099	Z: 0.731		G: 0.495		Z: 2.238*	
d *Citations in Books and Periodicals*												
Low	2	6	7	9	3	5	11	11	1	5	5	1
Moderate	3	7	14	12	7	12	29	22	1	1	8	13
High	0	1	0	4	1	7	10	13	0	1	13	17
	G: 0.149		Z: 0.533		G: 0.054		Z: 0.284		G: 0.474		Z: 1.976*	
e *Books Reviews*												
Low	5	11	6	2	2	13	13	2	2	4	5	1
Moderate	9	7	13	7	10	27	28	5	6	5	6	6
High	0	2	3	0	1	8	20	2	2	7	3	19
	G: 0.216		Z: 0.803		G: 0.177		Z: 0.901		G: 0.433		Z: 1.914*	
f *Abstracting and Indexing Services*												
Low	16	5	1	2	18	3	4	5	9	2	1	0
Moderate	22	7	5	2	37	14	13	6	9	3	3	8
High	3	1	0	1	20	8	2	1	0	0	18	13
	G: 0.113		Z: 0.356		G: -0.138		Z: -0.681			G: 0.682	Z: 3.799*	

Contd.

TABLE 4.23 *Contd.*

1	2	3	4	5	6	7	8	9	10	11	12	13
g *Consulting Experts*												
Low	3	2	13	6	2	9	11	8	2	4	6	0
Moderate	6	7	14	9	8	12	25	25	3	4	3	13
High	0	1	1	3	1	5	11	14	0	4	12	15
	G: 0.018		Z: 0.064		G: 0.201		Z: 1.080		G: 0.396		Z: 1.667*	
h *Attending Workshops and Seminars*												
Low	2	7	7	8	2	8	13	7	4	3	5	0
Moderate	6	8	13	9	11	14	28	17	3	1	9	10
High	1	1	1	2	0	9	12	10	0	1	8	22
	G: -0.079			Z: -0.228		G: 0.093	Z: 0.493		G: 0.724		Z: 4.013**	
i *Discussion with Colleagues*												
Low	2	11	4	7	0	7	12	11	2	4	3	3
Moderate	4	17	15	10	6	10	28	26	1	4	10	8
High	1	1	1	2	1	3	15	12	1	0	11	19
	G: 0.135		Z: 0.499		G: 0.062		Z: 0.317		G: 0.535		Z. 2.382**	

* Significance $P < .05$ ** Significance $P < .01$ (one tailed tests)

high. Kurskal and Goodman's Gamma was calculated separately for these three motivation groups. The resulting Gamma values showing the relations of ATI with source use frequency correspond to particular motivation group.

Analysis of the data (Table 4.23 a-i) reveal that for all the three primary sources of information viz., periodicals (G.0.482 $P < .05$), books (G. 0.487 $P < .05$) and theses (G. 0.495 $P < .05$) statistically significant attitude-behaviour relations are noticeable for the high motivation group. Significant positive relations are also noticeable for moderate group as to their use of books/research reports (G. 0.243 $P < .05$). Though all the other Gamma values are positive for the moderate motivation group and also for the low group with respect to use of periodicals and books, the relations are not statistically significant. It could be noticed that the Gamma values for the high motivation group are invariably higher than what was observed in the zero-order relations. Nonetheless the strength of association is also moderate.

As far as the secondary sources are concerned high motivation group consistently shows positive and statistically significant first order attitude-behaviour relations. The Gamma values explaining the strength of association for citation use (G. 0.474 $P < .05$), book reviews (G. 0.433 $P < .05$) and abstracts (G. 0.682 $P < .01$) vary from moderate to strong. That is, 47.4 per cent of differences in use of citations, 43.3 per cent in book reviews and as much as 68.2 per cent for abstracts is due to ATI. A consistent pattern does not emerge for the low and moderate groups. However, Gamma values show largely a positive ATI information source use association, despite their statistical non-significance.

As to the frequency of use of all the three non-bibliographic sources as well, the hitherto observed trend of high motivation group showing a positive and statistically significant relations hold good. The magnitude of association is moderate for consulting experts (G. 0.396 $P < .05$) and discussions with colleagues (G. 0.535 $P < .01$) explaining 39.6 per cent, and 53.5 per cent of the differences in the frequency of consulting experts and discussion with colleagues as a source of information respectively. The relations are strong, explaining 72.4 per cent of the differences as to workshops and seminars (G. 0.724 $P < .01$). Statistically significant ATI and information source use relations do not appear for the non-bibliographic source for the other two motivation groups.

Thus, the results reveal that the first order relations of attitude-behaviour on all the sources of information tend to be relatively strong for the high motivation group. The motivation for academic work is an important criterion, which when observed among those who are favourably inclined to information use more often results in frequent source use. In other words, strength of ATI and source use relations partially depend on the motivation. Relatively favourable ATI among the moderate and low group do not seem to result in information use behaviour in accordance with their attitudinal predisposition.

4.8.7 *Summary*

Motivation for the academic performance including various intrinsic and extrinsic motivating factors show a consistently positive and significant correlation with the ATI. *F* ratios also reveal that those with relatively higher motivation tends to possess more favourable ATI. The general trend of relationship of motivation and ATI is more or less consistent for different categorisation of the respondents including environmental affiliation and also on personal attributes. So much so interaction effect of independent variables is not significant on ATI. However, certain variations in the significance of the differences were not in the multiple comparisons.

Respondents with varying strength of motivation, classified as high, moderate and low, across the education levels reveal that Ph.D's with high motivation tend to posses a significantly favourable ATI and differ from all other groups. So also among the non-Ph.D's high group shows a statistical difference from the low group.

As to the respondents in different phases of their career strength of motivation has a definite bearing on the ATI for those in the middle and later phases of the career.

Despite a progressive trend of ATI going with motivation in all the positions, statistically significant differences are noticeable for only those in first two positions. Data do not show an interaction effect of position and motivation on ATI. A similar trend is also noticeable for motivation groups in University and Research and Training Institutions.

As to the strength of motivation as a conditional factor modifying the ATI and information source use relations, it has been found that high group of motivation consistently show positive and moderate to strong relations. The strength of the attitude-behaviour relations among the low and moderate motivation groups tends to be non-significant.

4.9 Job Satisfaction

4.9.1 *Job Satisfaction and ATI*

Industrial morale surveys over many years have asked the employees to rate the degree of 'adequacy' of various features of work situations. Job satisfaction studies conducted on the scientists working in organizations have shown moderate relations with the performance.

Satisfaction is a mental state of feeling. A person is satisfied with his job when his needs are fulfilled. When such a state of feeling is present in the scientists it can be expected that the interest in the academic process increases which may inturn induce a person to fulfil the job expectations. It could be assumed that in academic environment such a state of satisfaction could result in a favourable disposition to information use.

TABLE 4.24: Mean, S.D. and Correlation Coefficients between Job Satisfaction Items and ATI

	Mean	S.D.	*r*	
To make full use of present knowledge	4.16	1.12	0.15	P < .05
Opportunity for keep up to date	4.09	1.16	0.31	P < .01
Opportunity to write and publish	4.21	1.06	0.19	P < 0.1
A high degree of freedom in selecting research projects etc.	3.49	1.41	0.13	P < .05
Opportunity for promotion	3.37	1.36	0.10	(NS)
Adequate salary	3.69	1.31	0.08	(NS)
To work with colleagues of high competence	3.66	1.31	0.19	P< .01
Congenial colleagues	3.90	1.16	0.15	P < .05
To build professional reputation	3.80	1.18	0.23	P < .01
To work on difficult and challenging problems	3.52	1.26	0.13	P < .05
Attending professional meetings	3.48	1.36	0.10	(NS)
High degree of freedom in day-to-day activities	3.77	1.24	0.07	(NS)
To contribute to broad research knowledge	3.67	1.15	0.15	P < .05
Recognition of research by the organisation/faculty	3.39	1.25	0.21	P < .01
General satisfaction taking all these factors	3.45	1.29	0.19	P < .01
Total job satisfaction Score	55.62	12.46	0.19	P < .01

D.F. 260

Job satisfaction scale had 15 items focusing on various job factors. The scale had a theoretical range of 15-75. Observed scores for the study population extended from 17 to 75, with a mean of 55.62 and S.D. of 12.46. The distribution of respondents on the scale showed a negative skewness of -0.69 and a kurtosis of -1.11.

4.9.1.1. *Correlation of Job Satisfaction Scale Items with ATI*: Initially to examine relations of the job satisfaction items with the ATI product moment correlation was computed. Job satisfaction scores i.e. total of all the 15 items shows a correlation of 0.19 ($P < .01$) indicating that higher satisfaction is related to favourable ATI.

All the factors conceived to constitute job satisfaction show a positive relation with the ATI, confirming the trend observed for the total score. However, four of the fifteen items do not show a significant correlation. Three of these viz., opportunity for promotion, adequate salary and facilities for attending professional meetings are extrinsic environmental factors. It may be observed that as there are only a fewer rungs in the hierarchy to move up, even when the promotional opportunities are present it takes considerable number of years before such promotions materialise. So also, opportunities for attending professional meetings are more often available (in the typical Indian academic situation) for those in the higher rungs, lack of such facilities do not seem to seriously hamper the ATI among the respondents. Readiness to use information does not show significant relation with the feeling of adequacy of the salary one draws. Salary scales are, however, uniform in the four recognised positions of the hierarchy in all the organisations and do not vary as a reward for better performance. Again, high degree of freedom in day-to-day activities as opposed to freedom for selecting research projects/courses for teaching does not show a significant relation with ATI. In view of the varying aims and objectives of the organizations, exclusive freedom is rarely noticeable. This aspect does not seem to have significant bearing on the ATI either.

In the order of magnitude of correlation, among those factors which show significant relations with ATI, satisfaction on 'opportunity to keep up to date' stands first (r=0.31), followed by 'opportunity to build professional reputation' (r=0.23), 'recognition for research by the organization/faculty, (r=0.21), having competent colleagues, (r=0.19), facilities for writing and publishing research results (r=0.19).

Keeping up to date in ones field of specialisation is of prime importance in academic jobs, particularly when the focus is on research, failing which the esteem of the researcher in the peer group comes down. When the job functions provide for such an opportunity, ATI also tends to be favourable. So also, when the faculty recognises contributions of the staff and provides facilities for building up professional reputation by helping in teaching and publication activities through constructive criticism and encouragement, respondents also show further interest in such activities. The conducive environment facilitates them to hold favoùrable ATI. Satisfaction on the count of having competent colleagues within the organization can enthuse the fellow professionals to show greater interest in the academic activities, which, as the data indicates, bear a significant positive correlations with the ATI. Other factors which correlate at 5% level of significance are: feeling of satisfaction in terms of working on difficult problems, (r=0.13) having congenial colleagues, (r=0.15) freedom for selecting research problems (r=0.13) and also satisfaction interms of contributing to research knowledge, (r=0.15).

Thus, satisfaction on most of the items show a significant correlation with the ATI, wherein higher satisfaction is related to favourable ATI. Though a few items do not show significant results they are positive in their relations with the ATI.

4.9.1.2 *Job Satisfaction Groups and Their Relationship with ATI*: Data were analysed in another way to examine how the ATI behaves given a degree of satisfaction. Respondents in this analysis were categorised into high, moderate and low satisfaction groups based on the quartile one and three values. Those who had the job satisfaction score below the first quartile limit (Q_1 = 47) were identified as low and those with above the third quartile limit (Q_3 = 64) were called high group. The scores falling between these two ranges formed the moderate group.

From Table 4.25 it can be seen that the mean ATI scores shows an increasing trend from low to high group. Computed F ratio (F 6.41 $P < .01$) confirms the assumption that job satisfaction has a significant effect on the ATI of the social scientists. The t ratios reveal that significant differences are observable between moderate – low, and high-low satisfaction groups. Though high group has a slightly higher mean ATI score compared with moderate group they do not differ statistically.

Thus, relatively unfavourable ATI is discernible among those who have a low satisfaction, but moderate and high satisfaction seem to have a positive influence on the ATI of the respondents. As low satisfaction is the result of less conducive environment, often leading to lack of interest in job duties, it tends to bring in less favourable ATI.

TABLE 4.25: (a) Mean, S.D., (b) ANOVA Summary and (c) *t* Ratios for ATI *vis-a-vis* Job Satisfaction

(a) *Job Satisfaction*	N	Mean	S.D.	
Low	67	81.49	16.47	
Moderate	126	88.76	13.82	
High	69	89.38	14.55	
(b) *Source*	S.S.	D.F.	M.S.	F
Job satisfaction	2812.09	2	1406.05	6.41 $P < .01$
Error	56835.81	259	219.44	
Total	59647.89	261		
(c)				
Moderate - low	3.17 $P < .01$			
High - low	2.97 $P < .01$			
High - moderate	0.29 (NS)			

4.9.2 *ATI vis-a-vis Job Satisfaction and Environment*

It has been observed earlier that job satisfaction has a positive effect on the ATI. Analysis was carried out to examine whether this trend is noticeable in both the environments. In other words, the analysis aims at knowing the interaction effect of these variables on the ATI and also the individual effects of the two variables when the possible influence of one of the variables on the other is statistically controlled.

From Table 4.26 it could be noted that the magnitude of ATI tends to increase with the corresponding degree of job satisfaction in Universities and Research and Training Institutions. Computed analysis of variance confirms the significant influence of job satisfaction on the ATI. However, as has been observed in the other cases, effect of the job environment as such tends to be non-significant. The joint effect of the two variables over and above the two main effects is also not significant, implying that significant discrepancy in the magnitude of the ATI is not noticeable for the respondents in the two different environments but within the same group of job satisfaction.

TABLE 4.26: (a) Mean, S.D., (b) ANOVA Summary and (c) D.R.T. Results for ATI vis-a-vis Environment X Job Satisfaction

(a)

Environment	Job Satisfaction Low	Moderate	High
Universities	N 16 77.19 16.75	N 51 86.45 13.42	N 36 91.58 12.61
Research and Training Institutions	N 51 82.84 16.15	N 75 90.33 13.86	N 33 86.97 16.06

(b)

Source	S.S.(Adj.)	D.F.	M.S.	F
Job satisfaction	2992.21	2	1496.11	6.89 $P < .01$
Environment	191.51	1	191.51	0.88 (NS)
Job Satisfaction X Environment	1022.09	2	511.05	2.35 (NS)
Error	55622.20	256	217.27	

(c)

S.e.	14.74					
N	36	75	33	51	51	16
Mean	91.58	90.33	86.97	86.45	82.84	77.19

Mean scores underlined do not differ significantly at $P < .05$.

Duncan's Range Test worked out on ATI mean scores of six groups show that those with high job satisfaction tend to differ significantly in the ATI from those in the low group. This trend is common to respondents from University and Research and Training Institutions alike. In addition, moderate and low groups also show a significant difference in their ATI for those with university affiliation. In the case of Research and Training Institutions moderate group do not differ significantly from either low or high group. Within the same group of satisfaction respondents from two different affiliations do not tend to differ as to their readiness to use information.

It can be inferred from the results that among the three possible explanations of the variation in the dependent variable in the two way design, only job satisfaction seems to have a positive effect on the ATI. That is, higher satisfaction is found among those who have favourable attitudinal disposition to information. This trend is more or less consistent in both the job environments.

Job Satisfaction and Personal Attributes: The following sections presents the results of the two way analysis of variance when job satisfaction and one of the personal attributes are taken together The analysis aims to answer whether the effect of the job satisfaction on ATI is same for the different education, experience and position groupings of the respondents.

4.9.3 *ATI vis-a-vis Job Satisfaction and Education*

It has been noted that job satisfaction and education taken individually in analysis of variance show that ATI is a function of these variables. Analysis in the present context brings in these two variables together to know the variation in the main effects when the existing association in the independent variables is statistically corrected. So also, it examines the presence of the joint effect of the two variables on ATI over their individual main effects. Unlike most of the other cases a discrepancy in the trend of ATI scores is noticeable in the present context. Table 4.27 indicates that ATI mean scores do not progress with the increasing job satisfaction for Ph.D's and non-Ph.D's. However, Ph.D's tend to score more at different levels of job satisfaction compared with the non-Ph.D's.

The analysis confirms hitherto observed individual effects of education and job satisfaction on ATI when the sums of squares are adjusted to correct the error component introduced by the other variable (Job satisfaction or education) in the one way analysis. In addition, due to varying trends of ATI mean scores for Ph.D's and non-Ph.D's within the same group of satisfaction, the interaction effect of the two variables also tends to be significant. That is, the influence of each variable on ATI is different over the levels of other variables.

Further comparisons of the different groups show that Ph.D's in the low or high satisfaction group differ significantly from the non-Ph.D's. Moderately satisfied social scientists either with or without Ph.D. possess an overlapping intensity of predisposition to information use.

TABLE 4.27: (a) Mean, S.D., (b) Anova Summary and (c) D.R.T. Results for ATI vis-a-vis Job Satisfaction X Education

(a)

	Job Satisfaction		
Education	Low	Moderate	High
Non-Ph.D's	N 46 76.54 16.27	N 59 86.07 14.02	N 34 82.41 28.02
Ph.D's	N 21 92.33 10.70	N 67 91.13 13.19	N 35 96.14 12.78

(b)

Source	S.S.(Adj.)	D.F.	M.S.	F.
Education	6165.41	1	6165.41	32.09 $P < .01$
Job satisfaction	1445.74	2	723.37	3.77 $P < .05$
Education X Job Satisfaction	1486.28	2	743.14	3.87 $P < .05$
Error	49184.12	256	192.13	

(c)

S.e.	13.86					
N	35	21	67	59	34	46
Mean Scores	96.14	92.33	91.13	86.07	82.41	76.54

Mean scores underlined do not differ at $P < .05$

Ph.D's in different groups of satisfaction do not show a significant difference in their ATI. Non-Ph.D's, on the other hand, when they are less satisfied seem to possess a significantly less favourable ATI compared with the moderate group.

It may be inferred from the analysis that high satisfaction among the non-Ph.D's may be due to lesser expectations from the job which also seems to accompany with less favourable ATI. On the contrary when Ph.D's possess a low satisfaction which may be because of greater job expectations coupled with a proficiency at a higher level they tend to possess greater readiness to use information than the non-Ph.D's in different groups of satisfaction. This may also be due to relatively greater availability of opportunities for a change in the job for Ph.D's when they are less satisfied in their present job. However, to reap such opportunities one need to keep up to date in their field of specialisation and also involve in publishing activities so that they are 'visible' in the peer group. Non-Ph.D's with a higher satisfaction seem to show a contentment with what is available, which may be due to lesser expectations resulting in less favourable ATI. To add to this the nature of job duties for non-Ph.D's, particularly when they are in the lower positions in the hierarchy, may also have triggered this trend.

Thus, low satisfaction among those who have higher educational attainment seems to result in favourable ATI. This trend may be due to their need for bridging the gap between the job requirements and the provisions for the need fulfilment on job. When the availability is perceived to be less, it may make one to look for compensations by way of effective research and teaching or in similar activities which either facilitates a change in the job or leads to recognition in the same organization. This trend does not seem to recur among non-Ph.D's because of lesser proficiency resulting in lesser opportunities.

4.9.4 *ATI* vis-a-vis *Job Satisfaction and Experience*

This section examines the assumption that the combined effect of job satisfaction and experience is significant on ATI. The analysis also presents the individual effects of the two independent variables.

Table 4.28 shows that excepting a small deviation in the middle phase, wherein high satisfaction group shows a decline in their mean ATI, the general trend of relatively higher satisfaction inducing a favourable ATI in terms of higher mean score holds good for the break-up of the respondents based on their experience.

Analysis shows that even when the interaction is considered the main effects of the two variables remains significant. However, the interaction effect of these two variables does not seem to be significant indicating that experience and job satisfaction of the respondents act independently. The result also means that the effect of job satisfaction does not show significant deviations in different career phases. However, comparison of the ATI mean scores show that the three job satisfaction groups tend to differ significantly only for thosc in the initial phase of the career, where low satisfaction results in less favourable ATI. Despite a trend of increase in the mean scores reflecting the strength of ATI corresponding with the job satisfaction, the differences in the ATI scores are not significant in middle and later phases. Within high, moderate and low satisfaction groups ATI scores do not seem to differ significantly despite respondents being in different phases of one's career.

TABLE 4.28: (a) Mean, S.D., (b) Anova Summary and (c) D.R.T. Results for ATI *vis-a-vis* Job Satisfaction X Experience

(a)

	Job Satisfaction		
Education	Low	Moderate	High
Initial phase	N 21 75.81 10.88	N 20 81.30 9.68	N 17 86.71 8.87
Middle phase	N 34 83.11 17.19	N 45 88.96 15.77	N 25 87.32 18.10
Later phase	N 12 86.83 19.43	N 61 91.07 12.51	N 27 92.96 12.91

(b)

Source	S.S.(Adj.)	D.F.	M.S.	F.
Job satisfaction	1736.63	2	868.32	4.09 $P < .05$
Experience	2753.01	2	1376.51	6.48 $P < .01$
Job Satisfaction X Experience	370.58	4	92.65	0.44 (NS)
Error	53712.21	253	212.30	

(c)

S.e.	14.57								
N	27	61	45	25	12	17	34	20	21
Mean score	92.96	91.07	88.96	87.32	86.83	86.71	83.11	81.30	75.81

Thus, though satisfaction generally has a significant relations with the ATI, its effect is distinctly discernible among those in the initial phase with five year or less of academic experience. Despite low or moderate satisfaction in the later and middle phase, which seems to occur less often, respondents in these groups do not tend to possess less favourable ATI compared to the high group. Longer association with the academic profession seems to have, to a certain extent, compensated the effect of low satisfaction.

4.9.5 *ATI* vis-a-vis *Job Satisfaction and Position*

What is the nature of relations between ATI on the one hand and job satisfaction and position on the other? Do they have significant individual and interaction effect in the two way design? These are the questions enquired into in this section.

Classification of job satisfaction groups based on position showed that no observation was noticeable in now group among Professors/Directors. Therefore, for the purposes of analysis position 3 and 4 were combined. In the resulting bivariate table 4.29, it can be noted that excepting a slight deviation of high group possessing a lesser mean score than the moderate ones among Research Associates/Assistants, the general trend of increase in ATI mean scores can be observed in all the positions.

Analysis of the data indicate that only job satisfaction has a significant bearing on the ATI, even when the possible influence of being in a certain hierarchical position is corrected for. On the other hand despite position 3 and 4 being combined individual effect of the position on ATI does not tend to be significant. In addition, as the progression of the ATI mean scores for position groups seems to be more or less uniform, interaction effect of the two variables is also not statistically significant.

Multiple comparisons of the ATI means of the nine groups i.e., position groups classified according to the satisfaction, show that ATI has a significant relations with satisfaction only among the Research Associates, wherein low group possess a relatively less favourable ATI than the moderately satisfied ones. Analysis also reveal that higher job satisfaction seems to compensate the effect of being in higher position, as Lecturers/Assistant Directors with high satisfaction possess significantly more favourable ATI compared with low group among Readers/Deputy Directors.

It may be inferred from the analysis that interaction effect of these two variables is not significant on ATI. Effect of job satisfaction is discernible only among those in the position one – Research Associates/Assistants. As for the other positions despite a noticeable increase in the mean ATI scores in accordance with the respondents' job satisfaction, their significance is not statistically discernible.

TABLE 4.29: (a) Mean, S.D. (b) Anova Summary and (c) D.R.T. Results for ATI *vis-a-vis* Job Satisfaction X Position

(a)

	Job Satisfaction		
Position	Low	Moderate	High
	N 30	N 28	N 18
Research Associates/	77.93	89.25	84.39
Assistants	16.95	15.98	13.51
	N 24	N 38	N 17
Lecturers/	85.79	89.60	95.06
Assistant Directors	12.30	15.04	15.62
	N 13	N 60	N 34
*Readers/Deputy Directors and	81.77	88.00	88.97
Professors/Directors	19.81	11.71	13.70

* Positions viz., Reader and Professor/Director were combined as there were no observations in low group among Professors/Directors.

(b)

Source	S.S.(Adj.)	D.F.	M.S.	F.
Job satisfaction	2542.78	2	1271.39	5.85 $P < .01$
Position	1120.32	2	560.16	2.58 (NS)
Job Satisfaction X Position	708.01	4	177.05	0.81 (NS)
Error	55007.49	253	217.42	

(c)

S.e.	14.57								
N	17	38	28	34	60	24	18	13	30
Mean score	95.06	89.60	89.25	88.97	88.00	85.79	84.39	81.77	77.93

Mean scores underlined do not differ significantly at $P < .05$

4.9.6 *ATI and Information Source Use* vis-a-vis *Job Satisfaction*

It was within the purview of the research to examine the nature of first order relations of ATI and information source use when respondents are divided on their degree of satisfaction. The degree of job satisfaction is a situational variable which could affect ATI – source use relations. Accordingly the Gamma values were calculated to know the attitude-behaviour relations for low, moderate and high satisfaction groups separately. Table 4.30 a-i give the frequency distribution as to the source use *vis-a-vis* ATI for respondents in different job satisfaction groups and also the Gamma values.

The results of the analysis show that the association of ATI and the use rating of two of the primary sources viz., periodicals (G. 0.505 $P < .05$) and books (G. 0.679 $P < .01$) tends to be strong, statistically significant and positive for those who are highly satisfied with their job. As to the use of theses/dissertations none of the group show significant association. Though the strength of association is relatively high for this source for the highly satisfied respondents compared to those with moderate satisfaction, it is not statistically significant. Those who are either less or moderately satisfied consistently show a non-significant attitude-behaviour relations.

Consistently strong and significant positive association between ATI and source use is present for the high job satisfaction group with respect to the use of secondary sources of information. Gamma values in the context are 0.563 (citation in books/journals), 0.624 (book reviews) and 0.857 (abstracts) and all are significant at one per cent level. In addition, favourable ATI resulting in overt behaviour is noticeable for moderate satisfaction group in their use of abstracting journals (G. 0.341 $P < .05$). However, low satisfaction group shows non-significant association on all the secondary sources. Negative attitude-behaviour relations, though not significant, are also noticeable as to their use of abstracting/indexing sources.

The trend observed for those who are highly satisfied on primary and secondary sources of information also holds good on two of the three non-bibliographic sources viz., consulting experts (G.0.726 $P < .01$) and workshops and seminars (G. 0.600 P. < .01). The probabilities of favourable ATI resulting in frequent use of these two sources are to the tune of 72.6 per cent and 60.0 per cent. Significant first order relations are also noticeable as to the use of seminars/workshops as a source of information (G. 0.317 $P < .05$)

TABLE 4.30: Frequency Distribution and Gamma Values for ATI and Source use vis-a-vis Job Satisfaction Groups

	Job Satisfaction											
	Low N 67				Moderate N 126				High N 69			
	Use Frequency				Use Frequency				Use Frequency			
ATI	Not at all	Rarely	Moderately	Frequently	Not at all	Rarely	Moderately	Frequently	Not at all	Rarely	Moderately	Frequently
1	2	3	4	5	6	7	8	9	10	11	12	13
a *Periodicals*												
Low	0	5	11	10	0	3	16	11	0	7	1	2
Moderate	0	6	13	8	2	9	24	28	0	0	15	24
High	0	2	5	7	0	0	12	21	0	0	7	13
	G: 0.078		Z: 0.292		G: 0.296		Z: 1.497		G: 0.505		Z: 2.062*	
b *Books and Research Reports*												
Low	0	6	8	12	0	2	10	18	1	2	4	3
Moderate	0	4	11	12	1	4	22	36	0	3	8	28
High	2	2	1	9	0	0	7	26	0	0	2	18
	G: 0.083		Z: 0.311		G: 0.254		Z: 1.159		G: 0.679		Z: 2.873*	

Contd.

TABLE 4.30 *Contd.*

1	2	3	4	5	6	7	8	9	10	11	12	13
c *Theses and Dissertations*												
Low	7	11	7	1	4	11	12	3	1	5	0	4
Moderate	3	10	10	4	20	20	11	12	8	14	13	4
High	2	6	2	4	1	14	12	6	0	4	7	9
	G: 0.278		Z: 1.140		G: 0.109		Z: 0.592		G: 0.383		Z: 1.607	
d *Citations in Books and Periodicals*												
Low	3	7	12	4	1	6	6	13	2	3	5	4
Moderate	2	5	8	12	9	11	22	19	0	4	21	16
High	1	2	4	7	0	6	18	15	0	1	1	12
	G: 0.341		Z: 1.428		G: 0.037		Z: 0.193		G: 0.582		Z: 2.571*	
e *Books Reviews*												
Low	5	14	3	4	3	11	15	1	1	3	6	0
Moderate	2	8	15	2	16	13	25	9	7	18	7	7
High	2	4	7	1	1	13	14	5	0	0	5	15
	G: 0.250		Z: 1.015		G: 0.112		Z: 0.589		G: 0.624		Z: 3.185**	
f *Abstracting and Indexing Services*												
Low	13	5	4	4	22	5	0	3	8	0	2	0
Moderate	18	2	2	5	31	15	8	9	19	7	11	2
High	10	3	0	1	13	6	9	5	0	0	11	9
	G: -0.257			Z: -0.937		G: 0.341	Z: 1.838*			G: 0.857	Z: 6.441**	

Contd.

TABLE 4.30 *Contd.*

1	2	3	4	5	6	7	8	9	10	11	12	13
g *Consulting Experts*												
Low	3	4	10	9	0	11	15	4	4	0	5	1
Moderate	2	6	12	7	11	11	18	23	4	6	12	17
High	1	3	5	5	0	7	16	10	0	0	3	17
	G:-0.014			Z:-0.054		G: 0.170	Z: 0.912		G: 0.726		Z: 3.856**	
h *Attending Workshops and Seminars*												
Low	3	7	8	8	3	11	11	5	2	0	6	2
Moderate	2	6	10	9	11	9	26	17	7	8	14	10
High	1	5	4	4	0	6	13	14	0	0	4	16
	G:0.008		Z: 0.031		G: 0.317		Z: 1.774*			G: 0.600	Z: 2.827**	
Discussion with Colleagues												
Low	3	8	7	8	1	8	12	9	0	6	0	4
Moderate	0	9	8	10	8	11	21	23	3	1	24	11
High	1	3	3	7	1	1	15	16	1	0	9	10
	G: 0.205		Z: 0.814		G: 0.240		Z: 1.278		G: 0.346		Z: 1.369	

* Significance $P < .05$ ** Significance $P < .01$ (one tailed tests)

for the group of moderate satisfaction. None of the three groups tend to confirm the zero-order relations with regard to the source discussion with colleagues. However, it may be noted that the strength of the relations is more than what is observed in the zero-order, though are not significant in the context. Low satisfaction group, as was observed on primary and secondary sources, does not support the assumption of attitude-behaviour relations.

It can be concluded that the association of ATI and information source use also depends on the degree of satisfaction experienced in the job. The overall relations observed turn out to be strong on most of the sources for those who are highly satisfied. However, these relations are not confined to high group only, as the data bears out on two of the sources (abstracts/indexes, workshops/seminars) the attitude-behaviour relations are positive and significant among the moderately satisfied respondents also. Such relation consistently fail to emerge for those who are in the low satisfaction group. Thus, social scientists who are least satisfied do not show source use behaviour in accordance with their attitudinal disposition for the same. In other words, the favourable ATI resulting in frequent use of various sources of information is also conditional to the degree of job satisfaction.

4.9.7 *Summary*

Data bear out that job satisfaction has a positive effect on ATI. All the items in the job satisfaction scale shows a positive correlation with the ATI and excepting four items the others are statistically significant.

Interaction effect in the cases of environment and job satisfaction, experience and job satisfaction, and position and job satisfaction on ATI tends to be non-significant indicating that trend of relationship of ATI and job satisfaction for different position experience groups and also for different environments is largely same.

As to the experience groupings high satisfaction in the initial phase has a significant effect on the ATI, wherein they differ significantly from the low group. The trend of increasing ATI does not seem to be significant as the academicians put in more years of service in the profession.

Across the position groups as well, distinct relation of job satisfaction is discernible for Research Associates who are in the first rung of the job hierarchy, wherein moderately satisfied ones tend to be more favourable than the low group.

Education groupings of the respondents in different levels of satisfaction, show a significant interaction effect on the ATI. Analysis reveals that Ph.D's, probably because of their higher proficiency, tend to deviate from the normally observed trend when they fall in extreme groups of satisfaction. They also differ from non-Ph.D's who experience high or low satisfaction.

ATI and information source use relations to an extent depends on the degree of satisfaction experienced in the job. The overall relations observed turn out to be strong on most of the sources for those who are highly satisfied on their job. Moderately satisfied ones also show this tendency on two of the nine sources. Those who are least satisfied, despite their favourability to information use do not seem to behave as per their attitudinal disposition.

4.10 **Dedication to Job**

4.10.1 *Dedication to Job and ATI*

Four items relating to the work aspects in the organizational context were found to correlate in the pilot survey. These items were used to measure the intensity of job dedication. These items focused on the felt obligation to support the organizational goals, extent of involvement in the job duties, interest shown for research and teaching aspects of the job, and also feeling of challenge that is sensed in performing the assignments.

It is understandable that individual requirements and job provisions may not necessarily match one to one in any organization. For instance a social scientist interested in theoretical studies, in the job context of applied research may not entirely feel at home as to his job requirements. This necessitates a need adjustment to suit the organizational and group requirements. In the context of organizational behaviour in industries this concept is used to denote 'morale' and 'spirit of belongingness' when such a belongingness is present, it does not distort the individual's personal ideals. Whenever it is not present, it may lead to a lesser involvement in the job requirements and consequently may have a bearing on ATI and also information source use.

Scores for the four dedication items ranged from 4 to 20 on a five point scale. Observed dedication scores among the respondents also ranged from 4 to 20. Thus, the dedication extended from least to the most among the respondents. The mean score for the sample was 15.34 with a S.D. 3.34. The group as such leans towards higher side of the dedication.

4.10.1.1 *Correlation of Dedication Scale Items with the ATI*: To examine the relations of individual dedication items the scores of each items were separately correlated with that of ATI. The product moment correlations are shown in Table 4.31.

TABLE 4.31: Mean, S.D and Correlation Coefficients between Dedication Items and ATI

	Mean	S.D.	*r*	
Obligation for the organizational goals	4.24	1.13	0.26	P < .01
Involvement in research and teaching	3.94	1.03	0.13	P < .05
Interest shown in research and teaching	3.85	1.12	0.21	P < .01
Feeling of challenge in tesearch and teaching	3.32	1.34	0.16	P < .01
Total	15.34	3.34	0.17	P < .01
D.F. 260				

Correlation coefficients indicate that all the four items in the dedication scale correlate significantly with the ATI. That is to say each of the aspects – higher obligation, involvement, interest and challenge – occurs jointly with the more favourable ATI. So also the total of these items (dedication score) also correlate significantly with the ATI. Among the four items obligation felt to support organizational goals (r = 0.26 P < .01), shows a higher magnitude of relation followed by interest in the work (r = 0.21 P < .01), challenge experienced (r = 0.16 P < .01) and lastly involvement in the research and teaching activities (r = 0.13 P < .01).

4.10.1.2 *Dedication groups and their relation with ATI*: To examine the effect of different levels of dedication on ATI the respondents were grouped into high, moderate and low groups based on the quartile cut off points for the total score. Accordingly respondents with scores less than 13 (Q_1) were grouped as low and those with 18 (Q_3) and above as high, and those with scores between these two cut off points formed the moderate group.

TABLE 4.32: (a) Mean, S.D., (b) ANOVA Summary and (c) *t* Ratios for ATI *vis-a-vis* Dedication

(a) *Dedication*	N	Mean	S.D.	
Low	66	80.76	13.97	
Moderate	130	85.45	13.92	
High	66	96.55	13.86	
(b) *Source*	S.S.	D.F.	M.S.	F.
Dedication	8895.19	2	4447.59	22.70 $P < .01$
Error	50752.70	259	195.96	
Total	59647.89	261		
(c)				
Moderate - low	2.22 $P < .05$			
High - moderate	5.26 $P < .01$			
High - low	6.47 $P < .01$			

The mean scores of the ATI for the three dedication groups show an increase from low to high. The computed *F* ratio ($F = 22.70$ $P < .01$) is highly significant, indicating that dedication of the social scientists has a positive and definite influence on their ATI. Pairwise comparisons also show that significant differences appear between all the pairs, viz., high-moderate, high-low and moderate-low. It could be concluded from the analysis that the social scientists' dedication to their job duties has a significant and positive influence on the ATI.

4.10.2 *ATI* vis-a-vis *Dedication and Environment*

For the study population as such it has been observed that dedication has a significant and positive effect on ATI. But how far is this trend uniform in two job environments? The foregoing section examines this aspect. The individual effects of dedication and environment is also worked out. In the context the analysis adjusts the sum of squares so that the error introduced due to the association of the two independent variables is eliminated.

Table 4.33 presents the mean ATI scores for the low, moderate and high groups of dedication. An increasing trend of attitudinal intensity towards information is noticeable for respondents from the

Universities, and the Research and Training Institutions alike. The analysis to examine the significance of three possible ways of explaining the variation in the ATI, reveal that only one of these effects viz., that of independent variable dedication tends to be significant. Discrepancy in the ATI is not noticeable for those in the same groupings of dedication in their job, but with different institutional affiliation. The observed trend is consistent for both the groups which is shown in the non-significant interaction effect of the environment and dedication. Multiple comparisons of the groups reveal that those who are highly dedicated in universities and Research and Training Institutions tend to be significantly more favourable to information use compared with those in the low and moderate groups.

TABLE 4.33: (a) Mean, S.D., (b) ANOVA Summary and (c) D.R.T. Results for ATI *vis-a-vis* Environment X Dedication

(a)

	Dedication		
Environment	Low	Moderate	High
	N 18	N 54	N 31
Universities	78.06	85.30	94.52
	10.98	14.41	12.67
	N 48	N 76	N 35
Research and Training	81.77	85.57	98.34
Institutions	14.82	18.56	14.59

(b)

Source	S.S.(Adj.)	D.F.	M.S.	F.
Dedication	9116.09	2	4558.05	23.18 $P < .01$
Environment	232.29	1	232.29	1.18 (NS)
Dedication X Environment	191.43	2	95.60	0.49 (NS)
Error	50328.98	256	196.60	

(c)

S.e. 14.02

N	35	31	76	54	48	18
Mean score	98.34	94.52	85.57	85.30	81.77	78.06

(Underlined in print: 98.34 and 94.52; 85.57, 85.30, 81.77 and 78.06.)

Mean scores for the groups underlined do not differ at $P < .05$.

Thus, it can be concluded that dedication to job has a positive effect on the ATI, for the social scientists from university departments and Research and Training Institutions. Those who show higher dedication also tend to possess more favourable ATI.

Dedication and personal attributes: Preliminary analysis of the data showed that dedication to job and also education and experience tend to have a positive effect on ATI. In this section their combined effect on the dependent variable ATI is explored. That is, whether the effect of dedication on ATI is uniform for the sub-classification of the respondents on their personal variables.

4.10.3 *ATI* vis-a-vis *Dedication and Education*

In this section the analysis examines the effect of dedication on ATI for respondents in two education groups. Table 4.34 indicates that mean ATI score shows a progression from low to high groups for both Ph.D's and non-Ph.D's. Ph.D's in all the groups show higher mean score than the non-Ph.D's.

Two way analysis of variance confirms the significance of individual effects of education and dedication when the interaction sum of squares is also considered. However, the interaction effect of these two variables on ATI is not significant, indicating that significant deviation from the normal trend of increasing intensity of ATI with the dedication does not appear for the education groups. Combined effect of the two variables is additive in nature.

Further comparisons of the groups reveal that Ph.D's with high dedication also possess a more favourable ATI and differ from all other groups. Among the non-Ph.D's also high group possess a more favourable ATI and differ from the other two groups. Within the three dedication groups significant difference in favour of Ph.D's is present in high and moderate dedication groups. Ph.D's and non-Ph.D's with low dedication do not differ statistically in their ATI. Among the non-Ph.D's higher dedication tends to act as a compensation for Ph.D. degree, in that they show an overlapping intensity of ATI when compared with moderate and low groups with a higher educational attainment.

It could be concluded that dedication shows a significant effect on Ph.D's and non-Ph.D's. Among non-Ph.D's higher dedication seems to act as a compensation in place of higher educational attainment. The joint effect of these variables is additive in nature and hence the interaction F ratio is not significant.

TABLE 4.34: (a) Mean, S.D., (b) ANOVA Summary and (c) D.R.T. Results for ATI *vis-a-vis* Dedication X Education

(a)

	Dedication		
Education	Low	Moderate	High
	N 51	N 69	N 19
Non-Ph.D.	79.53	81.55	90.42
	14.53	14.32	16.48
	N 15	N 61	N 47
Ph.D.	84.93	89.87	99.02
	10.91	12.00	11.77

(b)

Source	S.S.(Adj.)	D.F.	M.S.	F.
Dedication	4914.46	2	2457.23	13.34 $P < .01$
Education	3550.09	1	3550.09	19.27 $P < .01$
Dedication X Education	29.37	2	14.69	0.08 (NS)
Error	47173.27	256	184.27	

(c)

S.e. 13.57

N	47	19	61	15	69	51
Mean score	99.02	90.42	89.87	84.93	81.55	79.53

Mean scores underlined do not differ significantly at $P < .05$.

4.10.4 *ATI* vis-a-vis *Dedication and Experience*

A similar analysis as was carried on in the earlier section was made to examine the effect of dedication on ATI for social scientists in different phases of their career. In the bivariate Table 4.35 it could be noted that mean ATI scores show a progression from low to high groups for respondents in middle and later phases. A deviation from this trend is noticeable for those in moderate groups in their initial phase, indicating that dedication may not have a similar effect in all the phases as far as its relation with ATI is concerned. Analysis confirms the individual effects of dedication and experience. The interaction effect of these variables is however, not statistically significant.

Nonetheless *F* ratio of 2.01 (nearing 5% level) calls for comparisons of different groups.

TABLE 4.35: (a) Mean, S.D., (b) ANOVA Summary and (c) D.R.T. Results for ATI *vis-a-vis* Dedication X Experience

(a)

	Dedication		
Experience	Low	Moderate	High
Initial phase	N 24 81.38 8.53	N 27 77.33 11.20	N 7 93.00 6.63
Middle phase	N 31 78.42 15.14	N 53 87.26 14.18	N 20 97.80 19.67
Later phase	N 11 86.00 17.97	N 50 87.92 13.32	N 39 96.54 10.75

(b)

Source	S.S.(Adj.)	D.F.	M.S.	F.
Dedication	6400.00	2	3200.00	16.90 $P < .01$
Experience	1333.28	2	666.64	3.52 $P < .05$
Dedication X Experience	1525.38	4	381.35	2.01 (NS)
Error	47894.05	253	189.31	

(c)
S.e. 13.76

N	20	39	7	50	53	11	24	31	27
Mean score	97.80	96.54	93.00	87.92	87.26	86.00	81.38	78.42	77.33

Mean scores underlined do not differ significantly at $P < .05$.

Multiple comparisons of the mean scores for nine groups show that high dedication group in middle and later phases differ significantly from the low group. A deviation from this trend is present for those in the initial phase wherein respondents with low dedication tend to possess more favourable ATI than the moderate group. This results in high and moderate group showing a difference and not high and low dedication groups.

Dedication is distinctly related with the ATI for those in the middle phase of their career. Among these respondents significant difference appear between low and moderate, moderate and high, and also high and low group. The trend of ATI is positive with the increasing levels of dedication. Within the three dedication groups significant difference does not appear for those in different phases, excepting for the moderate group where respondents in their initial phase tend to be less favourable to information use. Higher dedication acts as a compensation for the longer association with the attitude object as mean ATI scores for those in high group in initial and middle phase tends to be higher than those showing moderate or low dedication in later phase.

It could be inferred from the analysis that in all the phases higher dedication seems to have a positive influence on ATI. However, this is distinctly discernible among those in their middle phase. Deviation in the initial phase may be due to the routine nature of job assignment, particularly when they are in the lowest rung of the hierarchy. Thus, though interaction effect is partly present (nearing 5% level) it is not statistically significant.

4.10.5 *ATI* vis-a-vis *Dedication and Position*

Is the effect of dedication on ATI uniform for all the position groups? Analysis examining this trend and also main effects of the independent variables is presented in this section.

Table 4.36 reveals a progression of mean ATI scores from low to high groups in all the positions, excepting those in the highest position in the hierarchy wherein the low group score slightly higher than those who are moderately dedicated. Analysis confirm the individual effect of the dedication when interaction sum of square is deducted for arriving at the main effects. However, the influence of position and also the interaction of the position and dedication is not significant. Thus, the results confirm a broad similarity in influence of dedication on ATI for all the position groups.

Statistical comparison of the ATI mean scores show that high dedication group in all the positions tend to be more favourable in the ATI compared with respective low and moderate groups, excepting those in hierarchical position four, where the ATI mean score for high and low groups are not significant. However, across different positions moderate and low groups do not show statistical difference

TABLE 4.36: (a) Mean, S.D., (b) ANOVA Summary and (c) D.R.T. Results for ATI vis-a-vis Dedication X Position

Position	Dedication: Low	Dedication: Moderate	Dedication: High
Research Associates/ Assistants	N 37 80.11 14.96	N 29 82.66 15.79	N 10 100.40 14.37
Assistant Directors/ Lecturers	N 19 82.95 10.43	N 44 87.82 13.82	N 16 102.50 13.94
Deputy Directors/ Readers	N 8 78.00 17.15	N 41 87.29 12.90	N 24 91.75 14.00
Directors/ Professors	N 2 83.00 2.00	N 16 79.44 10.04	N 16 95.38 9.70

(b)

Source	S.S. (Adj.)	D.F.	M.S.	F.
Position	1231.24	3	410.41	2.13 (NS)
Dedication	8728.64	2	4364.32	22.69 $P < .01$
Position X Dedication	1438.29	6	239.72	1.24 (NS)
Error	48083.17	250	192.33	

(c)

S.e. 13.87

N	16	10	16	24	44	2	19	29	41	37	16	8
Mean Score	102.50	100.4	95.38	91.75	87.82	83.00	82.95	82.66	81.29	80.11	79.44	78.00

Means scores underlined do not differ significantly at $P < .05$.

in their intensity of ATI. The respondents in position two show relatively higher ATI mean score among high and moderate groups of dedication. Within the low, moderate and high groups significant differences mostly do not appear for different position groups. However, high and moderate groups of those in position two show a greater intensity of ATI as compared to their respective counterparts in position three and four. As respondents in high group in various positions tend to be more favourable than the moderate and low groups of the immediately next higher position, advantage gained by being in the higher position is compensated to a certain extent as far as the relations of dedication and ATI are concerned.

It can be concluded that dedication has more or less an uniform influence on the ATI of the respondents in all positions. ATI tends to be less favourable for those who show low or moderate dedication to their work. As significant deviations in this trend is not noticeable interaction effect is also statistically non-significant. On the contrary the two variables have an additive effect on the dependent variable.

4.10.6 *ATI and Information Source Use* vis-a-vis *Dedication to Job*

To what extent is the dedication which is shown to have a bearing on ATI is in itself a conditional factor affecting the ATI and information source use relations? The first order relations of ATI and information source use relations? The first order relations of ATI and information source use is worked out to examine the trend with the degree of dedication as the third variable.

Table 4.37 a-i show the frequency distribution regarding information source use and ATI for low, moderate and high groups of dedication. Kurskal and Goodman's Gamma worked out for these groups separately reveals that as far as the use of primary sources are concerned attitude-behaviour relations tend to be strong for the high dedication group for periodicals (G. 0.556 $P < .01$) and books/research reports (G. 0.696 $P < .01$). With regard to the use of theses/dissertations, the chances of favourable attitude and source use going together are moderate (G. 0.400 $P < .05$) and explain 40.0 per cent of the observed variations. On the contrary the low and moderate groups seem to have reduced the strength of zero-order relations as their Gamma values are consistently low and non-significant.

TABLE 4.37: Frequency Distribution and Gamma Values for ATI and Source use *vis-a-vis* Dedication to Job

ATI	Dedication											
	Low N 66				Moderate N 130				High N 66			
	Use Frequency				Use Frequency				Use Frequency			
	Not at all	Rarely	Mode- rately	Fre- quently	Not at all	Rarely	Mode- rately	Fre- quently	Not at all	Rarely	Mode- rately	Fre- quently
1	2	3	4	5	6	7	8	9	10	11	12	13
a *Periodicals*												
Low	0	4	10	11	0	6	11	11	0	5	7	1
Moderate	0	11	16	9	2	4	34	35	0	0	2	16
High	0	0	2	3	0	2	12	13	0	0	10	25
	G: 0.132		Z: 0.461		G: 0.148		Z: 0.712		G: 0.553		Z: 2.275*	
b *Books and Research Reports*												
Low	1	5	8	11	0	1	11	16	0	4	3	6
Moderate	0	5	12	19	1	6	26	42	0	0	3	15
High	0	0	3	2	0	2	7	18	2	0	0	33
	G: 0.160		Z: 0.548		G: 0.075		Z: 0.341		G: 0.696		Z: 2.739**	

Contd.

TABLE 4.37 *Contd.*

1	2	3	4	5	6	7	8	9	10	11	12	13
c *Theses and Dissertations*												
Low	4	11	9	1	6	13	5	4	2	3	5	3
Moderate	7	15	8	6	20	25	19	11	4	4	7	3
High	1	1	2	1	2	15	10	0	0	8	9	18
	G: 0.082		Z: 0.296		G: 0.051		Z: 0.263		G: 0.400		Z: 1.684*	
d *Citations in Books and Periodicals*												
Low	3	7	7	8	0	6	13	9	3	3	3	4
Moderate	3	6	15	12	8	11	32	24	0	3	4	11
High	0	1	1	3	0	7	14	6	1	1	8	25
	G: 0.212		Z: 0.782		G: -0.089		Z: -0.446			G: 0.491	Z: 1.979*	
e *Books Reviews*												
Low	4	14	3	4	4	6	17	1	1	8	4	0
Moderate	4	12	18	2	19	24	21	11	2	3	8	5
High	0	1	2	2	0	11	9	7	3	5	15	12
	G: 0.365		Z: 1.431		G: 0.114		Z: 0.599		G: 0.415		Z: 1.737*	
f *Abstracting and Indexing Journals*												
Low	15	3	2	5	18	4	4	2	10	3	0	0
Moderate	25	7	2	2	35	15	17	8	8	2	2	6
High	2	0	1	2	15	4	6	2	6	5	13	11
	G: -0.027		Z: -0.088			G: 0.089	Z: 0.486*			G: 0.564	Z: 2.669**	

Contd.

TABLE 4.37 *Contd.*

1	2	3	4	5	6	7	8	9	10	11	12	13
g *Consulting Experts*												
Low	3	2	13	7	4	7	10	7	0	6	7	0
Moderate	3	10	13	10	10	13	23	29	4	0	6	6
High	0	1	1	3	0	7	10	10	1	2	13	19
	G: 0.017		Z: 0.061		G: 0.160		Z: 0.840		G: 0.521		Z: 2.304*	
h *Attending Workshops and Seminars*												
Low	4	5	8	8	2	8	11	7	2	5	6	0
Moderate	2	13	12	9	11	10	34	20	7	0	4	7
High	0	0	2	3	1	11	8	7	0	0	11	24
	G: 0.129		Z: 0.473		G: -0.028		Z: -0.144			G: 0.693	Z: 3.747**	
Discussion with Colleagues												
Low	2	10	4	9	1	4	12	11	1	8	3	1
Moderate	1	9	14	12	7	10	35	23	3	2	4	9
High	0	1	1	3	3	1	12	11	0	2	14	19
	G: 0.232		Z: 0.855		G: 0.009		Z: 0.045		G: 0.543		Z: 2.480**	

* Significance $P < .05$ ** Significance $P < .01$ (one tailed tests)

The same trend of social scientists showing high dedication to job also showing a significant positive elations holds good for secondary sources. Chances of more favourable ATI associating with more frequent use of secondary sources such as citations in journals/books (G. 0.491 $P < .05$) and book reviews (G. 0.415 $P < .05$) gets a moderate support from the analysis and as to the abstracts as a source of information (G. 0.564 $P < .01$) the association is strong and positive. A consistent trend of relationship irrespective of the level of significance, is not noticeable for moderate and low dedication groups. Gamma value tend to be negative for low group in case of abstracts and it is negative for the moderate group on the source-citations in journals/books, implying that the source use does not correspond to the attitudinal disposition. However, in neither instance the relation is statistically significant.

The hitherto observed trend among the high dedication group is confirmed on the non-bibliographic sources as well. The attributable differences in non-bibliographic sources use to ATI extends to 69.3 per cent for workshop and seminars (G.693 $P < .01$, 54.3 per cent for discussions with colleagues (G. 0.543 $P < .01$) and 52.1 per cent for the source-consulting experts (G. 0.521 $P < .01$).

Moderate and low dedication group on the contrary show a non-significant attitude-behaviour relationship. As was noted earlier deviation in the direction of association is also noticeable for moderate group on the source-attending workshops and seminars.

The data consistently points out that high dedication, wherein respondents express greater degree of involvement, interest, challenge and also feel a sense of obligation for their work related activities, when associated with a favourable ATI tends to result in a consistently positive and significant overt behaviour corresponding with the expressed readiness to use information. However, despite such readiness, when the social scientists possess only moderate or low degree of dedication in their work, the source use behaviour does not seem to be consistent with the attitude. Thus, to a greater extent attitude-behaviour relations in the context is also conditional to the degree of dedication of the respondents to their job duties.

4.10.7 *Summary*

Dedication shown for the teaching and research assignment within the organization has a significant bearing on the ATI of the social scientists.

All the four items included as the measure of dedication show a positive and significant correlation with the ATI.

Break up of the dedication groups according to their education levels reveals that Ph.D's declaring high dedication differ from all the other groups in their ATI. Those with high dedication among the non-Ph.D's also show a similar trend within their sub-group.

The above observed trend holds good for the respondents in different experience groups or career phases. It is particularly so for the respondents in the middle and later phase.

Across the position groups also respondents showing a higher dedication tend to possess a more favourable ATI and differ significantly from other groups.

Analysis to examine the interaction effect of dedication with education, experience and position resulted in non-significant *F* ratio. The influence of dedication on the ATI is largely independent of the effect of other variables. In other words, personal variables do not interfere with dedication in their relations with ATI.

As was observed in the case of motivation, those who are highly dedicated to their job duties and with a more favourable ATI tends to involve in positive and significant overt behaviour corresponding with the expressed readiness to use information.

4.11 **Aspiration**

4.11.1 *Aspiration and ATI*

Aspirations are the goals set by individuals for achievement in a given activity. It has been noted earlier (Para 2.6) that aspirations whenever realistically set tend to correlate with the factors which facilitate in the accomplishment of the goals aspired. Higher goal achievement by academicians in the ladder of academic performance calls for more favourable ATI and also frequent use of information sources in accordance with their attitudinal disposition. Hence, it could be expected that higher level of aspiration has an influence on the attitudinal favourability of the social scientists. So also the information source use could be furthered by the level of aspiration. In other words, higher aspiration is expected to lead to a more favourable ATI and also facilitate ATI and source use relations.

In the context of this study cantril's pictorial ladder scale was used ascertain the social scientists' perception of their position in the wider academic context. Two anchoring points were defined as the stage in which the respondents enter the academic job (Rung '0') and the best that one can achieve in the academic profession (Rung '10'). A gap of three years was provided for setting their goal. Accordingly respondents indicated this present position in the ladder as they perceived it and also their goal for achievement three years hence. Neither the present nor the aspired position had any reference to their hierarchic position.

Against the theoretical range of 0 to 10 the observed range extended from 0 to 9 in the present and 0 to 10 in the future dimensions. The goal discrepancy i.e. the difference between future and present position also ranged from 0 to 7. Mean goal discrepancy was 1.68 with a S.D. of 1.24. For the respondents as a whole aspiration, in terms of goal discrepancy, was found to be significant (t = 21.94 P < .01).

TABLE 4.38: Mean, S.D. for the Aspiration Groups (Perceived Position on the Ladder) for the Present and Future Dimensions

		Future			
Aspiration		Low	Middle	High	Total
Present	High			N 49	N 49
			89.59	89.59	
				12.81	12.81
	Middle		N 58	N 90	N 148
			83.10	90.63	87.68
			17.46	14.91	16.21
	Low	N 29	N 33	N 3	N 65
		84.62	84.21	70.33	83.75
		11.37	14.07	29.93	14.44
Total		N 29	N 91	N 142	
		84.62	83.51	89.85	
		11.37	16.32	14.99	

4.11.1.1 *Aspiration (Arbitrary Cut off Points) and ATI*: Data on the present and future status were treated in two different ways to examine its relation with ATI. Initially an arbitrary cut off point was adopted, as is followed in aspiration studies (Muthayya, 1969). Those who rated themselves at or below the rung three of the ladder were designated as low group, 4 to 6 as the middle group, and 7 and above were called the high group. A similar classification of the responses concerning future position was also made. Merging of the perceived positions on the present and future dimensions show the movement of respondents from one group to another and those remaining in the same broad classification.

TABLE 4.39: (a) ANOVA Summary and (b) D.R.T. Results for Aspiration Groups '(Based on the Arbitrary cut off Points Recording the Mobility

(a)

Source	S.S	D.F.	M.S.	F.
Aspiration	3650.79	5	730.16	3.34 $P < .05$
Error	55997.10	256	218.74	
Total	59647.89	261		

(b)

S.e. 14.79

N	90	49	29	33	58	3
Mean Score	90.63	89.59	84.62	84.21	83.10	70.33

Means scores underlined do not differ significantly at $P < .05$.

Analysis based on these cut off points was carried on the ATI scores wherein the mobility of respondents from one group to another was taken into account. In all six groups were identified. Three of which showed a forward mobility (middle to high, low to middle and low to high) and the other three which remained in the same group.

Analysis of variance reveals a significant result (F 3.34 $P < .05$) indicating that the level of aspiration has an influence on the ATI of the respondents. Six groups showing different levels of aspiration were compared further using Duncan's Range Test to know the groups which differ significantly from one another. Analysis reveals that those who show a mobility from middle to high group tend to possess more favourable ATI and differ from those who remain in the same group. Such differences do not emerge for those who show mobility from the low group. In fact, a trend of decreasing mean ATI scores is noticeable as the respondents move from low to middle and high.

4.11.1.2 *Aspiration (Goal Discrepancy) and ATI*: Goal discrepancy, that is, the difference between future and present positions in the ladder scale extends from 0 to 7 for the response population. Information regarding the discrepancy is lost when the responses are classified as low, middle and high groups. In addition, discrepancy within the high group cannot be taken into consideration. To obviate this problem, respondents were classified based on their discrepancy scores.

TABLE 4.40: (a) Mean, S.D., (b) ANOVA Summary and (c) t Ratios for ATI *vis-a-vis* Aspiration (Goal Discrepancy)

(a)

Aspiration Goal discrepancy		N	Mean	S.D.
	0	41	81.51	14.80
	1	84	84.33	16.01
	2	79	90.29	13.81
	3 and above	58	90.55	13.55

(b)

Source	S.S	D.F.	M.S.	F.
Aspiration	3418.34	3	1139.45	5.23 $P < .01$
Error	56229.55	258	217.94	
Total	59647.89	261		

(c)

1-0	0.95 (NS)
2-1	2.54 $P < .05$
3-1	2.42 $P < .05$
2-0	3.22 $P < .01$
3-0	3.15 $P < .01$
3-2	0.11 (NS)

As there were only 12 observations having a discrepancy of four or more, they were grouped for the purposes of analysis with those who aspire to move three rungs higher. From Table 4.40 it could be noted that the mean ATI scores shows a progressive trend with the goal discrepancy. Computed *F* ratio (F 5.23 $P < .01$) indicate a significant influence of goal discrepancy scores on the ATI. Pairwise comparison of the four groups show that (Table 4.33 c) respondents having a discrepancy score 0 or 1 pair together as the *t* value between these groups is not significant. So also those with a discrepancy score 3 or 2 tend to overlap in their ATI. Significant differences appear on the other comparisons.

It can be inferred that there appears among the social scientists a general trend of favourable ATI going along with the higher aspiration. Two distinct groups viz., low (0-1) and high (2 and above) could be made based on the discrepancy scores as far as their relations with ATI is considered.

Of the two different treatments of aspiration data, though both show significant results, goal discrepancy method could be viewed as better of the two. It has also been noted that cut off points in certain cases may prove to be deceptive, in that though shift is present from lower rung to a higher one the response may fall in a group which is taken to be immobile (e.g. respondents in low group in present remaining in low in future dimension also, despite aspiring to move from rung 1 to 2 or 3). In addition, groups based on arbitrary cut off points were not conducive for analysis with further division on personal attributes because of very few or absence of respondents in particular cells. Due to these reasons for the purpose of further computation of aspiration data with personal variables high and low groups as recognised by the analysis taking goal discrepancy was considered.

4.11.2 *ATI* vis-a-vis *Aspiration and Environment*

It has been noted that aspiration for academic achievement has a significant effect on the ATI of the social scientists, wherein high aspirers also tend to possess more favourable ATI compared with the low group. ATI of the high and low groups were further classified into a bivariate Table 4.41 bringing respondents' institutional affiliation viz., University and Research and Training Institutions as an additional variable.

The analysis shows a significant F ratio for the aspiration. Even in the present sub-classification institutional affiliation in itself does not seem to have any bearing on the readiness to use information. In addition to this as the increasing trend of favourability to information use for those in both the environments is consistent with their level of aspiration the interaction effect of these variables is not statistically significant.

Duncan's Range Test carried out to compare the mean attitude scores of the four groups confirm that high aspirers in both the environments differ significantly from the low group. Statistical differences do not exist within the low and the high groups coming from University and Research and Training Institutions.

Thus, high goal intentions among the social scientists coming from two job environments consistently show a positive effect on their readiness to use information which is more or less an imperative for realising the projected level of aspiration.

TABLE 4.41: (a) Mean, S.D., (b) ANOVA Summary and (c) D.R.T. Results for ATI *vis-a-vis* Environment X Aspiration

(a)

Environment	Aspiration: Low	Aspiration: High
Universities	N 56 82.52 14.54	N 47 91.92 12.72
Research and Training Institutions	N 69 84.13 16.51	N 90 89.61 14.12

(b)

Source	S.S (Adj.)	D.F.	M.S.	F.
Aspiration	3192.30	1	3192.30	14.65 $P < .01$
Environment	6.90	1	6.90	0.03 (NS)
Aspiration X Environment	237.34	1	237.34	1.09 (NS)
Error	56206.86	258	217.86	

(c)

S.e. 14.76

N	47	90	69	56
Mean score	91.92	89.61	84.13	82.52

Mean scores underlined do not differ significantly at $P < 0.05$.

ATI vis-a-vis aspiration and personal attributes: In the following sections two-way analysis of variance is computed to know whether the effect of aspiration on ATI is same for those belonging to different education, experience and position groups. The analysis also examines the possible interaction of the two independent variables on ATI and the individual effects of the variables when the association of the independent variables is statistically controlled.

4.11.3 *ATI* vis-a-vis *Aspiration and Education*

This section explores the assumption that ATI is the function of aspiration and education taken individually and also the effect of aspiration on ATI tends to be significantly different for education groups i.e., the interaction effect of the two variables would be significant.

In the bivariate classification of ATI scores on aspiration and education level (Table 4.42), a trend of increasing mean scores for Ph.D's and non-Ph.D's alike could be noticed as they move from low to high level of aspiration. Analysis confirms the significant individual effects of aspiration and education when the possible mutual overlapping effect is corrected. However, interaction of these variables on ATI is not significant, implying that the effect of aspiration is same over all the levels of education and *vice versa.*

Multiple comparison of the mean ATI scores for the four group indicate that Ph.D's with higher aspiration differ significantly from the other three groups. It may be noted that Ph.D's who also have the higher aspiration, because of the facilitative advantage accompanying the higher educational attainment tend to possess a favourable ATI compared with other groups. So also among the non-Ph.D's significant difference is noticeable in favour of the high group. It has been observed earlier that Ph.D's generally possess a more favourable ATI than the non-Ph.D's. However, this difference is not noticeable when they show a low aspiration. In a way high aspiration among the non-Ph.D's brings in a greater readiness to use information which seem to bridge the gap between Ph.D's and non-Ph.D's to some extent. Thus, higher aspiration among the non-Ph.D's as far as its relation to ATI is concerned, compensates the advantages associated with the Ph.D. degree when such respondents show a low aspiration. It may also be inferred from the analysis that the combined effect of the two variables is additive in nature.

4.11.4 *ATI* vis-a-vis *Aspiration and Experience*

Respondents showing the low and high aspiration were further classified according to different phases of the career (based on their experience) to know the possible interaction effect of aspiration on ATI and also the joint effect of two independent variables.

TABLE 4.42: (a) Mean, S.D., (b) ANOVA Summary and (c) D.R.T. Results for ATI vis-a-vis Aspiration X Education

(a)

Environment	Aspiration: Low	Aspiration: High
	N 66	N 73
Non-Ph.D's	77.80	85.84
	15.59	13.59
	N 59	N 64
Ph.D's	89.68	95.61
	13.22	11.83

(b)

Source	S.S (Adj.)	D.F.	M.S.	F.
Aspiration	3244.05	1	3244.05	17.15 $P < .01$
Education	7578.06	1	7578.06	40.06 $P < .01$
Aspiration X Education	72.46	1	72.46	0.38 (NS)
Error	48800.58	258	189.15	

(c)

S.e. 13.75

N	64	59	73	66
Mean score	95.61	89.68	85.84	77.80

Mean scores underlined do not differ significantly at $P < .05$

A trend of increasing mean ATI scores could be noticed both with increasing aspiration and professional experience. Analysis shows significant main effects when the association between the independent variables is statistically adjusted. However, interaction effect of these variables as such is not significant, indicating that significant deviations from the observed trend do not appear for the respondents falling in three career phases. Comparisons of the mean ATI scores of six groups bring out that high and low aspirers show a significant difference in their ATI only in their middle phase. For those in the initial and later phase, despite a trend of higher ATI mean score from low to high group, statistically significant differences do not appear.

As far as the low aspirers in different career phases are concerned significant differences appear for those in later phase as compared to the other two groups. Within the high aspiration group statistical differences appear between those in initial phase and in the other two phases. Higher aspiration to a certain extent compensates the advantage of longer association with the attitude object, in that high aspirers in the initial phase and low aspirers in the middle and later phases tend to possess overlapping intensity of ATI. So also high aspirers in the middle phase and those in later phase do not show significant differences in their ATI.

TABLE 4.43: (a) Mean, S.D., (b) ANOVA Summary and (c) D.R.T. Results for ATI Score *vis-a-vis* Aspiration X Experience

(a)

Experience	Aspiration: Low	Aspiration: High
Initial phase	N 2 76.55 14.15	N 36 83.56 6.95
Middle phase	N 52 81.38 16,46	N 52 91.92 15.88
Later phase	N 51 88.41 13.79	N 49 93.84 13.13

(b)

Source	S.S (Adj.)	D.F.	M.S.	F.
Aspiration	2443.53	1	2443.54	12.14 $P < .01$
Experience	3075.22	2	1537.61	7.64 $P < .01$
Aspiration X Experience	343.99	2	171.99	0.86 (NS)
Error	51525.39	256	201.27	

(c)

S.e. 14.19

N	49	52	51	36	52	22
Mean score	93.84	91.92	88.41	83.56	81.38	76.55

Mean scores underlined do not differ significantly at $P < .05$

It can be inferred from the analysis that aspiration to move higher in the ladder of academic achievement has a significant influence on ATI for those in the middle phase of the career. In this phase of the career, because of sufficient professional experience and knowledge of the requirements, one would realise that achievement is assessed in terms of research output and such other information generation activities. High aspirers who need to involve in such activities show a significant difference in their ATI compared with the low group. Factors other than aspiration level seem to cloud the difference between the high and low aspirers for those in the initial and later phase of their career. Effect of these two variables is largely additive in nature.

4.11.5 *ATI* vis-a-vis *Aspiration and Position*

In this sub-section the computation was done to know the effect of aspiration for those in different hierarchical positions.

The classification of ATI scores based on aspiration and position largely confirms the general trend observed for the respondents. However, a deviation is noticeable for those in the highest position, wherein high aspiration group has a lesser ATI mean score (Table 4.44).

Despite such a deviation analysis confirms the significant main effect of aspiration when the effect due to association of position with the level of aspiration is statistically corrected. The individual effect of position and the interaction effect of position and aspiration are not significant. In the present classification the accounted variations in the ATI is due to level of aspiration alone.

Comparisons of the eight groups, computed to examine in greater detail the effect of aspiration on ATI for different position groups, reveal that significant difference between high and low group appear for only those in position one and three, with high aspirers possessing a more favourable ATI.

Among the high aspirers significant differences do not exist across four positions. Largely the same trend exists for low group, excepting for those in position one, who possess significantly less favourable ATI than those in position two and four.

Thus, the pattern of variation in ATI do not hold good for all positions. For those in position two and four both low and high group tend to possess ATI score which overlap with the mean score for the respondents as a whole and hence the effect of aspiration in not statistically significant. The key to the observed trend among those in position one and three is in the relatively lesser ATI mean score among the low aspirers which is much below the mean score for the response population (87.07). Low groups of the other two positions, on the other hand, have an ATI mean score slightly more than that of response population. Thus, low aspiration in position one and three accompany with considerably lesser attitudinal strength creating a wider gap between the two groups.

TABLE 4.44: (a) Mean, S.D., (b) ANOVA Summary and (c) D.R.T. Results for ATI vis-a-vis Aspiration X Position

(a)

Position	Aspiration: Low	Aspiration: High
	N 35	N 41
Research Associates/ Assistants	78.34	88.32
	15.53	15.98
	N 32	N 47
Lecturers/ Assistant Directors	87.56	91.02
	17.02	12.83
	N 35	N 38
Readers/ Deputy Directors	81.86	93.16
	14.74	11.58
	N 23	N 11
Professors. Directors	87.70	86.00
	12.29	12.42

(b)

Source	S.S (Adj.)	D.F.	M.S.	F.
Position	1349.07	3	449.69	2.12 (NS)
Aspiration	3148.07	1	3148.07	14.86 $P < .01$
Position X Aspiration	1306.20	3	435.40	2.06 (NS)
Error	53795.83	254	211.79	

(c)

S.e. 14.55

N	38	47	41	23	32	11	35	35
Mean score	93.16	91.02	88.32	87.70	87.56	86.00	81.86	78.34

Mean scores underlined do not differ significantly at $P < .05$.

4.11.6 *ATI and Information Source Use* vis-a-vis *Aspiration*

Level of aspiration is one of the important conditional factor which in itself may have an impact on the ATI and source use relations. The assumption in the context is that the higher level of aspiration facilitates ATI and information source use relations. This assumption was explored into with the help of partial tables prepared by dividing ATI and source use table on the basis of aspiration. Tables 4.45 a-i show the frequency distribution and Gamma values for high and low aspirers *vis-a-vis* ATI and source use.

The analysis reveals that ATI and use frequencies of all the three primary sources tend to be positive and significant among the high aspirers. Explained relations are to the tune of 32.5 per cent for periodicals use (G. 0.325 $P < .05$), 33.2 per cent for books/research reports (G. 0.332 $P < .05$) and 29.3 per cent in the case of theses/dissertations (G. 0.293 $P < .05$). Significant positive attitude-behaviour relations are also to be found among the low aspiration group. The Gamma values are 0.333 and 0.448 as to the use of periodicals and books/research reports respectively. Both these values are significant at 5 per cent confidence limit. The strength of observed relations for high as well as low groups are moderate. Thus, as far as the primary sources are concerned level of aspiration largely do not tend to affect the attitude-behaviour relations.

As to the use of secondary sources high aspirers consistently show statistically significant positive association with their ATI. However, Gamma values for citations (G. 0.315 $P < .05$), book reviews (G. 0.361 $P < .05$) and abstracts (G. 0.411 $P < .01$) show that the association is moderate. On the contrary among the low aspirers use of all the secondary sources show a non-significant association with the ATI. Nonetheless they are positive.

The trend of high aspirers showing a significant positive attitude and behaviour association holds good for the non-bibliographic sources as well. Gamma values for consulting experts (G. 0.462 $P < .01$), workshops/seminars (G. 0.495 $P < .01$) are moderate and ATI explains 46.2 per cent and 49.5 per cent of the differences in consulting experts and attending workshops/seminars respectively. As to the discussion with colleagues high aspirers not only tend to be positive and statistically significant (G. 0.564 $P < .01$) but also the association is strong explaining 56.4 per cent of the differences due to ATI. On the contrary among the low aspirers statistically significant ATI and

TABLE 4.45: Frequency Distribution and Gamma Values for ATI and Source use Relations *vis-a-vis* Aspiration

ATI	Aspiration							
	Low N 125				High N 137			
	Use Frequency				Use Frequency			
	Not at all	Rarely	Moderately	Frequently	Not at all	Rarely	Moderately	Frequently
1	2	3	4	5	6	7	8	9
a *Periodicals*								
Low	0	11	15	16	0	4	13	7
Moderate	1	6	24	26	1	9	28	34
High	0	1	8	17	0	1	16	24
	G: 0.333		Z: 1.754*		G: 0.325		Z: 1.705*	
b *Books and Research Reports*								
Low	1	5	13	23	0	5	9	10
Moderate	0	4	14	39	1	7	27	37
High	0	0	3	23	2	2	7	10
	G: 0.448		Z: 2.178*		G: 0.332		Z: 1.735*	

Contd.

TABLE 4.45 *Contd.*

1	2	3	4	5	6	7	8	9
c *Theses and Dissertations*								
Low	9	14	15	4	3	13	4	4
Moderate	12	19	13	13	19	25	21	7
High	0	11	11	4	3	13	10	15
	G: 0.174		Z: 0.949		G: 0.293		Z: 1.676*	
d *Citation in Journals and Books*								
Low	5	5	17	15	1	11	6	6
Moderate	6	7	26	18	5	13	25	29
High	0	3	12	11	1	6	11	21
	G: 0.109		Z: 0.561		G: 0.315		Z: 1.742*	
e *Books Reviews*								
Low	8	16	14	4	1	12	10	1
Moderate	13	13	21	10	12	26	26	8
High	3	5	11	7	0	12	15	14
	G: 0.233		Z: 1.291		G: 0.361		Z: 2.079*	

Contd.

TABLE 4.45 *Contd.*

1	2	3	4	5	6	7	8	9
f *Abstracting and Indexing Sources*								
Low	26	5	5	6	17	5	1	1
Moderate	30	13	8	6	38	11	13	10
High	9	3	11	3	14	6	9	12
	G: 0.236		Z: 1.249		G: 0.411		Z: 2.379**	
g *Consulting Experts*								
Low	5	6	17	14	2	9	13	0
Moderate	9	11	19	18	8	12	23	27
High	1	6	7	12	0	4	17	20
	G: 0.061		Z: 0.325		G: 0.462		Z: 2.771**	
h *Attending Workshops*								
Low	6	10	14	12	2	8	11	3
Moderate	8	8	24	17	12	15	26	19
High	1	6	12	7	0	5	9	27
	G: 0.080		Z: 0.426		G: 0.495		Z: 3.130**	
i *Discussion with Colleagues*								
Low	3	7	13	19	1	15	6	2
Moderate	5	11	21	20	6	10	32	24
High	2	3	10	11	1	1	17	22
	G: -0.027		Z: -0.141		G: 0.564		Z: 3.699**	

* Significance $P < .05$ ** Significance $P < .01$ (one tailed tests)

non-bibliographic source use is not noticeable. Moreover the relations tend to be negative for the source – discussion with colleagues.

Conclusion that can be drawn from the analysis is that the ATI and information source use relations are to a large extent also conditional to the level of aspiration. On all the sources of information attitude-behaviour relations are statistically significant and positive for the high group implying that more frequent source use and favourable ATI tends to occur jointly among the high aspirers. On the contrary significant association for the low group is noticeable only on two sources. Nonetheless, it may be noted that these two sources viz., books and periodicals are more frequently consulted ones.

On all the sources strength of association for high aspirers is more than what is present in the zero-order relations, which reveals that the low aspiration tends to suppress the strength of the ATI and source use relations. Thus, apart from ATI, level of aspiration is also an important variable in explaining the frequency of source use.

4.11.7 *Summary*

Analysis confirms that level of aspiration for academic achievement has a significant bearing on the ATI. This is borne out when data were considered taking goal discrepancy and also when arbitrary cut off points were adopted.

The trend of aspiration having an effect holds good for both Ph.D's and non-Ph.D's.

Within the different phases of the career significant differences appear for only those in the middle phase.

Position-wise classification of the high and low aspirers shows an effect of aspiration on ATI for only those in position one and three, wherein the high aspirers also tend to be more favourable compared in their respective low groups.

Aspiration and personal variables act independently in their effect on ATI, despite a few variations noted above. So the interaction of these variables is not significant. In case of education and experience the effect is additive in nature.

Thus, the data supports the assumption that higher level of aspiration has an influence on ATI. As far as the interaction effect is concerned the null hypothesis seems to hold good.

ATI and source use relations tend to be suppressed to a certain extent by the low aspiration. The Gamma values show that the strength of attitude-behaviour relations increase for high aspirers than what is observed for the group as a whole. Though low group also shows significant relations, it is confined to only two of the primary sources.

4.12 **Constraints in Information Use**

Information acquisition is not only a complicated process but also one impaired by many constraints which make this process difficult, time consuming, inefficient and ineffective. Effective handling of published information forms an integral and essential part of the academic achievement. Barriers which delay, disturb or destroy the flow of information – either with regard to quality or quantity – may result in its inefficient use.

Commonly experienced barriers in information use include: publishing delay, inferior quality of information, weak information search strategy and most important of all, the information congestion. The continuing expansion in the volume of published information demands a parallel increase in the information search and handling capacity of the user in addition to situational facilities for information use. INFROSS (Line, 1971, p. 159) study has noted that most frequent information problems encountered by the social scientists are those of access of information, poor library facilities and availability of relevant research literature in a foreign language.

In the present study nine of the commonly felt constraints in the information use were listed and the respondents were asked to indicate the degree of problem experienced by them on a four-point scale, wherein different degrees were defined as no problem, very little problem, considerable difficulty and extreme difficulty. Constraints included both situational ones such as getting information quickly enough, getting up to date material, locating suitable sources, qualified help to locate information sources and procedures in the libraries, and personal constraints such as finding time to look for or locate information, understanding statistics and research reports, availability of material in different languages. As it was observed in the pilot survey that many of the respondents do not use abstracting and indexing journals an item to know the degree of problem with respect to the knowledge of using abstracts and indexes was also included.

TABLE 4.46: Frequency Distribution of Respondents with Respect to their Degree of Constraints in Information Use

(N=262)

Constraints	Degree constraints			
	Extreme difficulty	Considerable problem	Very little problem	No problem
Finding time	15 (5.73)	87 (33.21)	52 (19.85)	108 (41.22)
Getting information quickly	58 (22.14)	89 (33.97)	56 (21.37)	59 (22.52)
Getting up to date material	86 (32.82)	96 (36.64)	46 (17.56)	34 (12.98)
Understanding statistics	10 (3.82)	58 (22.14)	77 (29.39)	117 (44.66)
Locating suitable sources	28 (10.69)	89 (33.97)	73 (27.86)	72 (27.48)
Qualified help to locate information	42 (16.03)	74 (28.24)	54 (20.61)	92 (35.11)
Knowing how to use abstracts and indexes	9 (3.44)	29 (11.07)	53 (20.23)	171 (65.27)
Material in different languages	107 (40.84)	51 (19.47)	35 (13.36)	69 (26.34)
Procedures in library	25 (9.54)	42 (16.03)	55 (20.99)	140 (53.44)

Distribution of the respondents on different scale points (Table 4.46) indicates that a greater proportion of respondents face no problem in finding time to look for and read information (41.22%), understanding statistics and research reports (44.66%). So also is the case with knowing how to use abstracts (65.27%) and procedures in libraries, wherein 53.44 per cent report to have no problem.

On the other side of the continuum are the constraints of extreme difficulty viz., availability of material in different languages and getting up to date material as expressed by 40.84 per cent and 32.82 per cent of the respondents respectively.

4.12.1 *Ranking of Constraints*

Ranking of the mean scores (Table 4.47) in which higher score indicates lesser degree of constraints reveal that getting up to date material in the field of their interest is the most difficult problem for the social scientists. This is followed by availability of material in different languages. Getting information quickly enough ranks third among the constraints. Situational constraints viz., locating suitable sources and qualified help to locate information ranks fourth and fifth respectively. As it has been observed earlier, finding time to read information, understanding statistics, procedures in libraries and lastly knowledge of using abstracting and indexing journals rank lower among the constraints in that order.

This trend largely confirms the findings of INFROSS study which states that social scientists have problem on the count of lack of information, material available in different languages and poor library facilities. However, it may be noted that for none of these nine constraints mean score is less than that of the midpoint – 2 – which indicates that social scientists within the study area do not face higher difficulty in information accessibility and use. This may be a reflection of the library facilities available to the respondents in the study area. It may also be noted that INFROSS study collected the data regarding the problems on open ended question and did not go into examining the degree of such constraints experienced by the respondents. However, what seems to be a paradox is the relative non-use of the abstracting and indexing services by a majority of the respondents. It cannot be attributed to the difficulty in knowing how to use abstracts, as majority of the respondents report otherwise.

4.12.2 *Constraints and Work Environment*

Data were analysed to examine whether the constraints experienced by the respondents differ in two different environment viz., for those working in Research and Training Institutions and Universities. As can be generally noticed Research Institutions have libraries with special collections meeting the needs of the particular clientele. In the Universities, on the other hand, the library caters to the larger number of clientele including students and staff. Thus, library collections of Research Institutions are qualitatively more need based than those of Universities. Research and Training Institutions also have an edge over their counterpart in regard to book-reader ratio. In addition, as has been noted earlier, Research and Training Institutions usually render in-house documentation services to its clientele which is not generally noticeable in University libraries.

TABLE 4.47: Mean and S.D. of the Constraints in Information use for the Total Sample and also mean, S.D. and *t* Ratios for Universities and Research and Training Institutions

Constraints	Mean and S.D.	Research & Training Institutions	Univer-sities	*t* ratio
Getting up to date material	2.11 1.01	2.24 1.01	1.90 0.96	2.72 $P < .01$
Material available in different languages	2.25 1.24	2.25 1.25	2.24 1.20	(NS)
Getting information quickly	2.44 1.07	2.60 1.05	2.19 1.04	3.11 $P < .01$
Locating suitable sources	2.72 0.98	2.83 0.97	2.57 0.98	2.11 $P < .05$
Qualified help to locate information	2.75 1.10	3.02 1.05	2.34 1.05	5.04 $P < .01$
Finding time to read information	2.97 0.98	3.01 0.99	2.91 0.95	(NS)
Understanding research reports and statistics	3.15 0.89	3.16 0.91	3.14 0.86	(NS)
Procedures in libraries	3.18 1.02	3.29 0.99	3.01 1.03	2.19 $P < .05$
Knowing how to use abstracts and indexes	3.47 0.83	3.43 0.89	3.53 0.72	(NS)

D.F. = 260

The *t* statistic computed (Table 4.47) reveals that on five of the nine constraints experienced by the respondents, those in the Research and Training Institutions face significantly lesser degree than the other group. Specific constraints on which difference is noticeable are: getting information quickly enough ($t = 3.11$ $P < .01$) getting up to date material ($t = 2.72$ $P < .01$), locating suitable sources ($t = 2.11$ $P < .05$) qualified help to locate information ($t = 5.04$ $P < .01$) and procedures in libraries ($t = 2.19$ $P < .05$). With regard to other constraints viz., finding time, understanding statistics, knowing how to use abstracts and that of foreign language, which are largely person-oriented, the two environments do not show any difference.

It may therefore be inferred that generally social scientists working in Research and Training Institutions have lesser degree of constraints than those in the University departments. The difference largely lies in situational factors. This is a reflection on the library facilities available in the Universities, which seems to be less conducive than that of Research and Training Institutions.

4.12.3 *Constraints and Information use*

One of the possible reasons for the low use of information sources could be the constraints the social scientists experience in the information gathering process. Despite the concerns frequently expressed about the various constraints hindering the information use, studies as to how far the user frustrations have upset the information flow are sparse. To examine this aspect of the information flow, data concerning the primary source use were analysed taking the degree of problems into consideration. Gamma statistic was worked out to test the assumption that the information source use would be less among those who experience higher degree of constraints.

Table 4.48a-h show the frequency distribution on different use categories *vis-a-vis* degree of constraints and also Gamma statistic values.

The results of the analysis reveal that the constraints do not tend to be associated with the information source use. This trend is consistent as far as the use of all the primary sources, with the exceptions of government publications use which is consulted more when it is not a constraint in locating the appropriate source (G. 0.221 $P < .05$) use of abstracts and indexes also tend to be less frequent when the constraint is of knowing to use them (G. 0.301 $P < .05$). Though Gamma values are positive in majority of the cases they are non-significant implying that the variations in the use frequency is not due to different degree of constraints experienced in the process. That is to say higher constraints do not necessarily mean less frequent information source use. In other words, constraints experienced in the acquisition of information do not necessarily seem to be the barriers which reduce the use of information sources.

TABLE 4.48: Frequency Distribution and Gamma Values Showing Degree of Constraints and Primary Source Relations

(N = 262)

Degree of Constraints	Use Frequency															
	Periodicals				Books/Research Reports				Theses/Dissertations				Government Publications			
	Not at all	Rarely	Moderately	Frequently	Not at all	Rarely	Moderately	Frequently	Not at all	Rarely	Moderately	Frequently	Not at all	Rarely	Moderately	Frequently
1	2	3	4	5	6	7	8	9	10	11	12	13	14	15	16	17
a *Finding time to look for or read information*																
Extreme Difficulty	0	1	10	4	0	1	7	7	3	6	2	4	0	4	5	6
Considerable Difficulty	2	10	22	53	2	8	18	59	15	30	26	16	9	24	24	30
A little problem	0	9	25	18	0	2	23	27	3	25	16	8	2	13	21	16
No problem	0	12	47	49	2	12	25	69	25	34	30	19	11	18	36	43
	G: -0.063		Z: -0.466		G: -0.001		Z: -0.006		G: -0.048		Z: -0.386		G: 0.071		Z: 0.563	

Contd.

TABLE 4.48 *Contd.*

1	2	3	4	5	6	7	8	9	10	11	12	13	14	15	16	17
b *Getting information quickly enough*																
Extreme Difficulty	2	10	17	29	3	6	7	42	14	18	15	11	8	18	13	19
Considerable Difficulty	0	7	42	40	0	6	31	52	11	38	23	17	3	17	38	31
A little problem	0	7	24	25	0	5	20	31	13	16	16	11	5	9	16	26
No problem	0	8	21	30	1	6	15	37	8	23	20	8	6	15	19	19
	G: 0.029		Z: 0.223		G: -0.075		Z: -0.542		G: 0.022		Z: 0.185		G: 0.054		Z: 0.448	
c *Getting up to date material*																
Extreme Difficulty	1	13	32	40	2	4	27	53	26	28	23	19	9	25	27	25
Considerable Difficulty	0	12	43	41	1	11	27	57	18	43	21	14	6	16	39	35
A little problem	1	3	15	27	0	3	8	35	8	10	18	10	5	6	12	23
No problem	0	4	14	16	1	5	11	17	4	14	12	4	2	12	8	12
	G: -0.083		Z: -0.624		G: -0.017		Z: -0.120		G: 0.093		Z: 0.801		G: 0.121		Z: 0.990	

Contd.

TABLE 4.48 *Contd.*

1	2	3	4	5	6	7	8	9	10	11	12	13	14	15	16	17
d *Understanding research reports and statistics*																
Extreme Difficulty	0	2	4	4	0	3	3	4	4	4	1	1	2	3	2	3
Considerable Difficulty	1	2	26	29	0	6	17	35	12	21	14	11	3	12	25	18
A little problem	1	11	36	29	1	8	27	41	16	24	24	13	9	15	28	25
No problem	0	17	38	62	3	6	26	82	14	46	35	22	8	29	31	49
	G: 0.047		Z: 0.342		G: 0.202		Z: 1.423		G: 0.133		Z: 1.064		G: 0.079		Z: 0.622	
e *Locating suitable sources*																
Extreme Difficulty	0	6	9	13	1	3	10	14	6	9	7	6	7	8	6	7
Considerable Difficulty	0	7	41	41	0	10	25	54	18	38	22	11	8	23	28	30
A little problem	1	11	33	28	0	7	23	43	10	25	22	16	5	15	26	27
No problem	1	8	21	42	3	3	15	51	12	23	23	14	2	13	26	31
	G: 0.071		Z: 0.586		G: 0.153		Z: 1.102		G: 0.108		Z: 0.901		G: 0.221		Z: 1.851*	

Contd.

TABLE 4.48 *Contd.*

1	2	3	4	5	6	7	8	9	10	11	12	13	14	15	16	17
f *Lack of qualified help to locate information*																
Extreme Difficulty	0	5	14	23	2	2	10	28	11	11	11	9	5	6	14	17
Considerable Difficulty	1	6	33	34	0	7	24	43	8	34	16	16	6	27	17	24
A little problem	0	8	22	24	0	7	13	34	11	16	16	11	8	10	18	18
No problem	1	13	35	43	2	7	26	57	16	34	31	11	3	16	37	36
	G: 0.068		Z: 0.517		G: 0.011		Z: 0.078		G: -0.028		Z: -0.234			G: 0.099		Z: 0.820
g *Procedures in libraries*																
Extreme Difficulty	0	1	11	13	1	1	6	17	2	10	5	8	5	4	6	10
Considerable Difficulty	1	2	14	25	1	5	12	24	9	15	13	5	3	12	13	14
A little problem	1	6	27	21	0	1	21	33	7	20	14	14	5	15	17	18
No problem	0	23	52	65	2	16	34	88	28	50	42	20	9	28	50	53
	G: -0.122		Z: -0.869		G: 0.001		Z: 0.006		G: -0.094		Z: -0.735			G: 0.097		Z: 0.749
h *Knowing how to use abstracts and indexes* *Abstracting/indexing sources*																
Extreme Difficulty	3	3	0	3												
Considerable Difficulty	23	0	3	3												
A little problem	32	12	7	2												
No problem	76	28	37	30												
	G: 0.301		Z: 2.084*													

* Significance $P < .05$ (one tailed test)

Appropriate question in the context perhaps is who experiences higher degree of constraints? In could be those who make use of the sources who experience the problems in the process which, however, do not seem to result in less frequent use of these information sources. Nonetheless, if these constraints are reduced by good library facilities, it may result in more effective source use. That is, when the social scientists get the required information quickly or librarians provide up to date material it may considerably reduce the strain in the search for such information. Facts, figures and research findings so available may facilitate social scientists to bring its applicability in their current research either as a methodological improvement or may act in support of their own findings. It may be recapitulated here that the respondents do not report an acute problem on any of the nine constraints as the mean ratings are higher than the mid-point moving towards 'a little' or 'no problem'.

Further analysis of the constraints in information use focuses on ATI and primary source use relations with constraints as the modifying situational factor.

4.12.4 *ATI and Information Source Use* vis-a-vis *Constraints*

4.12.4.1 *Finding Time to Look for the Read Information*: Table 4.49a-c presents the frequency distribution of ATI and source use separately for those who do not have any problem, a little difficulty and the last group is inclusive of those who experience considerable problem and extreme difficulty. Goodman and Kurskal's Gamma shows that the respondents who experience no problem in this regard also tend to show stronger attitude-behaviour relations. Gamma values tend to be positive and significant for all the three primary sources. Strength of association varies from moderate in case of periodicals (G. 0.50 $P < .01$) and theses (G. 0.343 $P < .05$) to strong for books (G. 0.587 $P < .01$). As to the other two groups experiencing relatively higher degree of constraints ATI and source use relations are statistically non-significant and in one case it is negative. Thus, the problem of finding time is also an important criterion in determining the attitude-behaviour relations in the context. The probability of favourable ATI and frequent primary source use occurring jointly is more for those who do not experience problems on this count.

TABLE 4.49: Frequency Distribution and Gamma Values for ATI and Primary Source use Relations *vis-a-vis* Constraint of Finding Time to look for or Read Information

ATI	Use Frequency: No problem N=108 — Not at all	Rarely	Moderately	Frequently	A little difficulty N=52 — Not at all	Rarely	Moderately	Frequently	Considerable/extreme difficulty N=102 — Not at all	Rarely	Moderately	Frequently
a *Periodicals*												
Low	0	6	12	5	0	1	7	8	0	8	9	10
Moderate	0	5	24	22	0	8	11	5	2	2	17	33
High	0	1	11	22	0	0	7	5	0	1	6	14
	G: 0.500		Z: 2.641*		G: -0.091		Z: -0.297		G: 0.377		Z: 1.753*	
b *Books and Research Reports*												
Low	0	6	8	9	0	1	4	6	1	3	10	18
Moderate	1	5	16	29	0	1	15	13	0	5	10	34
High	1	1	1	31	0	0	4	8	1	1	5	14
	G: 0.587		Z: 3.162		G: 0.185		Z: 0.543		G: 0.141		Z: 0.582	
c *Theses and Dissertations*												
Low	8	6	7	2	0	6	3	2	4	15	9	4
Moderate	16	16	11	8	3	14	9	3	12	14	14	9
High	1	12	12	9	0	5	4	3	2	7	5	7
	G: 0.343		Z: 1.852*		G: 0.129		Z: 0.411		G: 0.152		Z: 0.747	

* Significance $P < .05$ (one tailed tests)

4.12.4.2 *Getting Information Quickly Enough*

Distribution of ATI and source use taking four degrees of constraint in getting information quickly are presented in Table 4.50a-c, Gamma values indicate that those who do not have any problem in this regard show significant and positive relations with the extent of books and research reports use (G. 0.544 $P < .05$). However, as to the use of periodicals respondents who experience 'a little problem' show a strong positive attitude-behaviour relationship (G. 0.569 $P < .05$) implying that when the social scientists are concerned about the availability of information quickly, they show a stronger attitude-behaviour relations. None of the four groups show significant relations for the source – theses/dissertations. However, Gamma values are consistently positive and the strength of the first order relations for two groups is more than what is observed for the study population as a whole. The analysis though do not consistently bring out the varying strength of ATI and source use association it can be broadly inferred that those who experience either considerable or extreme difficulty in this matter do not tend to make use of the primary sources in accordance with their attitudinal disposition.

4.12.4.3 *Getting up to date Material*: Getting up to date material is the constraint which ranks first among the other problems experienced by the respondents. The analysis made from the contingency Table 4.51a-c reveals a trend which is different from what was observed so far. Unlike the other constraints, those who have no problem do not show significant association of ATI and source use. On the other hand respondents who experience considerable difficulty show significant and positive attitude and primary source use relations. Gamma values range from moderate in case of periodicals (G. 0.382 $P < .05$) and theses/dissertations (G. 0.466 $P < .01$) to strong in the case of books (G. 0.586 $P < .01$). No definite pattern is noticeable for other groups. However, excepting the use of theses by those who have 'a little problem' association is positive for the respondents who fall in the other groups.

4.12.4.4 *Understanding Statistics and Research Reports*: Wider application of statistics and such technical methods to data analysis andinterpretation among social scientists may itself be a constraint for those who are not equipped to comprehend such application in the

TABLE 4.50: Frequency Distribution and Gamma Values for ATI and Primary Source use Relations vis-a-vis Constraint of Getting Information Quickly Enough

	Use Frequency															
	No problem N=59				A little problem N=56				Considerable difficulty N=89				Extreme difficulty N=58			
ATI	Not at all	Rarely	Moderately	Frequently	Not at all	Rarely	Moderately	Frequently	Not at all	Rarely	Moderately	Frequently	Not at all	Rarely	Moderately	Frequently
a *Periodicals*																
Low	0	3	2	6	0	3	12	2	0	2	12	7	0	7	2	8
Moderate	0	5	13	11	0	3	10	15	0	4	18	19	2	3	11	15
High	0	0	6	13	0	1	2	8	0	1	12	14	0	0	4	6
	G: 0.334		Z: 1.186		G: 0.569		Z: 2.312*		G: 0.213		Z: 0.879		G: 0.254		Z: 0.882	
b *Books and Research Reports*																
Low	0	3	2	7	0	4	7	6	0	1	10	10	1	2	3	10
Moderate	1	3	12	12	0	1	10	19	0	4	16	21	0	3	3	24
High	0	0	1	18	0	0	3	6	0	1	5	21	2	1	1	8
	G: 0.554		Z: 2.107*		G: 0.456		Z: 1.597		G: 0.343		Z: 1.435		G: 0.053		Z: 0.155	
c *Theses and Dissertations*																
Low	2	2	5	2	7	4	4	2	1	13	5	2	2	8	5	2
Moderate	5	12	9	2	6	10	8	6	9	15	9	8	11	7	8	4
High	1	9	6	4	0	2	4	3	1	10	9	7	1	3	2	5
	G: 0.054		Z: 0.196		G: 0.412		Z: 1.606		G: 0.232		Z: 1.068		G: 0.154		Z: 0.574	

* Significance $P < .05$ ** Significance $P < .01$ (one tailed tests)

TABLE 4.51: Frequency Distribution and Gamma Values for ATI and Primary Source use Relations *vis-a-vis* Constraint in Getting up to date Material

ATI	Use Frequency															
	No problem N=30				A little problem N=46				Considerable difficulty N-96				Extreme difficulty N=86			
	Not at all	Rarely	Moderately	Frequently	Not at all	Rarely	Moderately	Frequently	Not at all	Rarely	Moderately	Frequently	Not at all	Rarely	Moderately	Frequently
a *Periodicals*																
Low	0	2	4	3	0	1	5	7	0	4	10	3	0	8	9	10
Moderate	0	2	7	7	1	2	5	9	0	7	22	24	1	4	18	20
High	0	0	3	6	0	0	5	11	0	1	11	14	0	1	5	10
	G: 0.417		Z: 1.175		G: 0.210		Z: 0.621		G: 0.382		Z: 1.719*			G: 0.319		Z: 1.377
b *Books and Research Reports*																
Low	0	3	1	5	0	2	2	9	0	4	8	5	1	1	11	14
Moderate	0	1	9	7	0	1	5	10	1	7	15	30	0	2	12	29
High	1	1	1	5	0	0	1	16	0	0	4	22	1	1	4	10
	G: 0.075		Z: 0.199		G: 0.479		Z: 1.366		G: 0.586		Z: 2.917*			G: 0.136		Z: 0.516
c *Theses and Dissertdtions*																
Low	1	4	3	1	3	2	5	3	5	8	4	0	3	13	7	4
Moderate	3	6	7	1	4	4	5	3	13	24	10	6	11	10	12	10
High	0	4	2	2	1	4	8	4	0	11	7	8	2	5	4	5
	G: 0.137		Z: 0.374		G: -0.136		Z: -0.458		G: 0.466		Z: 2.359*		G: 0.114		Z: 0.511	

* Significance $P < .05$ ** Significance $P < .01$ (one tailed tests)

published sources Respondents largely fall in three categories viz., those who have 'no problem', 'a little problem' and 'considerable difficulty'. Ten respondents who have expressed extreme difficulty were included with the group 'considerable difficulty' for the purposes of analysis.

The analysis of the contingency Table 4.52a-c reveal that ATI and source use relations tend to be relatively more for those who face 'no problem' as to understanding the statistical interpretations etc. The association is positive and significant for all the three sources viz., periodicals (G. 0.491 $P < .01$), books (G. 0.496 $P < .01$) and theses/dissertations (G. 0.477 $P < .01$). Gamma values, however, show moderate association. It may be noted that the strength of first order association is more for all the sources. Attitude-behaviour relations are affected by the constraints as the analysis reveal a non-significant results. Thus, those who do experience difficulty may not make frequent use of sources in accordance with their attitudinal disposition.

4.12.4.5 *Locating Suitable Sources*: Locating suitable sources when it is required for use is a situational constraints. The degree of problem faced on this count is a reflection on the library book stock and also their upkeep. It is more often observed that due to wrong shelving of books and the like readers face the problem. The distribution on the four degrees of this problem shows that only a small proportion of the respondents (N=28) feel it as an extreme difficulty constraining their information use behaviour. This group is merged with the one immediately next for the purposes of analysis. Three sets of contingency Table 4.53a-c were made incorporating the frequency of use of sources and ATI, on the condition of degree of problem experienced. Gamma values calculated for the three groups reveal that those who do experience 'a little problem' on this count show positive ATI and primary source use relations. Strength of association is moderate for periodicals (G. 0.471 $P < .05$) and strong in the other two cases (books G. 0.518 $P < .05$, theses G. 0.584 $P < .01$). Those who have no problem as to locating sources, though show positive association on all the three source, only in the case of use of books/research reports (G. 0.528 $P < .05$) the association tends to be significant. For respondents who do face considerable or extreme problem on this count, attitude-behaviour relations remain non-significant. This implies that despite favourable disposition to information use, probability of it associating with overt behaviour is not significant when greater degree of constraints are experienced as to locating sources for use. Thus, facilities for locating sources also affect the attitude-behaviour relations.

4.12.4.6 *Qualified Help to Locate Suitable Information*: In the wake of extensive literature output and greater specialisation qualified help in literature search would facilitate in source identification and use. Though availability of such help may not automatically increase the frequency of use it may be expected to facilitate those who also tend to be favourable to ATI. This assumption was tested by working out first order relations of ATI and primary source use taking the degree of constraint experienced on this count. The analysis shows (Table 4.54a-c) that those who do not have any problem either due to availability of help or because of good acquaintance with the available literature also tend to exhibit a positive and significant attitude-behaviour relations. The Gamma value is moderate for this group as to their use of periodicals (G. 0.391 $P < .05$) and strong with regard to the use of books (G. 0.616 $P < .01$). The respondent groups which do face varying degree of problems on this count do not show significant attitude-behaviour relations. However, this trend holds good as to the use of books and periodicals and not for the source theses/dissertations, where none of the groups show significant trend.

Thus, the availability of qualified help is more often than not an important criterion which facilitates attitude-behaviour relations. Despite relatively favourable ATI, when such help is not available, favourable ATI may not associate significantly with frequent use of the information sources. To a certain extent ATI and primary source use is conditional to the availability of qualified help.

4.12.4.7 *Procedures in Libraries*: The distribution of the respondents on the problem experienced with respect to procedural hindrances in the use of library show that relatively a few respondents experience extreme difficulty (N=25). More than 50 per cent of them have 'no problem'. The analysis of ATI and source use relations for the three groups experiencing different degrees of problem (Table 4.55) show that probability of favourable ATI and more frequent use of source use occurs when the social scientists have no problem in the libraries

TABLE 4.52: Frequency Distribution and Gamma Values for ATI and Primary Source use Relations *vis-a-vis* Constraint in Understanding Statistics and Research Reports

ATI	Use Frequency											
	No problem N=117				A little problem N=77				Considerable/extreme difficulty N=68			
	Not at all	Rarely	Moderately	Frequently	Not at all	Rarely	Moderately	Frequently	Not at all	Rarely	Moderately	Frequently
a *Periodicals*												
Low	0	9	6	6	0	6	13	9	0	0	9	8
Moderate	0	7	20	28	1	4	16	13	1	4	16	19
High	0	1	12	28	0	1	7	7	0	0	5	6
	G: 0.491		Z: 2.677*		G: 0.202		Z: 0.803		G: 0.039		Z: 0.127	
b *Books and Research Reports*												
Low	1	5	5	10	0	2	9	16	0	3	8	7
Moderate	0	1	17	37	1	5	13	16	0	5	11	23
High	2	0	4	35	0	1	5	9	0	1	1	9
	G: 0.496		Z: 2.406**		G: 0.056		Z: 0.211		G: 0.398		Z: 1.458	
c *Theses and Dissertations*												
Low	5	10	4	2	3	9	10	5	4	8	5	1
Moderate	8	24	18	5	12	6	11	6	11	14	5	9
High	1	12	13	15	1	9	3	2	1	3	5	2
	G: 0.477		Z: 2.702*		G: 0.136		Z: 0.587		G: 0.200		Z: 0.778	

* Significance $P < .05$ ** Significance $P < .01$ (one tailed tests)

TABLE 4.53: Frequency Distribution and Gamma Values for ATI and Primary Source Use Relations *vis-a-vis* Constraint in Locating Suitable Sources

ATI	Use Frequency											
	No problem N=72				A little problem N=73				Considerable/extreme difficulty N=117			
	Not at all	Rarely	Mode-rately	Fre-quently	Not at all	Rarely	Mode-rately	Fre-quently	Not at all	Rarely	Mode-rately	Fre-quently
a *Periodicals*												
Low	0	3	5	8	0	4	10	3	0	8	13	12
Moderate	1	4	11	19	1	7	15	13	0	4	26	28
High	0	1	5	15	0	0	8	12	0	1	11	14
	G: 0.274		Z: 1.018		G: 0.471		Z: 2.037*		G: 0.276		Z: 1.347	
b *Books and Research Reports*												
Low	1	2	5	8	0	3	7	7	0	5	10	18
Moderate	1	1	9	24	0	4	13	19	0	6	19	33
High	1	0	1	19	0	0	3	17	1	2	6	17
	G: 0.528		Z: 2.029*		G: 0.518		Z: 2.167*		G: 0.112		Z: 0.511	
c *Theses and Dissertations*												
Low	3	5	6	3	4	10	2	1	5	12	11	4
Moderate	8	11	10	4	6	11	13	6	17	22	11	10
High	1	7	7	7	0	4	7	9	2	13	7	3
	G: 0.201		Z: 0.847		G: 0.584		Z: 2.981*		G: -0.017		Z: -0.086	

* Significance $P < .05$ ** Significance $P < .01$ (one tailed tests)

TABLE 4.54: Frequency Distribution and Gamma Values for ATI and Primary Source use Relations vis-a-vis Constraint of Qualified help to Locate Suitable Information

ATI	Use Frequency															
	No problem N=92				A little problem N=54				Considerable difficulty N=74				Extreme difficulty N=42			
	Not at all	Rarely	Moderately	Frequently	Not at all	Rarely	Moderately	Frequently	Not at all	Rarely	Moderately	Frequently	Not at all	Rarely	Moderately	Frequently
a *Periodicals*																
Low	0	6	11	5	0	3	3	4	0	2	11	8	0	4	3	6
Moderate	1	6	15	24	0	5	13	10	1	4	17	18	0	0	7	8
High	0	1	9	14	0	0	6	10	0	0	5	8	0	1	4	9
	G: 0.391		Z: 1.810*		G: 0.387		Z: 1.349		G: 0.233		Z: 0.857		G: 0.299		Z: 0.902	
b *Books and Research Reports*																
Low	1	5	8	8	0	0	2	8	0	4	7	10	0	1	5	7
Moderate	1	2	15	28	0	6	8	14	0	2	15	23	0	1	3	11
High	0	0	3	21	0	1	3	12	0	1	2	10	2	0	2	10
	G: 0.616		Z: 3.120**		G: 0.035		Z: 0.102		G: 0.330		Z: 1.226		G: 0.161		Z: 0.435	
c *Theses and Dissertations*																
Low	5	10	6	1	2	5	2	1	1	8	8	4	4	4	3	2
Moderate	9	16	15	6	8	5	10	5	7	19	6	8	7	4	3	1
High	2	8	10	4	1	6	4	5	0	7	2	4	0	3	5	6
	G: 0.270		Z: 1.264		G: 0.261		Z: 0.955		G: -0.020		Z: -0.749		G: 0.430		Z: 1.577	

* Significance $P < .05$ ** Significance $P < .01$ (one tailed tests)

TABLE 4.55: Frequency Distribution and Gamma Values for ATI and Primary Source Use Relations vis-a-vis Constraint of Procedures in Libraries

	Use Frequency											
	No problem N=140				A little problem N=55				Considerable/extreme difficulty N=67			
ATI	Not at all	Rarely	Moderately	Frequently	Not at all	Rarely	Moderately	Frequently	Not at all	Rarely	Moderately	Frequently
a *Periodicals*												
Low	0	11	15	6	0	2	8	5	0	2	5	12
Moderate	0	11	24	36	1	3	13	13	1	1	15	11
High	0	1	13	23	0	1	6	3	0	0	5	15
	G: 0.485		Z: 2.924*		G: 0.015		Z: 0.047		G: 0.191		Z: 0.680	
b *Books and Research Reports*												
Low	0	9	9	14	0	0	8	7	1	1	5	12
Moderate	1	6	20	44	0	1	11	18	0	4	10	14
High	1	1	5	30	0	0	2	8	1	1	3	15
	G: 0.442		Z: 2.404*		G: 0.366		Z: 1.123		G: 0.127		Z: 0.445	
c *Theses and Dissertations*												
Low	7	14	8	3	2	4	6	3	3	9	5	2
Moderate	19	22	21	9	5	12	6	7	7	10	7	4
High	2	14	13	8	0	4	2	4	1	6	6	7
	G: 0.247		Z: 1.432		G: 0.089		Z: 0.309		G: 0.302		Z: 1.272	

* Significance $P < .05$ ** Significance $P < .01$ (one tailed tests)

TABLE 4.56: Frequency Distribution and Gamma Values for ATI and Abstracting and Indexing Source Use Relations vis-a-vis Constraint in Knowing How to Use them

ATI	Use Frequency											
	No problem N = 171				A little problem N = 53				Considerable/extreme difficulty N = 38			
	Not at all	Rarely	Moderately	Frequently	Not at all	Rarely	Moderately	Frequently	Not at all	Rarely	Moderately	Frequently
Low	23	6	5	4	10	3	1	1	10	1	0	2
Moderate	42	17	16	14	15	5	4	1	11	2	1	1
High	11	5	16	12	7	4	2	0	5	0	2	3
	G: 0.370		Z: 2.433**		G: 0.110		Z: 0.343		G: 0.347		Z: 0.939	

** Significance $P < .01$ (one tailed tests)

for easy consultation, borrowing etc. The strength of relations for periodicals (G. 0.485 $P < .01$) and books (G. 0.442 $P < .01$) are moderate. Gamma values, though positive, are non-significant for those who do experience problems in the libraries. Though first order relations show greater strength of association compared with what was observed in the zero-order, none of the three groups show statistically significant attitude-behaviour relation as to the use of theses/dissertations.

It can be inferred that ATI and primary source use relations are to a certain extent conditional to the degree of procedural problems experienced in the libraries. Wherever the facilities are not conducive, source use does not correspond with the attitudinal disposition.

4.12.4.8 *Knowing how to use Abstracts and Indexes*: It has been noted that only nine respondents experience extreme difficulty in knowing how to use abstracting and indexing sources. These respondents were grouped with the immediate next category for the purposes of analysis. The Gamma values reveal that those who are acquainted with the use of this secondary source when accompanied with a favourable ATI tend to make more frequent use. Gamma value of 0.370 ($P < .01$) implies that 37.00 per cent of the differences in the attitudinal disposition among those who do not face any problem. Despite a few possessing relatively favourable ATI the attitude-behaviour relations are not significant for those who face either 'a little problem' or 'considerable/extreme difficulty'. Thus, relative non-use of abstracting sources seems to be partly due to variations in the attitudinal favourability and partly because of constraint in knowing how to use them.

4.12.5 *Summary*

Social scientists in the study area do not face acute problem on any of the constraint that could hinder the information use. However, getting up to date material and material available in different languages seem to concern them more.

Social scientists in the University departments seem to face relatively greater problem, because of situational variations in the availability of information sources and services.

Constraints experienced in the acquisition of information do not necessarily seem to be the barriers which reduce the use of information sources. Data in most of the cases do not confirm that those who experience higher degree of constraints tend to use the sources less frequently compared with those who experience lesser degree of problems.

ATI and the use of primary sources is observed to be positive and significant when the social scientists experience 'no problem' on constraints such as – finding time to look for or read information, understanding statistics and research reports, qualified help to locate suitable material and procedures in libraries. However, those who show some concern about getting information quickly and also face 'a little problem' in locating sources bear positive and statistically significant ATI and source use relations. Thus, whenever the constraints are experienced by the respondents the strength of the attitude-behaviour relations are affected to the extent that it is often non-significant.

5

SUMMARY AND CONCLUSIONS

The need for the present study and a survey of the information use studies have been reviewed in the Chapter 1. Various concepts used in the study and the related studies in the context of scientific performance (wherever such studies are available) are reported in Chapter 2. Objectives, study population, methodology and also statistical techniques used are specified in Chapter 3. Results from the statistical analysis and their respective interpretations are presented in Chapter 4.

The purpose of the present chapter is to summarise the results.

5.1 Summary

The basic purpose of this study was to explore the attitudinal disposition of the social scientists towards information use, the relations of the attitude to information use behaviour and also the relations of selected personal and psychological attributes to ATI. Data for the study were derived from the survey conducted in social science departments of three universities and eight social science research and training institutions located in the twin cities of Hyderabad-Secunderabad.

5.2 Results and Conclusions

The hypotheses tested and the results arrived at have been summarised in Table 5.1.

In relation to the objectives laid down, major conclusion that can be drawn from the study relates to the nature and importance of the latent aspects of the information use behaviour by the social scientists. Though it is assumed in the information use studies that the scientists/academicians in general tend to be ready (i.e., invariably possessing a favourable attitudinal disposition) to make use of the information sources and make an attempt to keep abreast of the information published in various sources, it does not seem to be so in all the cases. This trend is more so in social sciences. Confining to one school of thought in understanding a given phenomenon, subjective evaluation of the research output, rationalisation of the information use habits and information requirements, which could be noted among social scientists are factors that need to be given a thought to in user studies. The present study of ATI examining this subjective evaluation among social scientists give a clue to their readiness to use information sources. In the context of this study the favourability of ATI of the response population is not very much pronounced, though it tends to be in the positive direction. With the mean score of 87.07 it borders the neutral point in the scale. There is ample scope for information scientists, information generators and also users of information sources in social sciences to reflect on this aspect.

TABLE 5.1: Summary of Results Supporting or not Supporting the Hypotheses

Hypotheses	Supported/ Not supported	Remarks
1. Attitude towards information has a positive effect on information source use.	Supported	Gamma values for nine of the twelve sources of information are found to be positive and sigficant. Strength of the relations are moderate. Gamma values are also positive for the other three sources.
2. Situational factors including psychological and personal attributes and also environments have a modifying effect on ATI and information source use relations i.e.,		
a. Higher the job satisfaction stronger the ATI and information source use relations.	Supported	Gamma values for those in the high group of job satisfaction are consistently significant and also strong. Moderate satisfaction group also shows positive and significant ATI — information source use relations on three of the sources.

(Contd.)

TABLE 5.1 *(Contd.)*

Hypotheses	Supported/ Not supported	Remarks
b. Higher the dedication stronger the ATI and information source use relations.	Supported	All the nine sources of information which have shown signification zero-order relations also seem to be conditional to high degree of dedication, as opposed to low and moderate ones. The observed relations for the high group are also strong for four of the sources.
c. Higher motivation to work facilitates ATI and information source use relations.	Supported	Moderate and low motivation among the social scientists hinder the ATI and source use relations. High strength of motivation on the contrary shows significant and positive attitude — behaviour relations. Three of these sources also bear strong statistical relations.
d. Higher level of aspiration facilitates ATI and source use relations.	Supported	For all the nine sources those with high level of aspiration also tend to show higher Gamma values. Low aspirers also share this significant, positive relationship as to the use of books/research reports and periodicals.
e. Higher educational attainment viz., Ph.D as opposed to non-Ph.D furthers ATI and information source use relations.	Supported	Gamma values for Ph.Ds are significant for seven of the nine sources. The magnitude of the relations are moderate.
f. Increase in professional experience improves ATI — and information source use relation.	Supported	Gamma values for five of the nine sources are positive and significant for those in the later phase and such relations are noticeable on three of the sources viz., books/research reports, periodicals and discussion with colleagues for those in the middle phase.

(Contd.)

TABLE 5.1 *(Contd.)*

Hypotheses	Supported/ Not supported	Remarks
g. ATI and information source use relations are facilitated by the increasing position in the hierarchy.	Not Supported	Contrary to the assumption significant and positive relations are observed on seven of the information sources for those in the position two. (A.Ds./ Research Officers, Lecturers) Research Associates show such relations on two sources and Readers/Deputy Directors on one source.
h. ATI and information source use relations are modified by the different job environments.	Supported	ATI and bibliographic source use relations are significant for those in Research and Training Institutions whereas significant relations for non-bibliographic sources are noticeable for those with university affiliation.
3. Various personal and psychological attributes have a positive effect on the ATI. That is:		
a. Higher job satisfaction is positively related to ATI	Supported	All the items in the job satisfaction scale show a positive product moment correlation coefficient with ATI and eleven of them are statistically significant. F ratios are also significant in both one way ANOVA and two way ANOVA's, wherein one of the other independent variables is introduced into the model and the effect of the same is corrected for. In all the cases F ratios are statistically significant.
b. Higher dedication is positively related to ATI	Supported	All the four items in the dedication measure show a positive and significant correlation coefficient. F ratios are significant at 0.01 level in one way and two way ANOVA's.

(Contd.)

TABLE 5.1 *(Contd.)*

Hypotheses	Supported/ Not supported	Remarks
c. Higher motivation to work is positively related to ATI.	Supported	Coefficient of correlation for all the items in the motivation scale and ATI is positive and significant. *F* ratios in one way and two way ANOVA's are significant at 0.01 level.
d. Higher level of aspiration is positively related to ATI.	Supported	Data were analysed in two ways. Goal discrepancy i.e., difference in future and present position in the ladder has a positive effect on the ATI as shown by the *F* ratio which is consistently significant at 0.01 level in one way and main effect of this variable in two way ANOVA's. Relations of the level of aspiration on ATI measured adopting arbitrary cut off points of the aspiration scale also reveal significant *F* ratio.
e. Higher educational attainment — Ph.D. as opposed to non-Ph.D. — is positively related to ATI.	Supported	*t* ratio for the two groups comraring the ATI mean scores and also main effect of education in two way ANOVA shows a highly significant effect of the education on ATI.
f. More years of professional experience is positively related to ATI.	Supported	*F* ratios in one way ANOVA is significant. So also the effect of experience in the two way ANOVA designs tested in this study.
g. Position in the hierarchy has a positive relation with the ATI.	Not supported	ANOVA results both in one way and two-way designs consistently show non-significant *F* ratio.
h. Attitudinal favourability towards information tends to differ for those in universities and Research and Training Institutions.	Not supported	*t* ratio comparing the difference between the two ATI means is not significant.

(Contd.)

TABLE 5.1 *(Contd.)*

Hypotheses	Supported/ Not supported	Remarks
4. Psychological and personal attributes show varying effect on ATI in different job environments or interaction effect of job environment taken in combination with one of the personal and psychological attributes is significant on ATI. That is:		
a. The trend of relationship of job satisfaction and environments.	Not Supported	Interaction effect in the two way ATI is different in two ANOVA is not significant. However, slight deviation in the progression of mean ATI scores is noticeable for those in Research and Training Institutions.
b. The trend of relationship of dedication and ATI is different in two environments.	Not Supported	Dedication has a similar effect on the ATI in both the job environments. Interaction of the two independent variables is not significant.
c. The trend of relationship of motivation and ATI is different in two environments.	Not Supported	Interaction *F* ratio is not significant.
d. The trend of relationship of aspiration and ATI is different in two environments.	Not Supported	Interaction *F* ratio is not significant.
e. The trend of relationship of educational attainment and ATI is different in two environments.	Supported	Interaction of the two variables is significant at 0.05 level. Non-Ph.D's in Research and Training Institution show a greater readiness to use information compared to the non-Ph.D's with the university affiliation.
f. The trend of relationship of professional experience and ATI is different in two environments.	Not Supported	Interaction effect is not significant.

(Contd.)

TABLE 5.1 *(Contd.)*

Hypotheses	Supported/ Not supported	Remarks
g. The trend of relationship of position in the hierarchy and ATI is different in two environments.	Not Supported	Interaction *F* ratio is not significant.
5. Psychological attributes taken individually show significantly varying effect on ATI when considered together with personal attributes or the interaction effect of psychological and personal attributes on ATI is significant. That is:		
1.a. The trend of relationship of job satisfaction and ATI is different for education groups.	Supported	Ph.D's, despite low job satisfaction tend to possess significantly more favourable ATI. Non-Ph.D's on the contrary show an increasing mean ATI score corresponding to their job satisfaction. Interaction *F* ratio is statistically significant.
1.b. The trend of relationship of job satisfaction and ATI is different for experience groups.	Not Supported	Interaction effect is not significant. The general trend of increase in ATI is noticeable for all the experience groups. However, significant difference in ATI from one group to another is noticeable for those in the middle phase.
1.c. The trend of relationship of job satisfaction and ATI is different for position groups.	Not Supported	Interaction effect is not significant. General trend of increasing mean ATI with job satisfaction is noticeable for all the position groups. Statistically significant difference for different groups of job satisfaction is noticeable for those in position one.
2.a. The trend of relationship. of dedication and ATI is different for education groups.	Not Supported	Interaction *F* ratio is not significant. A uniform trend of increasing mean ATI score is noticeable for Ph.D's and non-Ph.D's. High group in both the cases differ statistically from low and moderate dedication.

(Contd.)

TABLE 5.1 *(Contd.)*

Hypotheses	Supported/ Not supported	Remarks
2.b. The trend of relationship of dedication and ATI is different for experience groups.	Not Supported	Interaction *F* ratio is not significant. Though a deviation in the trend is noticeable for those in the initial phase the differences are not significant.
2.c. The trend of relationship of dedication and ATI is different for position groups.	Not Supported	All the positions show similar effect on ATI. Differences in the mean scores are significant between the high group and other groups for all the positions.
3.a. The trend of relationship of motivation and ATI is different for education groups.	Not Supported	Interaction effect is not significant. Motivation has similar effect for Ph.D's and non-Ph.D's.
3.b. The trend of relationship of motivation and ATI is different for experience groups.	Not Supported	The overall trend in the increase of mean ATI score is noticeable for all groups. the difference in favourability of ATI is significant in initial and middle phases.
3.c. The trend of relationship of motivation and ATI is different for position groups.	Not Supported	Significant deviation in the general trend is not noticeable among different positions. However, the difference in ATI mean scores is significant between different motivation groups for those in first two positions.
4.a. The trend of relationship of level of aspiration and ATI is different for education groups.	Not Supported	Higher level of aspiration for Ph.D's and non-Ph.D's induces more favourable ATI compared to the low aspirers in their respective groups. Interaction effect is not significant.
4.b. The trend of relationship of level of aspiration and ATI is different for experience groups.	Not Supported	Higher level of aspiration group tends to possess more favourable ATI in all the experience phases. The difference in the mean scores is significant for those in the middle phase.

(Contd.)

TABLE 5.1 *(Contd.)*

	Hypotheses	Supported/ Not supported	Remarks
4.c.	The trend of relationship of level of aspiration and ATI is different for position groups.	Not Supported	Interaction effect of position and aspiration is not significant. Mean ATI scores increase with the increase in level of aspiration for all the positions. The difference between low and high groups is noticeable for those in position one and three.
6.1	Constraints affect the information source use.	Not Supported	Almost all the Gamma values show non-significant relations between use of primary sources and degree of constraints experienced.
6.2	Constraints affect the ATI and information source use relations.	Supported	Gamma values are positive and significant when respondents experience 'no problem' on constraints such as: finding time, understanding statistics and research reports, qualified help to locate suitable material, and procedures in libraries. However, those who have expressed 'considerable difficulty' in getting information quickly and 'a little problem' as to locating suitable sources show significant attitude — behaviour relations.

ATI has been found to bear a significant and positive relation with most of the information sources considered in the study. The results suggest a need for recognising the intensive investigation of this latent aspect of the information use behaviour, i.e., ATI as one of the variables in user studies. It seems to have an intrinsic worth which may go a long way in explaining the observed source use pattern in social sciences, which is not very encouraging.

However, ATI is not the only factor which explain all the variance in information source use. Various situational factors facilitate or modify such relationship in explaining the observed attitude-behaviour link. The data indicate that in most of the cases strength of

ATI and information source use relations tend to improve when personal and psychological attributes are also considered in the analysis. That is, relatively higher job satisfaction, dedication, level of aspiration and motivation to work and also higher educational attainment and professional experience have been revealed to strengthen the attitude-behaviour relations. Only exception to this trend is the position in the hierarchy. Though position as such tends to modify the attitude-behaviour relations, it does not seem to go with the increasing position in the hierarchy. In addition to this, constraints in information use whenever experienced in relatively lesser degree, also seem to strengthen the relation of ATI and use of primary sources of information.

Considering the magnitude of attitude as such, significantly more favourable ATI is found among those who are relatively more satisfied in their job, more dedicated, and possess a higher level of aspiration and motivation to work. Higher educational attainment, i.e., Ph.D. as opposed to non-Ph.D. and more years of professional experience are also found to have a positive effect on ATI. On the other hand work affiliation i.e. working in university social science departments, where more work time is devoted to teaching as opposed to Research and Training Institutions, where research time is more, and also position in the hierarchy do not seem to have any bearing on the ATI.

The trend of personal and psychological attributes having a positive effect on ATI is shown to hold good in university departments and Research and Training Institutions alike. So also, the effect of psychological attributes tends to be more or less uniform, when they are subclassified based on the personal attributes considered in the study. Even when the overlapping effect of the two independent variables are statistically corrected (adjusted) in two way ANOVA, the main effect of the variables are in most cases statistically significant at 0.01 level (for example F ratio for motivation in one way ANOVA is 11.33. In two way ANOVA's when the analysis takes environment, education, experience and position also into consideration the F ratio for motivation works out to be 11.19, 9.48, 9.48, 12.69 respectively. In all the cases the results are significant at 0.01 level). The interaction effect on ATI, excepting in two cases viz., education X environment and education X job satisfaction, is invariably non-significant. So much so, the effect of the combination of any two independent variables on ATI, as far as the models examined, is largely additive in nature.

As there is a dearth of studies with the present focus, this research is explorative in nature. However, the results of this study point to the possible newer direction in which the information user research could continue. As information studies are largely the investigation into overt behaviour it is more appropriate to examine it from the angle of attitude towards the same by adopting measurement techniques employed in psychological studies. The user resistance could be better corrected by providing incentives facilitating attitude change for which attitude assessment studies give the basic clue.

APPENDICES

APPENDIX A

REFERENCES

Ackoff, R.L. and Halbert, M.H. (1958), *An operations research study of the scientific activity of chemists*. Cleveland, Case Institute of Technology.

Aiyepeku, Wilson O. (1983), Information transfer implications of development research administration in Nigeria. *Public Administration and Development,* 3, 161-172.

Ajzen, I. and Fishbein, M. (1973), Attitudinal and normative variables as predictors of specific behaviours. *Journals of Personality and Social Psychology*, 27, 41-57.

Ajzen, I. and Fishbein M. (1980), Understanding attitudes and predicting social behaviour. Englewood Cliff, N.J., Prentice-Hall.

Allen, T.J. (1969), Information needs and uses. *Annual Review of Information Science and Technology*, 4, 3-30.

Allen, T.J. and Cohen, S.I. (1966), *Information flow in an R & D Laboratory*. Cambridge, Mass. Massachusetts Institute of Technology.

Allport, G.W. (1953), The trend in motivational theory, in *Understanding Human Motivation*, ed. by Chalmers L. Stacey and Manfred F. De Martino. Cleveland, World Publishing Co., 1965, pp. 129-140.

Allport, G.W. (1967), Attitudes, in *Readings in Attitude Theory and Measurement*, ed. by Martin Fishbein. New York, John Wiley and Sons, pp. 3-13.

Amba, S. and Raghavan K.S. (1985), Information science in India: An analysis. *Library Science with a Slant to Documentation*.

Anand, Usha and Sohal, T.S. (1982), Measuring job satisfaction of scientists in an ICAR institute. *Asian Journal of Psychology and Education*, 9, 13-20.

Andrews, Frank ed. (1979), *Scientific productivity: The effectiveness of research groups in six countries*. Cambridge, Cambridge University Press.

Appel, J.S. and Guer, T. (1984), Bibliographic needs of social and behavioural sciences: report of a pilot survey. *American Be-*

havioural Scientist, 7, 51-54.

Arndt, Johan et al (1980), Information exchange among scientists: a two step socio-metric study. *Sociology*, 14, 141-148.

Artandi, S. (1973), Information concepts and their utility. *Journal of American Society for Information Science*, 24, 242-245.

Arvey, Richard D. and Dewhirst, H. Dudley (1979), Relationships between diversity of interests, age, job satisfaction and job performance. *Journal of Occupational Psychology*, 52, 17-23.

Atherton, Pauline (1975), Research in information science: an assessment (in *Perspectives in Information Science*, ed. by A. Debons and W.J. Cameroon, Leydon, Noordhoff) pp. 665-683.

Atkinson, J.W. (1964), *An introduction to motivation*. Princeton, N.J., Van Nostrand.

Atkinson, J.W. and Feather, N.T. (1966), *A theory of achievement motivation*. New York, Wiley.

Bagozzi, R.P. and Burukrant, R.E., Attitude organization and attitude behaviour relationship. *Journal of Personality and Social Psychology*, 37, 913-929.

Bath University (1972), *Experimental information service in social sciences 1969-1971: Final report*. Bath, Bath University Library.

Bath University (1973), *Analysis of requests to the National Children's Bureau's question and answer service*. Bath, Bath University Library.

Bath University (1974), *The relationship between usefulness and style of secondary publications: an experimental information service for planners*. Bath, Bath University Library.

Bath University (1980), *Towards the improvement of social science information systems: overview of research carried out 1971-1975*. Bath, Bath University Library.

Bealer, Robert C. and Kuvlesky, William P. (1968), On occupational aspirations and job attainments: a reply. *Rural Sociology*, 33, 353-356.

Bernel, J.B. (1959), The transmission of scientific information: a users analysis, (in *International Conference on Scientific Information*. Washington, 1958, Proceedings Vol. 1. Washington D.C., National Academy of Sciences, National Research Council) pp. 77-95.

Bernel, J.D. (1948), Preliminary analysis of pilot questionnaire on the use of scientific literature (in *Report of the Royal Society Scientific Information Conference* by Royal Society, London, Royal Society,

1948) pp. 589-637.

Blake, B. *et al* (1979), Inside information: social welfare practitioners and their information needs. *ASLIB Proceedings*. 31, 275-283.

Bogardas, Emoxy S., (1925), Measuring social distances. *Journal of Applied Psychology*, 9, 299-308. (Reprinted in *Readings in attitude theory and measurement*, ed. by Martin Fishbein. New York, John Wiley and Sons, pp. 71-76).

Borko, H. (1962), Determining user requirements for an information storage and retrieval system: a systems approach. (In *Information systems workshop,* ed. by C.P. Bourne. Washington D.C., Sparton Books) pp. 37-60.

Bourne, C.P. (1962), A review of the methodology of information system design. (in *Information systems workshop,* ed. by C.P. Bourne, Washington D.C., Sparton Books) pp. 11-35.

Brittain, J.M. (1970), *Information and its users: a review with special reference to the social sciences*. Bath, Bath University Press.

Brittain, J.M. (1975), Information needs and application of the results of users studies. (In *Perspectives in Information Science*, ed. by A. Debons and W.J. Cameroon Leydon, Noordhoff) pp. 425-435.

Brittain, J.M. (1979), Information services and the structure of knowledge in the social sciences. *International Social Science Journal*, 31, 711-728.

Brittain, J.M. (1982a), Pitfalls of user research and some neglected areas. *Social Science Information Studies*, 2, 139-148.

Brittain, J.M. (1982b), *The social sciences: the supply of one demand for documentation and data: a report to Unesco*. London, Ressendale.

Brittain, J.M. (1985), Relevance of social science output worldwide. *International Social Science Journal*, 37, 259-275.

Campbell, D.T. (1950), The indirect assessment of social attitudes. *Psychological Bulletin*, 47, 25-38.

Campbell, J.P. *et al* (1970), *Managerial behaviour, performance and effectiveness*. New York, McGraw Hill.

Campbell, J.P. and Pritchard, Robert D. (1976), Motivation theory in industrial and organizational psychology. (In *Handbook of Organizational Psychology* ed. by Marvin D. Dunnette. Chicago, Rand McNelly) pp. 63-130.

Caplan, N. (1975), The use of social science information by federal executives. (In *Social Research and Public Policies* ed. by G.M.

Lyons. The Darmoth OECD Conference, The Public Affairs Centre, Darmoth College, Hanover, New Hampshire) pp. 46-67.

Caplan, N. *et al* (1975), *The use of social science knowledge in policy decisions at the national level: a report of respondents.* Ann Arbor, University of Michigan.

Chaiken, Shelly and Stangor, Charles (1987) Attitudes and attitude change. *Annual Review of Psychology*, 38, 575-630.

Ching-Chih Chen (1982), *Information seeking: assessing and anticipating user needs*. New York, Neal-Schuman Publisher, Inc.

Clark, Alfred W. (1979), *Information use: a professional strategy.* Human Relations, 32, 503-522.

Clark, K.E. (1957), *American psychologists: a survey of growing profession.* Washington D.C., A.P.A.

Clifford, B. and others (1983), Information seeking: assessing and anticipating user needs. *Journal of Documentation,* 39, 130-132.

Cochran, W.G. and Coy, G.M. (1950), *Experimental designs.* New York, John Wiley, pp. 91.

Cole, Stephen and Cole, Jonathan (1973), *Social stratification in Science*. Chicago, University of Chicago.

Compton, Bertita E. (1965), The convention presentation: interwing an ultimate type of dissemination? *American Psychologist*, 20, 300-302.

Compton, Bertita E. (1973), Scientific communication (In *Handbook of Communication* ed. by Ithiel de Sola Pool *et al*. Chicago, Rand McNally College Publishing Co.) pp. 755-778.

Crane, Diana (1970), The nature of scientific and communication and influence. *International Social Science Journal*, 22, 28-41.

Davis, R.C. (1956). Commitment to professional values as related to the role performance of research scientists. Doctoral Dissertation, University of Michigan. (Quoted In *Scientists in organization: productive climates for research and development*, by Donald Pelz and Frank M. Andrews. New York, Wiley & Sons, 1966. p. 91.)

Defleur, M.L. and Westia, F.R. (1963), Attitude as a scientific concept. *Social Forces*, 42, 17-31.

Drever, J. (1956), *A dictionary of psychology*. Harmonds Worth, Penguin.

Drever, J. (1964), *A dictionary of psychology*. Middlesex, Penguin.

Edwards, A.L. and Kenney, K.C. (1946), A comparison of the Thurstone and Likert techniques of attitude scale construction. *Journal of Applied Psychology*, 30, 72-83.

Edwards, Allen L. (1969), *Techniques of attitude scale construction*. Bombay, Vakils.

Egan, Margaret and Henkle, Herman H. (1956), Ways and means in which research workers, executives and others use information. (In *Documentation in action*, ed. by Jesse H. Shera et al. New York, Reinhold Publishing Corporation) pp. 137-159.

Evans, M.G. (1969), Conceptual and operational problems in the measurement of various aspects of job satisfaction. *Journal of Applied Psychology*, 53, 53-101.

Farris, G.F. (1962), Congruency of scientists' motives with their organizations provisions for satisfying them, its relationship to motivation, affective job experiences, style of work and performance. Department of Psychology, University of Michigan. (As quoted in *Scientists in organization productive climate for research and development*, by Donald Pelz and Frank M. Andrews. New York, Wiley and Sons, 1966) p. 114.

Fazio, Russel H. and Zanna, Mark P. (1981), Direct experience and attitude-behaviour consistency. *Advances in Experimental Social Psychology*, 14, 161-202.

Fazio, Russel H. *et al* (1982), Attitude accessibility, attitude-behaviour consistency and the strength of object evaluation association. *Journal of Experimental Social Psychology*, 18, 339-357.

Ferguson, L.W. (1941), A study of the Likert technique of attitude scale construction. *Journal of Social Psychology*, 13, 51-57.

Fine, Sara (1984), Research on the psychology of information use. *Library Trends*, 32, 441-460.

Fishbein, M. and Ajzen, I. (1972), Attitudes and opinions. *Annual Review of Psychology*, 23, 487-544.

Fishbein, M. and Ajzen, I. (1974), Attitude towards object as predictors of single and multiple behavioural criteria. *Psychological Review*, 81, 59-74.

Fishbein, M. and Ajzen, I. (1975), Beliefs, attitude, intention and behaviour. Reading, Mass., Addison-Wesley.

Ford, G. (1977), *User studies: an introductory guide and a select bibliography*. Sheffield, University of Sheffield, Centre for User Studies.

Freedman, Jonathan *et al* (1970), *Social psychology*. Englewood Cliffs, N.J. Prentice Hall.

Gardner, John W. (1940), The use of the term level of aspiration. (*in Understanding human motivation*, ed. by Chalmers L. Stacey and

Manfred F. Demartino. Cleveland, World Publishing Co.) pp. 323-329.

Garvey, William D. (1979), *Communication: the essence of science.* Oxford, Pergamon Press.

Garvey, W.D. and Compton, B.E. (1967), A programme of research in scientific information exchange: orientation, objectives and results. *Social Science Information*, 6, 213-237.

Garvey, W.D. and Griffith, B.C. (1963), *Reports of the American Psychological Association's project on scientific information exchange in psychology*. Washington D.C., A.P.A.

Garvey, W.D. and Griffith, B.C. (1964), Scientific information exchange in psychology. *Science*, 146, 1655-1658.

Garvey, W.D. and Griffith, B.C. (1964b), The structure, objectives and findings of a study of scientific information exchange in psychology. *American Documentation*, 15, 258-267.

Garvey, W.D. and Griffith, B.C. (1965a), Reports of the American Psychological Association project on scientific information exchange in psychology. Washington D.C., A.P.A.

Garvey, W.D. and Griffith, B.C. (1965b), Scientific communication: the dissemination system in psychology and a theoretical framework for planning innovations. *American Psychologist*, 20, 157-164.

Garvey, W.D. and Griffith, B.C. (1966), Studies of social innovations in scientific communication in psychology. *American Psychologist*, 21, 1019-1036.

Garvey, W.D. *et al* (1970), Some comparison of communication activities in the physical and social science (in *Communication among scientists and engineers* by Carnot E. Nelson and Donald K. Pollock. Lexington, Heath Lexington Books) pp. 61-84.

Garvey, W.D. *et al* (1971), A comparison of scientific communication behaviour of social and physical scientists. *International Social Science Journal*, 23, 256-272.

Garvey, W.D. *et al* (1974), The dynamic scientific information user, *Information Storage and Retrieval*, 10, 115-131.

Glaser, Berney G. (1964), Organizational scientists: their professional careers. New York, Bobbs-Merrill Co.

Glaser, Berney G. (1965), Differential association and the institutional motivation of scientists. *Administrative Science Quarterly*, 10, 82-92.

Goldenson, Robert M., ed. (1984), *Longman dictionary of psychology and psychiatry*. New York, Longman.

Griffith, B.C. and Garvey, W.D. (1964), Systems in scientific information exchange and the effects of innovation and change. *Proceedings of the American Documentation Institute*, 1, 191-200.

Griffith, B.C. and Garvey, W.D. (1966), The national scientific meeting in psychology as a changing social system. *American Behavioural Scientist*, 10, 3-8.

Guilford, J.P. and Fruchter, Benjamin (1978), *Fundamental statistics in psychology and education*. Tokyo, McGraw-Hill, Kogakusha Ltd.

Guttman, Lewis (1944), A basis for scaling qualitative data. *American Sociological Review*, 9, 139-150.

Guttsman, W.L. (1966), The literature of social sciences and provisions for research in them. *Journal of Documentation*, 22(3), September, 1986, 186-194.

Haag, D.E. (1984), Barriers limiting the usefulness of published information in the research environment. *Special Libraries*, 75, 214-220.

Hall, D.T. and Lawler, E.E. (1969), Unused potential in research and development organizations. *Research Management*, 12, 339-354.

Haller, A.O. (1968), On the concept of aspiration. *Rural Sociology*, 33, 484-487.

Harriman, P.L. ed. (1946), Twentieth century psychology. New York.

Helmreich, Robert et al (1978), Achievement motivation and scientific attainment. *Personality and Social Psychology Bulletin*, 4, 222-226.

Herner, Saul (1954), Information gathering habits of workers in pure and applied science. *Industrial and Engineering Chemistry*, 46, 228-236.

Herner, Saul (1962), Determination of user needs for the design of information systems. (in *Information systems workshop: the designers responsibility and his methodology*. Washington D.C., Spartan Books)

Hogeweg-De Haart, H.P. (1983), Characteristics of social science information: a selective review of the literature. Part-I. *Social Science Information Studies*, 3, 147-164.

Hogeweg-De Haart, H.P. (1984), Characteristics of social science information: a selective review of the literature, Part-II. *Social Science Information Studies*, 4, 15-30.

Hoppock, R. (1935), *Job satisfaction*. New York, Harper.

Hulin, C.L. and Blood, M.R. (1968), Job enlargement, individual differences and worker responses. *Psychological Bulletin*, 69, 41-55.

Huse, E.F. and Bowditch, J.L. (1977), *Behaviour in organizations: a systems approach to managing*. Reading, Mass., Addison-Wesley.

Indian Association of Special Libraries and Information Centres (IASLIC) (1965), *Users and library and information services*. IASLIC Special Publication No. 5 pt. 1. Calcutta, IASLIC.

Javerlin, Kalervo and Repo, Aatto J. (1982), Knowledge work augmentation and human information seeking. *Journal of Informaion Science*, 5, 79-86.

Jhansi Rani, Ghanta (1985), Scientific productivity of agricultural scientists: an activity analysis approach. Doctoral Dissertation, Andhra Pradesh Agricultural University.

Karki, M.M.S. (1982), Information needs of Indian industry. *Annuals of Library Science and Documentation*, 29, 8-11.

Kast, F.E. and Rosenzweig, J.E. (1979), *Organization and management: a systems approach*. New York, McGraw-Hill Book Co.

Katy, O. (1960), The functional approach to the study of attitudes. *Public Opinion Quarterly*, 224, 163-204.

Katy, D. and Scotland, E.A. (1959), Preliminary statement to a theory of attitude structure and change. (in *Psychology: a study of science* by New York, McGraw Hill Book Co., u.3)

Kent, A.K. (1984), The specialised journals: the raw materials for innovation. (in *Information and innovation* ed. by B.T. Stern. Amsterdam, North-Holland Press) pp. 95-100.

Kilpatrick, F.P. and Cantril, H. (1960), Self-anchoring scaling: a measure of individuals' unique reality world. *Journal of Individual psychology*, 16.

Kerman, A.K. (1974), *The psychology of motivation*. Englewood Cliffs, N.J., Prentice-Hall.

Kornhauser, W. (1962), *Scientists in industry: conflict and accommodation*. Berkeley, University of California Press.

Kramer, Clyde Young (1956), Extension of multiple range test to group means with unequal number of replications. *Bio-metrics*, 12, 307-310.

Kretch, D. and Crutchfield, R.S. (1948), *Theory and problems of social psychology*. New York, McGraw Hill.

Kretch, D. et al. (1962), Individual in society. New York, McGraw Hill Book Co.

Krikelas, James (1983), Information seeking behaviour patterns and concepts. *Drexel Library Quarterly*, 19, 5-20.

Krishna Kumar (1973), Research libraries in developing countries. Delhi, Vikas.

Kuruna, S. (1986), Productivity of scientists and engineers. *Indian Educational Review*, 21, 106-110.

Lapiere, R.T. (1934), Attitudes vs actions. *Social Forces*, 13, 230-237.

Lawler, E.E. (1969), Job design and employee motivation. *Personnel Psychology*, 22, 426-435.

Lawler, E.E. and Hall, D.T. (1970), Relationship of job characteristics to job involvement, satisfaction and intrinsic motivation. *Journal of Applied Psychology*, 54, 305-312.

Lazarfeld, P.F. and Reitz, J.G. (1975), An introduction to applied sociology. New York, Elsevier.

Lee, Sang M. (1971), An empirical analysis of organizational identification. *Academy of Management Journal*, 14, 213-226.

Lewin, Kurt (1936), Psychology of success and failure. (in *Understanding human motivation* ed. by Chalmers L. Stacey and Manfred F. Demartino. Cleveland, World Publishing Co., 1965) pp. 317-322.

Likert, Rensis (1967), The method of constructing an attitude scale (in *Readings in attitude theory and measurement,* ed. by Martin – Fishbein. New York, John Wiley & Sons) pp. 90-95.

Lin, Nan et al (1970), A study of the communication structure of science (in *Communication among scientists and engineers*, ed. by Carnot E. Nelson and Donald K. Pollock. Lexington, Heath Lexington Books) pp. 23-60.

Lindquest, E.F. (1968), Statistical analysis in educational research. Boston, Hengh Mifflin Co.) pp. 251-252.

Lindsley, Donald S. (1957), Psycho-physiology of motivation (*in* Jones, Marshall R. ed. *Nebraska symposium on motivation*. Lincoln University of Nebraska. p. 48.

Lindzey, G. and Aronson, E. eds. (1985), *The handbook of social psychology*. Vol. 1,2. New York, Random House, 810p. 3rd ed.

Line, M.B. (1963), Students attitude to the University library. *Journal of Documentation*, 19, 100-117.

Line, M.B. (1969), Information requirements in the social sciences: some preliminary considerations. *Journal of Librarianship*, 1, 1-19.

Line, M.B. (1971a), The information uses and needs of social scientists: an overview of INFROSS. *ASLIB Proceedings*, 23, 412-434.

Line, M.B. *et al* (1971b), *Investigation into information requirements of the social sciences: information requirements of college and education lecturers and school teachers.* Bath, Bath University Library.

Line, M.B. *et al* (1971c), *Investigation into information requirements of the social sciences*; Research report No. 1. Information requirements of researchers in the social sciences. Bath, Bath University Library. v.1. text v.2 tables.

Locke, E.A. (1968), Towards a theory of task motivation and incentives. *Organizational Behaviour and Human Performance*, 3, 157-189.

Locke, E.A. (1969), What is job satisfaction? *Organizational Behaviour and Human Performance*, 4, 309-336.

Locke, E.A. (1970), Job satisfaction and job performance: a theoretical analysis. *Organizational Behaviour and Human Performance*, 5, 484-500.

Locke, E.A. (1976), The nature and causes of job satisfaction (in *Handbook of industrial and organizational psychology*, ed. by Marvin D. Dunnette, Chicago, Rand McNelly) pp. 1297-1347.

Locke, E.A. et al (1970), Studies of the relationship between satisfaction, goal setting and performance. *Organizational Behaviour and Human Performance*, 5, 135-158.

Lodahl, T. and Kejner, M. (1965), The definition and measurement of job involvement. *Journal of Applied Psychology*, 49, 24-33.

Luthans, F. (1977), *Organizational behaviour.* New York, McGraw Hill Book Co.

Lutz, Gene M. (1984), *Understanding social statistics.* New York, McMillan Publishing Co.

McArthur, L.A. *et al* (1969), Acting on an attitude as a function of self percept and inequality. *Journal of Personality and Social Psychology*, 12, 295-302.

McCurrey, Michael W. and Edwards, Shirley A. (1972), Hierarchies of scientist goal objects: individual characteristics and performance correlates. *Journal of Applied Psychology*, 56, 271-272.

McCurrey, Michael W. and Edwards, Shireley A. (1973) Organizational climate conditions for effective research scientists role performance. *Organizational Behaviour and Human Performance*, 9, 439-459.

Mc Guire, William J. (1969), The nature of attitudes and attitude change. (in *Handbook of social psychology* ed. by Gardner Lindzey and Elliot Aronson, Reading Addison-Wesley Publishing

co., 1969, Vol. 3) pp. 136-314.
Mc Iver, John P. and Carmines, Edward G. (1981), *Unidimensional scaling*. Beverly Hills, Sage Publications.
Mc Kelvey, B. Sekaran V. (1977), Toward a career based theory of job involvement: a study of scientists and engineers. *Administrative Science Quarterly*, 22, 281-305.
Marzocco, Frank N. (1975), Human dimensions of information need. (in *Perspectives in information science*, ed. by Antony Debons and William J. Cameron. Leydon, Noordhoff, 1975) pp. 75-92.
McGuire, W.J. (1986), The vicissitudes of attitudes and similar representational constructs in Twentieth Century psychology. *European Journal of Social Psychology* 16, 89-130.
Meadows, A.J. (1974), Communication in science. London, Butterworths.
Menzel, Herbert (1958), *The flow of information among scientists: problems, opportunities and research questions*. Springfield, NTIS.
Menzel, Herbert (1960), *Review of studies in the flow of information among scientists*. New York, Columbia University, Bureau of Applied Social Research.
Menzel, Herbert (1964), The information needs of current scientific research. *Library Quarterly*, 34, 4-19.
Menzel, Herbert (1966), Scientific communication: five themes from social science research. *American Psychologist*, 21, 999-1004.
Mick, Colin M. et al (1980), Towards usable user studies. *Journal of American Society for Information Science*, 347-356.
Miller, John B. (1980), The role of managerial and professional motivation in the career success of management professors. *Academy of Management Journal*, 23, 487-508.
Miller, Lynn E. and Grush, Joseph E. (1986), Individual differences in attitudinal versus normative determination of behaviour. *Journal of Experimental Social Psychology*, 22, 190-202.
Misshauk, Michael J. (1970), Importance of environmental factors to scientists, engineers. *Personnel Psychology*, 49, 319-323.
Mitchell, Terence R. (1979), Organizational behaviour. *Annual Review of Psychology*, 30, 243-281.
Murphy, G. and Likert, Rensis (1937), Public opinion and the individual. New York, Harper.
Murthy, A.T. (1972), Use of bibliographical tools. *Indian Librarian*, 26, 182-186.
Muthayya, B.C. (1971), *Farmers and their aspiration*. Hyderabad,

NICD.

Nagpaul, P.S. and Pruthi, S. (1979), Problem solving, new idea generation in R & D: the role of information. *Communication, R & D Management*, 9(3), July 1979, 147-149.

Newcomb, T.M. (1952), *Social psychology*. London, Tavistok.

Newcomb, T.M. et al (1965), *Social psychology: the study of human interactions*. New York, Holt.

Orr, R.H. (1961), The metabolism of new scientific information: a preliminary report. *American Documentation*, 12, 15-19.

Orr, R.H. et al (1964), The bio-medical information complex viewed as a system. *Federation Proceedings*, 23, 1133-1145.

Ostrom, T. (1984), Attitude theory (in *Encyclopedia of psychology*, ed. by Raymond J. Corsion. New York, John Wiley & Sons) v.1. pp. 100-102.

Pagano, Robert R. (1981), *Understanding statistics in the behavioural sciences*. St Paul, West Publishing Co.

Paisley, W.J. (1965), *The flow of (behavioural) science information: a review of research literature*. Stanford, Institute of Communication Research, Stanford University.

Paisley, W.J. (1968), Information needs and uses. *Annual Review of Information Science and Technology*, 3, 1-30.

Pareek, Udai and Chattopadhyay, S.N. (1965), Measuring level of aspiration of farmers through a perspective technique. *Indian Journal of Social Work*, 25, 363-373.

Parkar, Edwin B. and Paisley, William J. (1966), Research for psychologists at the interface of scientist and his information system. *American Psychologist*, 21, 1061-1071.

Paterson, R.E. (1946), The use of adjusting factors in the analysis of data with disproportionate sub-class numbers. *Journal of American Statistical Association*, 41, 334-346.

Pelz, Donald C. (1956), Some social factors related to performance in a research organization. *Administrative Science Quarterly*, 1, 310-325.

Pelz, Donald C. and Andrews, F. Michael (1962), Organizational atmosphere, motivation and research contribution. *American Behavioural Scientist*, 6, 43-47.

Pelz, Donald C. and Andrews, F. Michael (1966), Scientist in organizations: productive climates for research and development. New York, Wiley.

Pratt, Allan D. (1980), Information and emmerphosis: an attempt at definition. (*in* theory and application of information research: proceedings of the second international research forum on information science, 3-6, August 1977. *Royal School of Librarianship*, Copenhagen, ed. by Ole Harso and Leif Kajbery. London, Mansell), pp. 30-33.

Price, Derek J. De. S. and Beaver, Donald De B. (1966), Collaboration in an invisible college. *American Psychologist*, 21, 1011-1018.

Project INISS: final report on the innovation programme. 1978-1980. Sheffield, Sheffield University, Department of Information Studies, 1980.

Pruthi, S. and Nagpaul, P.S. (1978), Communication patterns in small R & D projects. *R & D Management*, 8(2), April, 53-58.

Rajagopalan, T.S. and Rajan, T.N. (1984), Use of information in science and research with emphasis on national development: some Indian experiences. *International Forum on Information and Documentation*, 9, July, 3-9.

Rajan, J.V. and Subramanian, S.K. (1969), Creativity in scientific institutions: the problem of job incentives. *Indian Journal of Public Administration*, 15, 410-421.

Rees, A.M. (1963), Information needs and patterns of usage (in *Information retrieval in action*, by Centre for Documentation and Communication Research, School of Library Science, Western Reserve University) pp. 17-23.

Regan, Dennis T. and Fazio, Russel (1977), On the consistency between attitude and behaviour: look to the method of attitude formation. *Journal of Experimental Social Psychology*, 13, 28-45.

Roberts, Norman (1982), A search for information man. *Social Science Information Studies*, 2, 93-104.

Rokeach, Milton (1968), Attitudes, (in *International Encyclopedia of Social Sciences*. New York, Macmillan Company and the Free Press) Vol. 1, pp. 449-458.

Rokeach, M. and Kliejunas, P. (1972), Behaviour as a function of attitude toward object and attitude toward situation. *Journal of Personality and Social Psychology*, 22, 194-201.

Rosenberg, Victor (1981), Cultural and political traditions and their impact on the transfer and use of scientific information. *Information Services and Use*, 1, 75-80.

Rouse, William B. and Rouse, Sandra H., Human information seeking and design of information systems. *Information Processing and Management*, 20, 129-138.

Sahai, S.N. (1971), Reading trends of library users in Bihar. *Unesco Bulletin for Libraries*, 25, 151-157.

Sample, J. and Warland, R. (1973), Attitude and prediction of behaviour. *Social Forces*, 51, 292-304.

Sangameshwaran, S.V. and Gopinath, M.V. (1977), CFTRI documentation services: a user survey. *Annals of Library Science and Documentation*, 24, 147-153.

Sangameshwaran, S.V. and Gopinath, M.V. (1977), Food science and technology information services (FOSTIS): users assessment of CFTRI documentation services. *Library Science with a Slant to Documentation*, 14, 129-135.

Schrader, A. (1983), Toward a theory of library and information science. Dissertation submitted for the degree doctor of philosophy in the school of Library and Information Science, Indiana University. 2 pts.

Schuman, H. and Johnson, M.P. (1976), Attitudes and behaviour. *Annual Review of Sociology*, 2, 161-207.

Shantamani, V.S. (1982), A comparative study of R & D Units with special reference to motivation, involvement and level of aspiration. *Asian Journal of Psychology and Education*, 9, 1-12.

Shaw, R.R. (1956), *Pilot study on the use of scientific literature by scientists.* Washington D.C., National Science Foundation, 1956.

Shera, J.H., *Foundations of education for librarianship*. New York, Becker & Hayes, 1972.

Sherif, C.W. *et al*, Personal involvement, social judgement and action. *Journal of Personality and Social Psychology*, 27, 311-328.

Sherif, M. and Sherif, C.W. (1956), *An outline of social psychology.* New York, Harper & Row.

Shukla, Aditya N. (1972), The concept of extension education: a study in psycho-physical methods. (in *Studies in extension education*, ed. by P.R.R. Sinha. Hyderabad, NICD) pp. 9-19.

Singh, S.N. (1979), Assessing information needs and uses: a state of the art report. *Herald of Library Science*, 18, 38-45.

Slamecka, V. (1982), The inclination towards information use. (in *Information and the transformation of society*, ed. by G.P. Sweeney. Amsterdam, North Holland) pp. 63-70.

Skelton, Barbara (1971), *Comparison of results of science user studies with investigation into information requirements of the social sciences*. Bath, Bath University Library.

Slocum, John, W. and Cron, William L. (1985), Job attitudes and performance during three career stages. *Journal of Vocational Behaviour*, 26, 126-145.

Snyder, Mark and Kendzierski, Deborah (1982), Acting on one's attitude: procedures for linking attitude and behaviour. *Journal of Experimental Psychology*, 18, 165-183.

Sri Chandra (1970), Scientists: a social-psychological study. New Delhi, Oxford.

Stacey, Chalmers L. and Demartino, Manfred F. (1965) Understanding human motivation. Cleveland, World Publishing Co.

Steinfalt, Thomas M. and Infante, Dominic A. (1976), Attitude-behaviour relationships in communication research. *Quarterly Journal of Speech*, 62, 267-278.

Stolte-Heiskanen, Veronica (1979), Externally determined resources and the effectiveness of research units. (in Andrews, Frank M. ed. *Scientific productivity: the effective uses of research groups in six countries*. Cambridge, Cambridge University Press) pp. 121-153.

Stouffer, Samel A. *et al* (1950), Measurement and prediction. (in *Studies in Social Psychology in World War II*. Vol. IV. Princeton, Princeton University) pp. 60-90.

Streatfield, D.R. *et al* (1981), A problem based training approach to information for practitioners. *Libri*, 31, 243-257.

Streatfield, D. (1983), Moving towards the information user: some research and its implications. *Social Science Information Studies*, 3, 223-240.

Strenstrom, P. and Mc Bride, R.B. (1979), Serial use by social science faculty. *College and Research Libraries*, 40, 426-431.

Sudhakara Rao, B.S. and Subramaniam, J.B. (1981), Information for small industry: a survey. *Sedme*, 8, 1-14.

Summers, Edward G. *et al* (1983), Measuring users affective response to information: development and validation of the attitude towards information scale (ATIS). *Social Science Information Studies*, 3, 109-120.

Summers, Edward G. *et al* (1983a), The effect of personal, professional and psychological attributes and information seeking behaviour on the use of information sources by educators. *Journal of the American Society for Information Science*, 34, 75-85.

Tai, Simon W. (1978), *Social Science statistics: its elements and applications*. Santamonica, Goodyear Publishing Co.

Thurstone, L.C. and Chave, E.J. (1929), The measurement of attitude (Reprinted in *Readings in attitude theory and measurement,* ed. by Martin Fishbein. New York, John Wiley & Sons) pp. 77-89.

Tittle, C.R. and Hill, R.J. (1967), Attitude measurement and prediction of behaviour: an evaluation of conditions and measurement techniques. *Sociometry*, 30, 199-213.

Tobin, Jayne Culver (197), A study of library "use studies". *Information storage and Retrieval*, 10, 107-113.

United Nations Educational Scientific and Cultural Organisation (1981), *Guidelines on studies of information users* (Pilot version) Paris, UNESCO.

Urquhart, D.J. (1948), The distribution and use of scientific and technical information. (in *Royal Society Scientific Information Conference*. London, Royal Society) pp. 408-409.

Uytterschaut, L. (1966), Literature searching methods in social science research: a pilot enquiry. *American Behavioural Scientist*, 9, 23-26.

Vishwanathan, C.G. (1976), *Elements of information science*. New Delhi, Today and Tomorrow Printers.

Vitales, M.S. (1953), Motivation and morale in industry. New York, W.W. Norton (as quoted in the *Nature and causes of job satisfaction*, ed. by Marvin D. Dunnette, Chicago, Rand McNelly, 1976), p. 1300.

Vollmer, Howard M. (1965), *Work activities and attitudes of scientists and research managers: data from a national survey*. Menlopark, Stanford Research Institute. (pp. 203-204 questionnaire)

Vroom, Victor H. (1964), *Work and motivation*. New York, John Wiley & Sons.

Wanous, John P. and Lawler, Edward E. (1972), Measurement and meaning of job satisfaction. *Journal of Applied Psychology*, 56, 95-105.

Warner, L.G. and Defleur, M.L. (1969), Attitude as an interactional concept: social constraint and social distance as intervening variables between attitude and action. *American Sociological Review*, 34, 153-169.

Weigel, R.H. and Newman, L.S. (1976), Increasing attitude-behaviour correspondence by broadening the scope of the behavioural measure. *Journal of Personality and Social Psychology*, 33, 793-802.

Wersig, G. and Windel, G. (1985), Information science needs a theory of information actions. *Social Science Information Studies*, 5, 11-23.

Wert, James E. *et al* (1954), *Statistical methods in education and psychological research*. New York, Appleton Century.

White, B. (1969), *Information provision in town and country planning: a research report*. London, Library Association.

Wicker, A.W. (1971), An examination of 'other variables' explanation of attitude-behaviour inconsistency. *Journal of Personality and Social Psychology*, 19, 18-30.

Wilson, Patrick and Farid, Mona (1979), On use of records of research. *Library Quarterly*, 49, 127-145.

Wilson, T. *et al* (1982), Models of the information user: progress and prospects in research. (in *Information and the transformation of society*, ed. by G.P. Sweeney. Amsterdam, North-Holland Co.) pp. 361-367.

Wilson, T.D. (1981), On user studies and information needs. *Journal of Documentation*, 37, 3-15.

Wilson, T.D. (1981), Sociological aspects of information science. *International Forum on Information and Documentation*, 6, 13-18.

Wilson, T.D. (1984), The cognitive approach to information seeking behaviour and information use. *Social Science Information Studies*, 4, 197-204.

Wilson, T.D. and Streatfield, D.R. (1979), Information needs in local authority social science departments: a second report on project INISS. *Journal of Documentation*, 35, 120-136.

Wilson, T.D. and Streatfield, D.R. (1981), Structured observation in the investigation of information needs. *Social Science Information Studies*, 1, 173-184.

Wernimont, D.F. (1966), Intrinsic and extrinsic factors in job satisfaction. *Journal of Applied Psychology*, 50, 41-50.

Wood, D.N. and Bower, C.A. (1969), The use of social science periodical literature. *Journal of Documentation*, 25, 108.

Yates, B. (1984), Information needs of human beings. *International Forum on Information and Documentation*, 9, 24-28.

APPENDIX B

1. Name ....

2. Are you (tick one)
   — Male
   — Female

3. Date of birth (tick one)
   — August 1960 or later
   — July 1960 to August 1955 — July 1940 to August 1935
   — July 1955 to August 1950 — July 1935 to August 1930
   — July 1950 to August 1945 — July 1930 or earlier
   — July 1945 to August 1940

4. Highest degree (tick one)
   — Doctor's (Subject area :
   — M. Phil. (Subject area :
   — Master's (Subject area :

5. If your highest degree is not doctor's, are you presently working for doctoral degree?

   Yes .... No ....

6. In what year was your highest degree awarded?

   ....

7. What is your total research and teaching experience? (tick one)

   — Up to 5 years — 21 to 25 years
   — 6 to 10 years — 26 to 30 years
   — 11 to 15 years — 30 years and above
   — 16 to 20 years

8. What is your official designation? (tick one)

   — Professor — Director
   — Reader — Deputy Director
   — Lecturer — Assistant Director
   — Research Associate/Assistant
   — Others (specify)..

9. Of your total work time (at office or otherwise) about what proportion do you normally spend on the following type of activities (if it fluctuates strike an average. Enter nearest 10%).

Per cent of time

Teaching and training ....
Research ....
Research guidance ....
Administrative work ....
Others (specify) ....

Total should add 100%

10. a. If you are conducting research are you conducting it

Individually? :- — Yes — No
With others? :- — Yes — No

b. If with other researchers
How many?
What is your status in them?: Project leader ....
Project associate ....
Others (specify) ....

11. **MOTIVATION**

Listed below are different kinds of opportunities which an academic job might offer. If you were to seek a job how much importance would you personally attach to each of these:

Items	Check below how important each item is to you in your work
To make full use of my present knowledge and skills	– Extremely important – Quite important – Somewhat important – Not very important – I can't say
Opportunity to keep up - to date on new scientific developments in the field	– Extremely important – Quite important – Somewhat important – Not very important – I can't say
Opportunity to write and publish research findings	– Extremely important – Quite important – Somewhat important – Not very important – I can't say

Contd.

Items	Check below how important each item is to you in your work
A high degree of freedom in selecting research projects to work on and teaching assignments	— Extremely important — Quite important — Somewhat important — Not very important — I can't say
Opportunity for promotion into higher position	— Extremely important — Quite important — Somewhat important — Not very important — I can't say
An adequate salary	— Extremely important — Quite important — Somewhat important — Not very important — I can't say
To work with colleagues of high competence	— Extremely important — Quite important — Somewhat important — Not very important — I can't say
To have congenial colleagues	— Extremely important — Quite important — Somewhat important — Not very important — I can't say
To build up professional reputation	— Extremely important — Quite important — Somewhat important — Not very important — I can't say
To work on difficult and challenging problem	— Extremely important — Quite important — Somewhat important — Not very important — I can't say

Contd.

Items	Check below how important each item is to you in your work
Attending professional meetings in my field	— Extremely important — Quite important — Somewhat important — Not very important — I can't say
A high degree of freedom in day-to-day research and teaching activities	— Extremely important — Quite important — Somewhat important — Not very important — I can't say
To contribute to broad research knowledge in the field	— Extremely important — Quite important — Somewhat important — Not very important — I can't say

12. **JOB SATISFACTION**

Listed below are the facilities that an academic job usually offers. To what extent are you satisfied on each of these aspects in your pesent job.

Items	Check below how important each item is to you in your work
To make full use of my present knowledge and skills	— Yes, definitely — Yes, I think so — No, I don't think so — No, definitely not — I can't say
Opportunity to keep up to date on new scientific developments in the field	— Yes, definitely — Yes, I think so — No, I don't think so — No, definitely not — I can't say
Opportunity to write and publish research findings	— Yes, definitely — Yes, I think so — No, I don't think so — No, definitely not — I can't say

Contd.

Items	Check below how important each item is to you in your work
A high degree of freedom in selecting research projects to work on and teaching assignments	— Yes, definitely — Yes, I think so — No, I don't think so — No, definitely not — I can't say
Opportunity for promotion into higher position	— Yes, definitely — Yes, I think so — No, I don't think so — No, definitely not — I can't say
An adequate salary	— Yes, definitely — Yes, I think so — No, I don't think so — No, definitely not — I can't say
To work with colleagues of high competence	— Yes, definitely — Yes, I think so — No, I don't think so — No, definitely not — I can't say
To have congenial colleagues	— Yes, definitely — Yes, I think so — No, I don't think so — No, definitely not — I can't say
To build up professional reputation	— Yes, definitely — Yes, I think so — No, I don't think so — No, definitely not — I can't say
To work on difficult and challenging problem	— Yes, definitely — Yes, I think so — No, I don't think so — No, definitely not — I can't say

Contd.

Items	Check below how important each item is to you in your work
Attending professional meetings in my field	— Yes, definitely — Yes, I think so — No, I don't think so — No, definitely not — I can't say
A high degree of freedom in day-to-day research and teaching activities	— Yes, definitely — Yes, I think so — No, I don't think so — No, definitely not — I can't say
To contribute to broad research knowledge in in field	— Yes, definitely — Yes, I think so — No, I don't think so — No, definitely not — I can't say
Has your organisation/ faculty generally given your research/the recognition it deserves	— Yes, definitely — Yes, I think so — No, I don't think so — No, definitely not — I can't say
Taking everything into consideration how satisfied are you in general in your job	— Yes, definitely satisfied — Yes, I think I'm satisfied — No, I don't think I'm satisfied — No, definitely not satisfied — I can't say

13. **DEDICATION**

To what extent do you feel obliged in supporting the goals of your organisation:

- Strong obligation
- Moderate obligation
- Slight obligation
- No obligation
- I can't say

Contd.

Some individuals are completely involved in their research and teaching work — absorbed by it day and night, for others this work is simply one of the several interests. How involved are you in your work?

- Not much involved
- Somewhat involved
- Involved
- completely involved
- I can't say

How interesting do you find your present research/teaching work?

- Hardly interesting
- Somewhat interesting
- Interesting
- Very interesting
- I can't say

How challenging do you find your present work in the sense of demanding concentration, intelligence etc?

- Not at all challenging
- Somewhat challenging
- Challenging
- Very challenging
- I can't say

14. Please rate, as best as you can, each of the following sources of information according to the extent of your use during your current research and teaching by encircling the appropriate number:

	Not used									Most used
Periodicals	0	1	2	3	4	5	6	7	8	9
Books and research reports	0	1	2	3	4	5	6	7	8	9
Theses and dissertations	0	1	2	3	4	5	6	7	8	9
Government publications and other official documents	0	1	2	3	4	5	6	7	8	9
Citations and bibliographies in book and periodicals	0	1	2	3	4	5	6	7	8	9
Book reviews	0	1	2	3	4	5	6	7	8	9
Abstracting and indexing services	0	1	2	3	4	5	6	7	8	9

Reading list, bibliographies produced by library staff	0	1	2	3	4	5	6	7	8	9
Primary data collected through surveys or experiments	0	1	2	3	4	5	6	7	8	9
Consulting with experts or authorities	0	1	2	3	4	5	6	7	8	9
Participating in workshops, seminars, courses etc.	0	1	2	3	4	5	6	7	8	9
Discussions with colleagues in your institution or out side	0	1	2	3	4	5	6	7	8	9
Others (specify)	0	1	2	3	4	5	6	7	8	9

15. Among the following please indicate the degree of the problems you face in making use of the information:

	No problem	Very little problem	A little diffi- culty	Extreme diffi culty
Finding time to look for or read information				
Getting information quickly enough				
Getting up to date material				
Understanding research reports and statistics				
Locating suitable sources				
Lack of qualified help to locate information				
Knowing how to use indexes/ abstracts etc.				
Material available in different languages				
Procedures in libraries				
Others (specify)				

16. LEVEL OF ASPIRATION

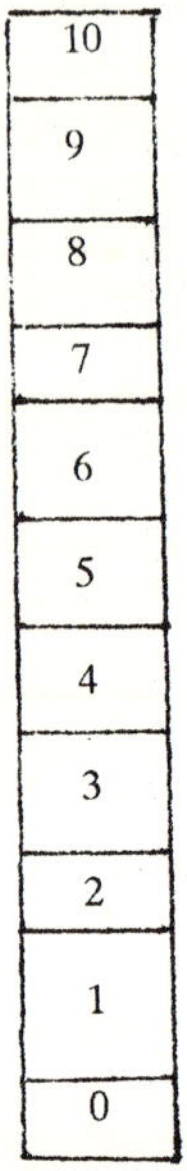

Here is a ladder with ten rungs. The lowest rung (0) can possibly indicate the place a person graduates into when he takes up an academic job after his studies. The highest rung (10) can possibly indicate the best one can possibly achieve in the academic life, like making substantial original contributions in the field of specialisation, propounding a new theory etc. which guarantees international reputation. The remaining rungs falling in between represent different phases in one's academic career. Imagine your academic career representing the different rungs in the ladder and indicate.

Where would you place yourself at the present moment of time: Rung No. ....

Where do you think you would be three years from now: Rung No. ....

ATTITUDE TOWARDS INFORMATION

What is your opinion on the following statements? Your answer is correct if you express your sure opinion. This is not a test and you are not to be graded. PLEASE DO NOT OMIT ANY ITEM. In each case encircle the letter or letters which represent your own ideas about each statement.

SA — Strongly Agree
A — Agree
U — Undecided
D — Disagree
SD — Strongly Disagree

1. Personal experiences are always more educative than published information.	—	SA	A	U	D	SD
2. Research reports dealing with different cultural context rarely carry worthwhile information for us.	—	SA	A	U	D	SD
3. Presentation of information in statistical terms poses difficulties in understanding.	—	SA	A	U	D	SD
4. Intellectual curiosity is satisfied mostly through reading.	—	SA	A	U	D	SD

5. Factual information rarely gets recorded in the research reports.	—	SA	A	U	D	SD
6. It is better to do something else than spend the time in academic reading.	—	SA	A	U	D	SD
7. As an individual reads more his understanding of the reality would increase.	—	SA	A	U	D	SD
8. Few people have adequate time to go through the required information	—	SA	A	U	D	SD
9. Published information influences the value system of the individuals.	—	SA	A	U	D	SD
10. Most research reports are monotonous to read through.	—	SA	A	U	D	SD
11. An effective teacher is not always one who up-dates his information.	—	SA	A	U	D	SD
12. Findings in social sciences are usually confirmatory rather than contributory.	—	SA	A	U	D	SD
13. In social science research ideas borrowed from other published sources are rarely acknowledged.	—	SA	A	U	D	SD
14. After a certain stage most academicians lose their interest in academic reading, for it fetches them nothing.	—	SA	A	U	D	SD
15. Research conclusions are rarely different from common man's understanding.	—	SA	A	U	D	SD
16. Peer group appreciation is mostly ensured to those who are well read in their respective discipline.	—	SA	A	U	D	SD
17. Elaborate procedures in libraries more often restrict their use.	—	SA	A	U	D	SD
18. In most cases it is extraneous factors and not extensive reading which ensures academic reputation.	—	SA	A	U	D	SD
19. Information acquisition fosters scientific attitude among the people.	—	SA	A	U	D	SD
20. Most people do not abide by the copy right laws.	—	SA	A	U	D	SD
21. Social research reports are often fabricated.	—	SA	A	U	D	SD
22. Information up-dating is not essential for success in teaching jobs these days.	—	SA	A	U	D	SD

23. Published information is useful only for research purposes and is rarely of significance in practical life. — SA A U D SD
24. The nature of many academic jobs does not demand regular information seeking. — SA A U D SD
25. Available information on many social research topics is so confusing that it is better not to take notice of many of them. — SA A U D SD
26. Social scientists need not necessarily look through all the available information in their areas of specialisation. — SA A U D SD
27. Many of the literature guides are so confusing that they seem to scare the users away. — SA A U D SD
28. Computer information retrieval would only prove an uneconomical investment in our situation. — SA A U D SD
29. However much one aspires it is often other factors and not wide reading which help in the academic jobs. — SA A U D SD
30. Even if most of the current research reports are over looked it hardly matters in academic jobs these days. — SA A U D SD
31. Published reviews of researches are often based on personal likes and dislikes. — SA A U D SD
32. Information up-dating is not always an important criterion for decision making in matters relating to academic work. — SA A U D SD
33. Voracious readers are rarely innovative in their jobs. — SA A U D SD
34. There is nothing of practical value in acquiring published information. — SA A U D SD
35. Social research is often duplicated due to the absence of information about the research already conducted. — SA A U D SD
36. New job opportunities are rarely available to those who are widely read in their respective disciplines. — SA A U D SD

37. Many research reports arrive at wide generalisations on the basis of inadequate date.	SA	A	U	D	SD
38. Cultural richness of a country is mostly reflected in the information base (in terms of libraries, archives) it has.	SA	A	U	D	SD

APPENDIX C

Attitude Items Used in the Preliminary ATI Scale and the Results of the Statistical Analysis Relating to the Pilot Survey

Items	*t* ratio	Correlation Co-efficients		Remarks
		Item to total correlation	Corrected Item to total correlation	
1	2	3	4	5
It is better to do something else than spend the time in academic reading.	3.67**	.57**	.55**	Selected to the final scale.
Research information is not valued by our policy makers.	1.89	.20	.18	
Information up-dating is more valuable than what most people think.	1.25	.25	.24	
Money spent on books and journals in libraries may rather be used for other purposes.	1.06	.19	.18	
Research reports dealing with a different cultural context rarely carry worth while information for us.	4.18**	.56**	.54**	Selected.
Findings of the social research are usually confirmatory rather than contributory.	5.86**	.56**	.55**	Selected.
Research conclusions are rarely different from common man's understanding.	3.50**	.51**	.48**	Selected.
Quality of research often depends on the affectiveness with which information in books and journals are used.	0.37	.01	-.02	
Information up-dating is not essential for success in teaching jobs these days.	3.49**	.57**	.55**	Selected.

Contd.

1	2	3	4	5
Accessibility to information by the academicians would facilitate their intellectual competition.	0.58	.08	.06	
Computer information retrieval would only prove an uneconomical investment in our situation.	4.51**	.48**	.45**	Selected.
Research progress would be considerably fast when the wide array of information on the topic is readily available.	2.55*	.33*	.31*	
Innovative ideas often come through reading the available information.	2.11*	.32*	.30*	
Social scientists need not necessarily look through all the available information in their areas of specialisation.	4.01**	.58**	.56**	Selected.
Even if most of the current research information is over looked it hardly matters in academic jobs these days.	5.44**	.55**	.53**	Selected.
Information is useful only for research purposes and is rarely of significance in practical life.	3.98**	.57**	.55**	Selected.
Only those reports which are widely cited by the other researchers are of academic worth.	2.60*	.37**	.34*	
Information up-dating is not always an important criterion for decision making in matters relating to academic work.	3.56**	.50**	.48**	Selected.
Information up-dating does not assure contributions to the academic thinking.	2.32*	.30*	.33*	
Personal experiences are always more educative than published information.	3.65**	.50**	.48**	Selected.
As an individual reads more his understanding of the reality would increase.	2.86**	.42**	.39**	Selected.
Information influences the value system of the individual.	2.82**	.53**	.51**	Selected.
Reading makes a full man.	2.34*	.37**	.34*	
Wide reading helps not only in job but also life in general.	2.05*	.28*	.31*	

Contd.

1	2	3	4	5
Effective use of information often facilitates social change.	2.21*	.33*	.31*	
Information acquisition fosters scientific attitude among the people.	3.64**	.54**	.52**	Selected.
Regular reading is essential for proper appreciation of social controversies.	1.79	.39**	.37**	
Recorded information is the best method to preserve the culture for posterity.	1.88	.28	.26	
A good bibliographic information base would be a valuable national resource.	2.33*	.46**	.45**	
Scholarship of an academician is often reflected in his wide readings.	2.32*	.41**	.39**	
Most people do not try to get a piece of information when it is not easily available.	1.32	.29*	.27*	
Information about negative aspects of the social issues need not be given much importance.	-1.13	-.18	-.21	
It is not immediate utility of information to oneself but knowing what is happening in the world is what is usually expected.	0.41	.14	.12	
There is nothing of practical value in acquiring published information.	4.53**	.64**	.63**	Selected.
Reading in many instances turns out to be a bad habit.	2.48*	.44**	.42**	
Being called a 'book worm' is not a compliment to any person.	2.25*	.33*	.30*	
Efforts for acquiring information would loose its significance to a person soon after it serves the immediate purpose it is intended to.	1.96	.23	.20	
Cultural richness of a country is mostly reflected in the information base (in terms of libraries etc.) it has.	2.87**	.40**	.38**	Selected.
Prolific information out put reflects active academic involvement in the social progress.	2.21*	.42**	.40**	
Discussions with professional colleagues are usually enough of a source for gathering current research information.	0.79	.19	.15	
Information provided in research abstracts can rarely give a good picture of the study.	1.34	.38**	.38**	

Contd.

1	2	3	4	5
One can be a successful teacher just by making use of a few standard texts.	2.51*	.39**	.35*	
Data in statistical sources are often unreliable.	2.56*	.38**	.36*	
Encyclopaedia are supposed to contain gist of the total information, yet most people hardly find the need to consult them.	0.97	.15	.13	
Subject dictionaries rarely come of use in normal academic work.	2.45*	.32*	.30*	
Consulting social science information sources published in India is not necessary when international sources are easily accessible.	1.82	.40**	.38**	
Bibliographies are usually out dated and incomplete to provide the required information.	1.08	.27*	.24	
Most of the international social science bibliographic sources are nominally useful, for they are biased towards the developed countries.	2.17*	.28*	.25	
Government publications usually contain obsolete information.	2.06*	.27*	.24	
Mimeographed publications are always preliminary writings.	1.54	.31*	.29*	
Bibliographies are of little use when references listed in them are not accessible.	0.57	.22	.19	
For those who keep in touch with the important journals in their field of interest, abstracting and indexing sources come of little use.	1.28	.18	.16	
Much of the information in journals would be of only archival value when they are received late by the libraries.	0.57	.19	.16	
Presentation of information in statistical terms poses difficulties in understanding.	2.78**	.46**	.44**	Selected.
In most cases information seeking habit depends on the nature of academic atmosphere in the faculty/Institute.	2.37*	.45**	.43**	
Few people have adequate time to go through the required information.	2.96**	.48**	.45**	Selected.
Most research reports are monotonous to read through.	3.75**	.53**	.51**	Selected.

Contd.

1	2	3	4	5
Getting a translation of the original when it is in a language not understood is often a difficult proposition.	0.41**	.09	.07	
Information output is so fast that it is difficult to keep pace with it.	-0.16	.15	.09	
It is too much of a strain to collect all the available information on a particular topic.	1.21	.28*	.25	
Reading does nothing but strains the eyes.	1.30	.24	.23	
Elaborate procedures in libraries more often restrict their use.	3.20**	.39**	.36**	Selected.
It is very expensive to request for a reprint when the original article is not accessible.	1.61	.27	.24	
Though specific information is known to exist it is difficult to find it when it is required.	0.89	.20	.17	
Usually available books in the libraries are out dated and they rarely carry worth while information.	2.66*	.35*	.33*	
Lack of without qualified help to use most of the sources end up being unused.	1.27	.20	.18	
Many of the literature guides are so confusing that they seem to scare the users away.	3.90**	.51**	.55**	Selected.
Social research is often duplicated due to the absence of information about the research already done.	2.85**	.47**	.45**	Selected.
The nature of many academic jobs does not demand regular information seeking.	9.87**	.70**	.68**	Selected.
Available information on many social research topics is so confusing that it is better not to take notice of many of them.	6.44**	.60**	.58**	Selected.
It is difficult to assess the need for extent of information on a topic of research in a short time.	0.73	.09	.07	

Contd.

1	2	3	4	5
Intellectual curiosity can be satisfied mostly through reading.	3.27**	.46**	.44**	Selected.
Regular reading is the main contributor to academic success.	2.12*	.39**	.37**	
An effective teacher is not always one who up-dates his information.	3.63**	.49**	.47**	Selected.
Information seeking behaviour of an academician is the reflection of his commitment to the profession.	2.71*	.32*	.30*	
As one acquires more information one gets confidence for intellectual participation, irrespective of his job status.	2.06*	.37**	.35*	
Reading encourages to think in the right lines.	0.24	.09	.07	
Time spent on reading is a wise investment for individual progress.	2.08*	.36**	.37**	
Reading beyond a basic limit comes in the way of original thinking.	2.08*	.36**	.34*	
After a certain stage most academics loose interest in academic reading for it fetches them nothing.	3.51**	.52**	.49**	Selected.
Feeling of inefficiency is experienced by most of the academicians when they don't keep in touch with the recent research in their specialised area.	1.54	.28	.26	
Peer group appreciation is mostly ensured to those who are well read in their respective discipline.	4.02**	.44**	.42**	Selected.
In most cases it is extraneous factors and not extensive reading which ensures academic reputation.	7.74**	.53**	.51**	Selected.
Eagerness to know the current research in one's field of interest contributes largely to the satisfaction on academic jobs.	1.12	.22	.19	
Voracious readers are rarely innovative in their jobs.	4.14**	.61**	.59**	Selected.
Regular information seeking is the best way to ensure an inflow of challenging opportunities for social scientists.	2.13*	.32*	.30*	
New job opportunities are rarely available to those who are widely read in their respective disciplines.	4.37**	.60**	.57**	Selected.

Contd.

1	2	3	4	5
Significant contributions in social sciences have come from thinkers and not by voracious readers.	-0.19	.03	.00	
Through understanding of the current research often ensures affiliation with the colleagues who are well recognised in the concerned field of research.	1.67	.33	.31*	
However much one aspires it is often other factors and not wide reading which help in the academic jobs.	4.11**	.43**	.41**	Selected.
Factual information rarely gets recorded in the research reports.	4.26**	.59**	.57**	Selected.
Mostly references in the reports are desired readings and not actual readings.	2.55*	.33*	.30	
In social science research ideas borrowed from other sources are rarely acknowledged.	2.78**	.39**	.37**	Selected.
Most people do not abide by the copy right laws.	3.51**	.45**	.43**	Selected.
Many research reports arrive at wide generalisations on the basis of inadequate data.	6.00**	.60**	.58**	Selected.
Social research reports are often fabricated.,	3.69**	.48**	.46**	Selected.
Published reviews of researches are often based on personal likes and dislikes.	2.86**	.42**	.40**	Selected.

D.f. Correlation Co-efficient 48
t ratio 26

** Significance P < .01
* Significance P < .05

APPENDIX D

ATI Scale Items and Results of the Statistical Analysis for the Final Survey Data

Items	Correlation Co-efficients		
	t ratio	Item to total correlation	Corrected Items to total correlation
1	2	3	4
Personal experience are always more educative than published information.	3.28**	.30**	.24**
Research reports dealing with different cultural context rarely carry worthwhile information for us.	3.42**	.21**	.18**
Presentation of information in statistical terms posses difficulties in understanding.	5.06**	.38**	.29**
Intellectual curiosity is satisfied mostly through reading.	1.96*	.12	.09
Factual information rarely gets recorded in the research reports.	7.95**	.47**	.43**
It is better to do something else than spend the time in academic reading.	5.52**	.32**	.22**
As an individual reads more his understanding of the reality would increase.	3.47**	.29**	.23**
Few people have adequate time to go through the required information.	4.34**	.34**	.25**
Published information influences the value system of the individuals.	1.81	.13*	.10
Most research reports are monotonous to read through.	11.80**	.59**	.53**
An effective teacher is not always one who updates his information.	8.34**	.37**	.30**
Findings in social sciences are usually confirmatory rather than contributory.	8.37**	.44**	.40**
In social science research ideas borrowed from other published sources are rarely acknowledges.	8.10**	.43**	.41**
After a certain stage most academicians lost their interest in academic reading, for it fetches them nothing.	8.00**	.48**	.43**

(*Contd.*)

1	2	3	4
Research conclusions are rarely different from common man's understanding.	9.79**	.47**	.41**
Peer group appreciation is mostly ensured to those who are well read in their respective discipline.	2.27*	.13*	.08
Elaborate procedures in libraries more often restricts their use.	4.47**	.32**	.23**
In most cases it is extraneous factors and not extensive reading which ensures academic reputation.	8.20**	.51**	.45**
Information acquisition fosters scientific attitude among people.	5.95**	.36**	.27**
Most people do not abide by the copy right laws.	4.73**	.20**	.17*
Social research reports are often fabricated.	9.57**	.60**	.55**
Information updating is not essential for success in teaching jobs these days.	6.63**	.13*	.13*
Published information is useful only for research purposes and is rarely of significance in practical life.	9.99**	.56**	.49**
The nature of many academic jobs does not demand regular information seeking.	7.11**	.52**	.41**
Available information on many social research topics is so confusing that it is better not to take notice or many of them.	5.95**	.51**	.48**
Social scientists need not necessarily look through all the available information in their areas of specialisation.	5.25**	.40**	.39**
Many of the literature guides are so confusing that they seem to score the users away.	6.61**	.49**	.41**
Computer information retrieval would only prove uneconomical investment in our situation.	5.74**	.40**	.37**
However much one aspires it is often other factors and not wide reading which help in the academic jobs.	8.35**	.56**	.51**
Even if most of the current research reports are overlooked it hardly matters in academic jobs these days.	8.81**	.63**	.52**

Contd.

1	2	3	4
Published reviews of researches are often based on personal likes and dislikes.	9.45**	.63**	.51**
Information updating is not always an important criterion for decision making in matters relating to academic work.	7.46**	.49**	.41**
Voracious readers are rarely innovative in their jobs.	5.77**	.53**	.40**
There is nothing of practical value in acquiring published information.	4.64**	.44**	.30**
Social research is often duplicated due to the absence of information about the research already done.	4.27**	.31**	.24**
New job opportunities are rarely available to those who are widely read in their respective disciplines.	8.64	.52**	.47**
Many research reports arrive at wide generalisations on the basis of inadequate data.	6.02**	.33**	.23**
Cultural richness of a country is mostly reflected in the information base (in terms of libraries, archives) it has.	1.37	13*	.10

* Significance P< .05

** Significance P < .01

INDEX

CICIL LIST

CONCEPTS IN COMMUNICATION, INFORMATICS & LIBRARIANSHIP

(CICIL)

General Editor: **S.P. AGRAWAL**

CICIL-1 Development of Library Services in India: Social Science Information
S.P. Agrawal Rs. 150

CICIL-2 Development of Documentation in India: Social Science Information
S.P. Agrawal Rs. 250

CICIL-3 UNESCO and Social Sciences: Retrospect and Prospect
S.P. Agrawal and **J.C. Aggarwal** Rs. 250

CICIL-4 INDIANA : A Bibliography of Bibliographical Sources
M.K. Jain Rs. 200

CICIL-5 Dimensions of Library and Information Science: Kaula Festschrift
V. Venkatappaiah (Eds.) Rs. 600

CICIL-6 Book Numbers: Some Indian Methods
M.P. Satija and **S.P. Agrawal** Rs. 100

CICIL-7 National Policy for University Libraries in India: Problems and Perspectives
N.B. Inamdar and **L.S. Ramaiah** (Ed.) Rs. 250

CICIL-8 Media Utilisation for the Development of Women and Children
B.S. Thakur and **Binod C. Agrawal** Rs. 150

CICIL-9 Terrorism: An Annotated Bibliography
Susheela Bhan (Ed.) Rs. 275

CICIL-10 Transnational Library Relations: The Indo-American Experience
M.B. Konnur Rs. 175

CICIL-11 Geography of Marketing and Commercial Activities in India (Documentation on Research Information)
R.S. Dixit Rs. 130

CICIL-12 Information India 1988: Global View
S.P. Agrawal and **J.C. Aggarwal** Rs. 200

CICIL-13 Women's Education in India: Historical Review, Present Status and Perspective Plan
S.P. Agrawal and **J.C. Aggarwal** Rs. 360

CICIL-14 Cultural Communication in India: Role and Impact of Phonograms
J.M. Ojha Rs. 220

CICIL-15 Second Historical Survey of Educational Development in India: Select Documents 1985-1989
S.P. Agrawal and **J.C. Aggarwal** Rs. 490

CICIL-16 Documentation Encyclopaedia of UNESCO and Education
J.C. Aggarwal and **S.P. Agrawal** Rs. 800 (set of 2 parts)

CICIL-17 Attitude Towards Information: A Study of Post-Graduate Teachers and Researchers in Social Sciences
N.G. Satish Rs. 450

CICIL-18 Librarianship and Bureaucratic Organisation: A Study in the Sociology of Library Profession in India
P.K. Jayaswal Rs. 175

CICIL-19 Literature Search
K.A. Isaac Rs. 150

CICIL-20 Child Education in India: Index to Scholarly Writings in Indian Educational Journals and Newspapers since independence
S.P. Agrawal and **Naresh Kanta** Rs. 100

CICIL-21 Lok Sabha and Vidhan Sabha Elections in India 1989 & 1990: Process and Results with Comparative Study of Manifestos
S.P. Agrawal and **J.C. Aggarwal** Rs. 250

CICIL-22 Islamic Studies in India: A Survey of Human, Institutional and Documentary Sources
Mohamed Taher Rs. 180

CICIL-23 Panchayati Raj: An Annotated Bibliography
N.B. Inamdar, N.G. Satish and **Anil Takalkar** 290

CICIL-24 Information India 1989-90: Global View
S.P. Agrawal and **J.C. Aggarwal** Rs. 500

CICIL-25 First Handbook of Psychological and Social Instruments
Udai Pareek and **T. Venkateswara Rao** Rs. 500

CICIL-26 Educational and Social Uplift of Backward Classes: At What Cost and How? Mandal Commission and After
S.P. Agrawal and **J.C. Aggarwal** Rs. 275

CICIL-27 Mass Media and New Horizons: Impact of TV & Video an Urban Milieu
H.R. Trivedi Rs. 180

CICIL-28 Indian Writings on Education : An Indicator to Indian Educational Journals Grouped by Subject Deseriptors 1979 to 1986 (in two parts)
S.P. Agarwal Rs. 900 (per set)

CICIL-29 Nation in Crisis
S.P. Agrawal and **J.C. Aggarwal** Rs. 200

CICIL-30 Information India 1990-91: Global View
S.P. Agrawal and **J.C. Aggarwal** Rs. 500

CICIL-31 Development of University Libraries in India after Independence
O.P. Gupta Rs. 270

CICIL-32 Handbook on Child : With Historical Background
Pramila Pandit Barooah Rs. 320

CICIL-33 Weaker Section in Indian Society : Undiscovered Past, Uncertain Present and Unpredictable Future : Index to Writings in Indian Scholarly Journals and 10 National Newspapers Classified under 1500 Descriptors 1886-1990
S.P. Agrawal and **Rajeev Kumar Sharma** Rs. 600

CICIL-34 Communication Informatics and Librarianship in India : An Introductory Guide to Publications Based on a Survey of Libraries in Capital City of India
S.P. Agrawal and **Pushpa Rani Sharma** Rs. 720

CICIL-35 Problems of Collection Development in Special Libraries
M.S. Sridhar Rs. 225

CICIL-36 National Information Resources for Social Sciences in India : Mobilisation, Dispersal and International Enhancement
S.P. Agrawal Rs. 225

CICIL-37 Modern History of Punjab : A Look Back into Ancient Peaceful Punjab Focusing Confrontation and Failures Leading to Present Punjab Problem, and a Peep Ahead : Relevant Select Documents
J.C. Aggarwal and **S.P. Agrawal** Rs. 400

CICIL-38 India Information Sources : Economics and Business
Kyllikki Ruokonen and **Manohar Lal** Rs.

CICIL-39 Educational Planning in India : With a Slant to Educational Financing and Administration, Vol. 1, Reports of Committees and Commissions, Five Year Plans, Statistical Tables
J.C. Aggarwal and **S.P. Agrawal** Rs. 650

CICIL-40 Integrated Library System : Two Case Studies : Latin America and India
Maria Luiza Rigo Pasquarelli, Rosaly Favero Krzyanowski, Ines Maria M. Imperatriz and S.P. Agrawal Rs. 160

CICIL-41 Social Science Information in India: Effort towards Bibliographical Control
S.D. Vyas Rs. 300

CICIL-42 Higher Education in India Since Independence: U.G.C. and Its Approach
O.P. Gupta Rs. 360

CICIL-43 Government and Politics in India: A Bibliographical Study of Contemporary Scenario Chronicling Rajiv Gandhi Era
S.P. Agrawal and **Rajeev Kumar Sharma** Rs. 500

CICIL-44 Second Handbook of Psychological and Social Instruments
D.M. Pestonjee Rs. 300

CICIL-45 Development/Digression Diary of India; 3D Companion Volume to Information India: 1990-91
S.P. Agrawal Rs. 200

CICIL-46 Development/Digression Diary of India; 3D Companion Volume to Information India: 1991-92
S.P. Agrawal Rs. 300

CICIL-47 Information India 1991-92: Global View
S.P. Agrawal and **J.C. Aggarwal** Rs. 500

CICIL-48 Committees and Commissions in India 1974, A Concept's Project, Compiled by a team of professionals guided by **Virender Kumar** (Vol. 12) Rs. 450

CICIL-49 Committees and Commissions in India 1975, A Concept's Project, Compiled by a team of professionals guided by **Virender Kumar** (Vol. 13) Rs. 450

CICIL-50 Committees and Commissions in India 1976, A Concept's Project, Compiled by a team of professionals guided **Virender Kumar** (Vol. 14) Rs. 450

CICIL-51 Committees and Commissions in India 1977, A Concept's Project, Compiled by a team of professionals guided by **Virender Kumar** (Vol. 15) (in four parts) Rs. 450 each

CICIL-52 Committees and Commissions in India 1978, A Concept's Project, Compiled by a team of professionals guided by **Virender Kumar** (Vol. 16) (in two parts) Rs. 450 each

CICIL-53 Subject Guide to Communication, Informatics and Librarianship in India (Based on a Survey of Library Holdings in Capital City of India)
S.P. Agrawal and **Pushpa Rani Sharma** Rs. 400

CICIL-54 Restructurring of Library and Information Science Curriculum
A. Tejomurty Rs. 250

CICIL-55 Committees and Commissions in India 1979, A Concept's Project, Compiled by a team of professionals guided by **Virender Kumar** (Vol. 17) (in two parts) Rs. 450 each

CICIL-56 Committees and Commissions in India 1980, A Concept's Project, Compiled by a team of professionals guided by **Virender Kumar** (Vol. 18) (in two parts) Rs. 450 each

CICIL-57 Third Historical Survey of Educational Development in India
S.P. Agrawal and **J.C. Aggarwal** Rs. 700

CICIL-58 Model Library Legislation
Velaga Venkatappaiah Rs. 400